# Middle School LITERACY CENTERS

## CONNECTING STRUGGLING READERS TO LITERATURE

Lynette Prevatte

Middle School Literacy Centers


Cover, Book Design, and Layout | Mickey Cuthbertson

Library of Congress Cataloging-in-Publication Data

Prevatte, Lynette, 1970-
Middle school literacy centers : connecting struggling readers to literature / Lynette Prevatte.
p. cm.
Includes bibliographical references.
ISBN-13: 978-0-929895-98-7 (pbk.)
ISBN-10: 0-929895-98-3 (pbk.)
1. Reading (Middle school) 2. Classroom learning centers. 3. Young adult literature--Study and teaching (Middle school) I. Title.
LB1632.P74 2007
428.4071'2--dc22
2007013624

ISBN-13: 978-0-929895-98-7
ISBN-10: 0-929895-98-3

10 9 8 7 6 5 4 3 2

Maupin House Publishing, Inc.
2416 NW 71st Place
Gainesville, FL 32653
1-800-524-0634 / 352-373-5588
352-373-5546 (fax)
www.maupinhouse.com
info@maupinhouse.com

Publishing Professional Resources That Improve Classroom Performance

# Dedication

Dedicated to my husband, Jody, who is more supportive and loving than I deserve.
To my children, Justin and Sydney—when you smile, you give me everything!

# Acknowledgments

I am so grateful for the inspiration and wisdom of my Uncle Steve, who taught us all to appreciate reading and a good education, and teachers like my mother-in-law, Judy Prevatte, who do the job because they love children.

My deepest gratitude to Valerie Hauser and Melanie Ward for the confidence, the suggestions, and the Saturday breakfasts. A special thank you to Marilyn Durant, Trey Lee, Natalie Sommer, and Dood Wood—filled with passion and brilliant ideas!

Much appreciation to all of my colleagues at Lewis Middle. How lucky I am to have found such a loving and supportive family.

To Dr. Dennis Carroll and The College Board for setting me on a path that would take me to places I never imagined I could go.

Thank you to Emily Gorovsky. Every first-time writer should be so lucky to have such a patient and professional editor.

And most importantly, to the reading and English teachers who, despite the many challenges, never waiver from what is important. Your dedication humbles me; it is a privilege to share with you this resource. I look forward to dynamic dialogues.

# Table of Contents

# Introduction

There they were—twenty-seven eighth graders—all level one, all present for the beginning of a new year of English. Back then, reading teachers were new to middle school, and for most of these kids, I *was* the reading teacher.

Postures varied. Some slumped. Some sat misleadingly straight. Others made no pretense at all and, as soon as they found their seats, the "been there, done that" portion of the group settled into a nap-like state.

As the weeks progressed, we did a lot of talking. Not unlike any other year, the conversations seemed one-sided. Me: "Why do you think you struggle with reading?" Student: "I don't know." Me: "Do you understand how important reading is?" Student: "Yes." Me: "Why is it important?" Student: "If I don't do better, I'll work at McDonalds."

With each passing day, I could never really tell who was winning the war. I mean, it's a little difficult to lead a battle when your warriors aren't sure who they are fighting, what the enemy looks like, or even where the battlefield is located. Yet, every day, I'd arm myself with the confidence that my leadership was making a difference, that my best efforts would result in success for each of those students (despite the posture they chose).

We marched through the calendar—one dry lesson after another: main idea, cause and effect, author's purpose . . . if it would be tested, I would make sure it was covered. We wrote about what we read. We spoke about what we read. I felt like we should have been the poster children for literature-rich classrooms.

And finally, one morning—one quiet fall morning—I looked around the room. By all appearances, they were busy. I had delivered an amazing lesson, and each student was dutifully completing some attractively arranged worksheet, much like the day before and the day before that. My colleagues who valued order and quiet would have called this a "good" class. But, something was missing. Something was terribly wrong. My class was boring.

For all of my efforts to make the lessons meaningful, I left out the largest factor—the kids. The kids were disconnected from the literature, and I had managed to take the "meaning" out of "meaningful." My lessons weren't promoting learning—they were promoting completion, and if I thought I was encouraging these kids to love literature, I was living in a fantasy land for sure.

So, I stopped the class, and we had another talk. I can remember the day well, and I'll never forget the gist of the conversation. Me: "Do you understand what it means to 'read well?'" Class: "Sure. It's those kids who read out loud and they don't go slow or mess up words." Me: "Do you *want* to read better?" Class: "I already know how to read." Me: "So, you don't care?" Class: "No, I just don't want to make a bad score on the test." Me: (pause) "When was the last time you remember *liking* to read?" Class: (long silence—and finally, a hand) "Well, when I was in elementary school, my teacher set up reading centers. Each center had directions, and you worked at your own pace." Another voice added, "Yeah! I remember! We would fight to get to the best center first, and the teacher would rotate us around the room so we got to do each one."

As I listened to the students reminisce, my head began to spin. Each of their recollections added a new dimension to my growing list of issues to consider: preparation, movement, time management, noise level, and assessment. Middle schoolers can be guilty of judging the quality of a class by the amount of "fun" they are having, and I have always stood firm in my belief that I am not here to entertain for the sake of fulfilling that expectation. I just needed to find a way to marry the best practices to a format that might seem palatable to an adolescent who is reluctant to read. Literacy centers were the solution.

## Inspiration Comes to Life

I won't lie about my intentions. I wasn't out to create methodology or improve on the pedagogy of literacy. I really just wanted to pump some life into my students. That class typified kids all over the country: low performing, with little interest and lots of experience with failure. In the data-driven environment our system had created, I could give each of them lots of information: "You aren't reading on grade level," "You are in danger of being retained," and "Statistics show that if we don't get you turned around before age fifteen, you are doomed to a lifetime of operating as a functional illiterate." But how useful was any of this? Did it motivate them or show them how to improve?

The latest research seemed more promising. Educators, like Janet Allen and Chris Tovani, were helping teachers to understand why kids struggled with reading, and their expertise provided teachers with an arsenal of tactics to confront the problems head on. Moreover, research showed that reading strategies really did help kids learn to read more effectively, and teachers were finding that literacy had less to do with reading words and more to do with *how* their students read, organized, and responded to what they read. I realized that all of this could be taught within the literacy-center format, addressing the problems of struggling readers while promoting a love for literature at the same time.

## What You'll Find in This Book

**Chapter One** lays out six accepted premises about adolescent learning that must be taken into consideration when planning the activities for your literacy centers.

**Chapter Two** explains the Big Ten areas of reading that students must master to become successful readers and that literacy centers should be built around: main idea, cause and effect, compare and contrast, vocabulary in context, sequence of events, literary devices, fact and opinion, reference and research, author's purpose, and summarizing. **Chapter Two** also includes cross-indexes of ten well-known strategies your students can apply in the centers to master the Big Ten skills while connecting with literature. Each strategy includes an explanation and application ideas, as well as a list of centers where that strategy is best integrated.

**Chapter Three** offers helpful answers to some of the most frequently asked questions regarding organizing, managing, and assessing centers.

**Chapter Four** provides forty literacy centers built around the Big Ten skills (four centers for each of the ten skills), plus a bonus set of four centers focusing on standardized testing must-have skills. Each center includes teacher directions, student directions, and worksheets. The targeted goals for students, preparation needed, and a list of suggested materials are included on the teacher directions, as well as any special considerations to note for that center. The student directions are divided into three sections: "Focus on the Skill" (a warm-up exercise), "Practice the Skill," and "Take It to the Next Level," all of which are included on the teacher directions as well. Students will also see a rubric on their directions sheet so that the exact requirements for each center are made clear. The worksheets follow the same format as the student directions and include "Focus on the Skill," "Practice the Skill," and "Take It to the Next Level."

# Chapter One
## Laying the Foundations

## Consider All Angles

Middle-school literacy centers are not dressed-up versions of primary-school centers. They are based on the unique needs of the middle-level age group, and they are centered around age-appropriate literature that requires evaluation, analysis, and reasoning.

As with all age groups, the path to effective reading instruction has to begin with goal-making. For literacy centers to work in a middle-school classroom, the objectives for learning need to be based on the following accepted premises about adolescent learning:

1. Adolescent learning is unique; therefore, effective reading instruction in middle school should focus on appropriate developmental skills: purpose, comprehension, fluency, phonemic awareness, vocabulary, and writing.
2. Differentiated instruction is valuable to a middle-school classroom.
3. Middle-school-aged students must be exposed to a variety of literature and positive experiences with text.
4. Any type of successful reading instruction is going to consider the learning styles of the students.
5. There are linguistic differences between boys and girls that may affect reading proficiency.
6. Teacher expectation affects whether or not an adolescent will care about what is taught.

### 1. Adolescent learning is unique; therefore, effective reading instruction in middle school should focus on appropriate developmental skills: purpose, comprehension, fluency, phonemic awareness, vocabulary, and writing.

The word "literacy" involves "reading, writing, and other symbolic communication" (Alvermann, 2001). Unlike emergent and developing readers, a struggling adolescent reader may not have sufficient groundwork for proficiency. Fortunately, we have a greater understanding for how to help adolescents build confidence and aptitude, but educators must understand their unique needs.

**Kids have to know why they need reading.** The generally accepted word is "purpose," and just as teaching "author's purpose" is an important skill for acquiring comprehension, I believe it's important to teach "purpose for literacy" so kids understand why they should invest their time and attention.

Without a doubt, informed readers pay more attention. Every year, my lowest-performing class is filled with kids who lack literacy skills at a young age. The more startling truth is the fact that most of their parents lacked the same skills. My prevailing question at the beginning of every year is "How many of you have heard your parents say they hope you will not have to work as hard as they do?" I have yet to see a class where at least two-thirds of the students didn't raise their hands.

Show them the statistics. Share what you know.

Studies have shown that good adolescent readers were read to when they were younger, own books or subscribe to magazines, and see the adults in their lives (parents, teachers, and significant role models) reading on a regular basis. I share this with my students for two reasons: First, because they need to recognize what happened in their own lives. To a fourteen-year-old, reading is "not cool." How did they come to that conclusion? Has that conclusion been a benefit to them? Secondly, I want them to always think about literacy as a responsibility, one they can pass on. I have had many former students come back to visit with their own children (my babies with new babies) and they want me to know about the books they've been reading to them at night. All I can think is, "They were listening!"

We also know that there may be a direct correlation between literacy and wealth. While we may not know for sure if the wealthy read for pleasure, we do know that the majority of people who buy books from bookstores hold diplomas. Technical programs, licensure exams, and specialized certification are alternatives to college, and middle-school kids need to know that some of the fastest-growing, well-paying jobs will all require effective reading skills, even if they don't require college degrees: computer systems analyst—$67,520; database administrator—$61,950; physical therapist—$61,560; network systems and data communication analyst—$61,250 (Morsch, 2006).

However, the greatest purpose for literacy may be about becoming a good, capable human being. It's the difference between knowing how to read a map and trusting someone to tell you the right way to go. It's being able to read instructions, learning something new because you want to grow and improve, and having the option of making choices because you know there is something better. Above salary and paychecks, literacy provides confidence, self-esteem, and opportunity. Without understanding the purpose for being literate, an adolescent may never buy into the need to improve.

**Comprehension is the most difficult component of adolescent literacy.** Adolescents who struggle to read do not always grasp the scope of their dilemma. In their minds, they can read the words, so what is the problem? Finding the main idea, making connections to what they read with other text, and differentiating reliable and unreliable information can be challenging; and, often times there doesn't seem to be a point. Remember, adolescents are caught up in the concrete stage of development. Learning has to smack them in the face. In order for that to happen, comprehension has to be broken down into smaller pieces (fact and opinion, compare and contrast, inference, etc.)—and it must be clear how those pieces fit into the larger picture.

**Fluency cannot be overlooked, no matter how much an adolescent begs you to try.** In the younger grades, struggling readers may have hidden behind a perceived shyness, a quiet nature, or an obvious embarrassment. By the time they get to the middle grades, those same students are terrified to read aloud. Through repeated, guided, and independent reading, an adolescent reader must be taught how to recognize errors and acknowledge they need help.

As teachers, we have to create an environment that is safe and non-threatening. It's a constant struggle to instill trust, and in the past few years I began to announce, "This class is just like Las Vegas. What happens in Mrs. Prevatte's class stays in Mrs. Prevatte's class." The class may giggle, but somewhere down deep I get the feeling many of them hope it's really true.

**Phonemic awareness is not just for the little people.** I am constantly meeting teachers who are amazed that their middle-school students can't pronounce words. The fact of the matter is there are a lot of adolescent readers who do not possess the skills to decode sounds. They have to be re-taught how to translate text into sounds. Words that present phonemic challenges can only be recognized with frequent practice and opportunities to recognize those words in context. The days of "Sound it out" cannot end in elementary school.

**Vocabulary, vocabulary, vocabulary!** I always relate the ability to read, recognize, and use new words to owning a key to the world. The more words you learn, the more doors you can unlock—and the more people with whom you can converse. When presented with an unfamiliar word, my students are the first to say, "Mrs. Prevatte, that's a big word." But more often than not, they will follow that comment with "What does it mean?"

At this age, adolescents are poised for learning strategies to identify and learn new words, and they genuinely want to understand words in context. By exploring etymology, prefixes, suffixes, and root words, meaning can be discovered. Through synonyms, antonyms, homonyms, and homophones, relationships among word meanings are created. Furthermore, as words are learned, they must be practiced in writing and conversation. A quote by Evelyn Waugh captures the sentiment perfectly: "One forgets words as one forgets names. One's vocabulary needs constant fertilizing or it will die."

**Writing pulls everything together.** If you're looking at literacy as a building, writing is the mortar that holds the bricks together. Writing is more than just spelling, punctuation, and usage; it's about engaging the content. Today's middle schoolers write far more than their predecessors ten years ago, and they seem to readily recognize words like "details," "examples," and "support"—doing a far better job discerning expository (informational) from persuasive.

Adolescent readers have to be given time to reflect on what they read, and they have to be taught how to respond to questions effectively. They should begin to approach writing situations with attention to audience—choosing to elaborate or remain concise. Their writing experiences should be diverse and require them to look at what they read from a variety of perspectives. They should think about how they want to organize their thoughts, and graphic organizers should be a part of their everyday lives, in all of their classes.

Because reading and writing go hand in hand, it's easy to see why a struggling reader may be hesitant to commit words to paper. Small steps are better than no steps, so a teacher who is willing to provide constructive feedback has to be a part of the routine.

## 2. Differentiated instruction is valuable to a middle-school classroom.

But, what is differentiated instruction? When I first heard the phrase, I was presenting a workshop to high-school AP teachers. We were discussing the importance of taking a difficult concept—*argumentation*—apart and giving kids an opportunity to experience the term in many different ways: individually reading a speech, determining the message of the speech in a small group, and debating the author's purpose as a whole class. As I took them through a variety of engaging activities, a veteran teacher spoke out: "Oh my gosh. This is differentiated instruction!"

The National Center on Accessing the General Curriculum (NCAC) says the following:

> "Differentiated instruction applies an approach to teaching and learning so that students have multiple options for taking in information and making sense of ideas. The model of differentiated instruction requires teachers to be flexible in their approach to teaching and adjusting the curriculum and presentation of information to learners rather than expecting students to modify themselves for the curriculum. Classroom teaching is a blend of whole-class, group, and individual instruction. Differentiated instruction is a teaching theory based on the premise that instructional approaches should vary and be adapted in relation to individual and diverse students in classrooms." (Hall, 2002)

The concept of centers is an exercise in differentiated instruction. I just don't think it would be fair to discuss literacy centers without making it clear how much is dependent upon teachers' ability to accept differentiated instruction as a viable part of reading instruction. As a former skeptic, I can safely tell you that I too was afraid to unleash my students into the unknown realm of the "small group." By all accounts, many teachers will tell you that this is a situation for chaos. Again, I suppose the bottom line has to be about what is best for students.

Yes, we're talking about the same concept as the centers you remember from grade school—busy kids learning with a purpose. However, these are hardly the matching games and felt-board activities you might be imagining. Literacy centers allow students to move beyond the traditional instructional formats, and each center can challenge students of varying grade levels and ability to engage in meaningful lessons that go far beyond what you can achieve in a whole-class situation. Literacy centers are NOT miniature warehouses for storing the students who are not working directly with the teacher. The teacher is an active part of the process—interacting with students to promote comprehension and thoughtful analysis.

Centers create energy, and with some groundwork and consistency, students will recognize their structure and regulation as sure as if the seats were lined up in neat rows and the overhead stood at the front of the room. Keep in mind that there have to be definite goals, and classroom management is a must. Differentiated instruction isn't about throwing down a checkered flag and watching your students race around the room; it is about understanding that no two students are alike and that every child deserves the opportunity to feel like he or she has choices and can manage his or her own learning.

### 3. Middle-school-aged students must be exposed to a variety of literature and positive experiences with text.

If the teacher I am today could talk to the teacher I was ten years ago, one of the first tips I would impart is the importance of connecting kids to literature. Back then, high-stakes testing was new to education, and the only goal (much like today) was to get kids to pass the test. Every publisher was scurrying to put together practice tests and skills-based workbooks to fulfill a need. My students began to expect every story we read to be followed by multiple-choice and extended-response questions. I can remember being troubled by the fact that my students seemed to answer the questions well in the classroom but then weren't able to duplicate their success when it came to test taking. Perhaps it was that we hadn't found the right "program" or literature series. Maybe we weren't using the right materials.

My very good friend and colleague, Marilyn Durant, helped me realize the absurdity of my thinking: "Those books are preparing kids for a test. We're preparing kids for life." I've never met anyone who talks the talk and walks the walk like Durant: reading to her students every single day, allowing kids to take her beloved young adult novels home without a check-out or return policy, and sharing her favorite poems, short stories, and picture books like *The Mysteries of Harris Burdock* by Chris Van Allsburg, *Barn Dance* by Bill Martin Jr. and John Archambault, and *The Jolly Postman* by Allan Ahlberg with the biggest, baddest, most unlikely fans of children's literature you can imagine—all the while attending to the very skills I had fretted about teaching. You only have to pass through her classroom once to notice the thousands of books that line the shelves; believe me, her students know that literature holds meaning.

While I cannot dispute the need for exposing students to the format, necessary verbiage, and testing strategies, I have strong feelings about reducing literacy instruction to a packaged program. Sure, it's easier to run off a worksheet that guarantees cause and effect will be covered, but if you ask your students what cause and effect is, will they bring up page 47 of the test practice book? No, cause and effect is better illustrated in Walter Dean Myers's short story, "The Treasure of Lemon Brown," where a teenage boy is forced to acknowledge that the definition of "treasure" holds a different meaning than what he may have assumed after an old homeless man reveals his heart-wrenching tale of love and loss.

Now, I've actually taught workshops to teachers who have argued that they "do not have time to read" anymore. What a terrible thought. I have worked with adolescents—tough ones—for a long time. There is nothing more rewarding to me than when a child I haven't taught in ten years says hello to me in the mall and asks if I remember when we read *Cheaper by the Dozen* by Frank B. Gilbreth, Jr. and Ernestine Gilbreth Carey or *The Pearl* by John Steinbeck. My love for books became so transparent that when a student from another classroom delivered *The Other Boleyn Girl* by Philippa Gregory as a "Secret Santa" gift to a colleague, one of the students in her class said, "Oh, your Secret Santa must be Mrs. Prevatte. That's her favorite book." How my heart leapt when I heard that story!

In my classroom, books are part of our everyday lives. I try to model my passion for reading and I'm all about the book talk: "You guys, I just finished *Inkheart* by Cornelia Funke last night, and I have to tell you what I thought!" When I buy new books for the classroom library, I like to take time out to talk about the titles I chose and why. If a student has expressed interest in a particular genre or favorite author, I keep an eye open for titles that I can suggest—middle schoolers love to know that you are paying attention. Our media specialist purchased book stands, and I display the newest titles for a short time before putting them on the shelf (building frenzy for something that is perceived as limited and new). As a matter of fact, it was the principal's idea to make the stands available, as she had read a study about how consumers will choose books more readily when their covers face forward over the spine of a book on a bookshelf.

If you've taught middle-school students for even a short time, you know they will do flips for a reward. My students who finish a novel put their names on tickets (you can find rolls of them in most stores' school supply sections), and I sporadically draw several names from a fish bowl for small candies, stickers, or bookmarks. All of my students know about my "Accelerated Reader" folder—a folder filled with the individual printouts of AR tests showing students have read a title and passed a corresponding test. Those students qualify for king-size candy bars, and I only draw from that file twice a semester. On the wall, I keep a chart of the state's suggested novel titles, and everyone knows to write their name and check off the book on the chart to be invited to a special ice cream party in the spring.

Literacy centers should promote reading; inasmuch, we should keep in mind that struggling readers rarely come into contact with text away from the classroom. This is a perfect opportunity to expose kids to rich literary experiences, and kids love to see variety: excerpts from novels, picture books, short stories, transcripts from National Public Radio (NPR), letters to the editor, articles from magazines (*Newsweek*, *Time*, *Teen People*, etc.), historical letters, journal entries, and speeches. Recently, I've rediscovered how important reference sources have become to literacy, and the resources for centers designed for reference and research skills are immense: atlases, dictionaries, thesauruses, almanacs, and encyclopedias, just to name a few.

### 4. Any type of successful reading instruction is going to consider the learning styles of the students.

When you are building a literacy center, always keep in mind the three main styles of learning: visual, auditory, and kinesthetic. Understanding the learning styles of the students we teach is not new to the classroom, but it can be easily overlooked. Literacy centers offer teachers a tool for helping kids to learn about their strengths and limitations as learners, and there is certainly a benefit to helping kids understand how they learn best. Personally, I have always been a visual learner, and I have to really make myself *listen* when information is new and unfamiliar. When I share this with my students, I want them to understand that, if I don't understand something, I can't make the excuse, "Well, I'm just not good at listening." It's my responsibility, as it is theirs, to be in touch with individual learning styles and make the effort to improve the weaknesses.

In order for students to achieve such an understanding about themselves, a teacher must provide opportunities for exercising a balance of learning styles within a literacy center. That may be as simple as analyzing tone words from an excerpt of a novel, discussing what those words imply about where and when the story takes place, and drawing a sketch with details that shows an understanding of the story's setting. Each part of the activity requires a different learning style, and your students will love and hate different aspects of the assignment according to their own preferences. For example, I will invariably hear an auditory learner complain, "I can't draw," and there's merit to that complaint. My job as the facilitator is to make them aware of the goals and provide feedback: "It's not the artistic quality of the drawing that's important. I want to see the details you chose to show what you understand."

I know it seems like a lot to worry about, but it's really more about being aware. Paying attention to learning style isn't about creating custom-built lessons for each student in the class, but it is about making the attempt to balance lessons that reflect the varying needs of the students. The "learning-style methodology" (Farkas, 2003) has a positive affect on achievement, and when a teacher uses the multi-sensory instructional approach, there's a better chance of reaching a greater number of students.

### 5. There are linguistic differences between boys and girls that may affect reading proficiency.

Before I delve into the "how" of literacy centers, let me finish the "why" with a little food for thought. Over the years, I noticed one consistent feature of my low-performing classes—on average, they have a ratio of two boys for every girl. At some point, I began to pay attention to the discrepancy and started looking for real-time statistics to see if there was a correlation to my classroom. The National Assessment of Educational Progress (NAEP) reports consistently show a greater percentage of boys than girls in the U.S. fail to read at *basic* levels. Further studies revealed that boys are two times more likely than girls to be diagnosed with learning disabilities and twice as likely to be placed in special-education classes. Some experts contend that the needs of boys are not being met in today's classrooms, and the issue of literacy is near the center of their argument.

Again, the difference between boys and girls is an issue that is worth discussing with kids. Every year, I ask "Who talks more—boys or girls?" You won't be surprised to hear that girls unanimously get the vote. It becomes somewhat of a comedy routine. We go through the whole scenario. Cindy is on the phone with Trey, and she's asking him a million questions about his day: "Did you see Sarah's outfit? Why didn't you say 'hi' to me in P.E.? Are you going to the dance Friday?" On the other end of the line, Trey responds, "Uh-huh...I don't know...Yep." At this point, the girls are giggling, and the boys are shaking their heads. I confidently step forward and raise my hand. "Girls, I have a terrible announcement to make about your conversations with boys. They may not even be listening." The girls scan the room, their eyes questioning their male counterparts and, again, the boys nod in agreement. "Seriously, Mrs. P.," an outspoken boy in the class said one year, "sometimes, I just put the phone down and play video games. They don't even notice and keep talking."

Reading and writing are related to language (linguistics). You won't be surprised to know that boys posses better gross motor skills and 3D visualization and girls are more linguistic and process emotions faster. What may surprise you is there may not be a gender difference in speaking rate or articulation rate. Yes, the girls might be speaking more in middle school, but it's not necessarily because the boys lack *ability*.

> "Dr. Deborah Tannen, a linguistics professor at Georgetown University, found that girls want to make connections through conversation, while boys use conversation to gain status. For boys, conversations are contests they are always trying to win. Girls talk to build rapport with others and to explore their own feelings and opinions. They discuss relationships, people, and experiences. Boys view conversations as ways to exchange information or solve problems. They discuss news, sports, and subjects not directly related to themselves." (Gard, 2000)

So, what does this have to do with literacy centers? I found that centers can really address the issue of how adolescent boys acquire literacy. Adolescent boys have two strikes against them when it comes to classroom learning: 1) by nature, they're more active, and 2) they may not be able to use their brains as efficiently as females their own age (Tyre, 2006). If boys have the opportunity to engage in activities that possess a kinesthetic component in a setting that does not require an immediate response, struggling male adolescent readers may feel a sense of accomplishment. Effective literacy instruction can't be about which gender is better, but it must acknowledge that the two are very different from one another indeed.

### 6. Teacher expectation affects whether or not an adolescent will care about what is taught.

Literacy centers are not traditional. In my experience, I had to really work to feel comfortable including them in my class—and this has made me exhausted on certain days. But, you know what my students ask on the way out the door? "When are we going to do that again?" They're excited by the opportunity to do something different, and I'm astonished to learn that they are capable of so much more than I may have once expected.

Whenever I talk about rigor in the classroom, I have to think back on my own education. When did I really try? The obvious answer: when the work was interesting or relevant. If kids see relevance, they will engage, but that doesn't mean they will master the skills the first, second, or even twentieth time (look at what test scores show us about comprehension over time). Keep in mind, the number one factor for success with literacy centers is *teacher expectation*. If you communicate (verbally or otherwise) that the centers are too difficult, the terms are too advanced, the students can't behave, etc., well, everything you expect will come true.

Learning is a process, and sometimes, helping kids to "get it" has more to do with *coaching* than *teaching*. You have to reflect on the bigger pictures. Were the students engaged? Did they sense the spirit of the format? Are you more aware of your students' specific strengths and weaknesses now? If you want to increase the opportunities for success with literacy centers, then make sure you have addressed the unique needs of your students: all levels of text, interesting themes, and a variety of activities that address learning style and multiple intelligences.

As with anything related to student learning, expectation is everything. I cannot stress to you how easily a great lesson can be sabotaged by a teacher who doesn't believe her students can do the work. Behavior, ability, attention—they are all challenges to literacy centers. But, if you see those challenges as insurmountable barriers, then it's nearly impossible to prove you wrong.

## The Next Step

Now that you've considered why you should use literacy centers, you are ready to focus not only on the skills your students must practice, but the strategies they must apply to master those skills. Chapters Two and Three provide the skill and strategy information you need to create and maintain effective literacy centers.

# Chapter Two
# Strategies for Creating Centers around the "Big Ten" Areas of Reading

## What Are the "Big Ten" Areas of Reading?

To make literacy centers as effective and meaningful as possible, you have to narrow the scope to the most needed skills. I call these the "Big Ten": main idea, cause and effect, compare and contrast, vocabulary in context, sequence of events, literary devices, fact and opinion, reference and research, author's purpose, and summarizing. These skills appear again and again in many state reading standards and on assessment tests, and they're also the skills middle-school students must master to become successful readers. The forty literacy centers in Chapter Four are built around the Big Ten (four centers for each of the ten skills), providing the basic *structure* for the literacy-center program. The *substance* comes from the strategies students will apply to practice and eventually master these skills.

## Combining the Strategies with the Literature

Middle-school-aged kids like analogies to help them make sense of their world, and I tell students that working with text is like meeting a new friend. When you first meet a person, you're **activating background or prior knowledge**: "Have I met this person before? What have I heard about this person? What impression do I get from this person's conversation, actions, or dress?" The first step in a meaningful literary experience is the "first impression" of the material. This first impression might require students to brainstorm or talk about a certain topic without stopping for one minute.

Continuing with the "new friend" comparison, using literacy **strategies** is analogous to the "getting-to-know-you" phase of a friendship. These strategies aid in comprehension before, during, and after we read. Just as we use common phrases to get to know our friends—"How are you? What's up? What are you doing?"—we can use reading and writing strategies as "conversation starters." Within those strategies are graphic organizers, or tools to help us assemble thoughts and ideas. These strategies and tools point us in the right direction and give us a framework for understanding what we read, almost the same way those first questions for a new friend help us begin to discuss issues that are personal and require more thought and consideration.

While it is important to meet and get to know your friend, the real test of friendship is the **application.** Middle-school kids like the phrase "got your back," and they'll tell you that a real friend is someone who shows he or she is looking out for you. That's the proof for them—the confirmation that someone is going to be there when you need them. However, until you've reached that step in your relationship—helped a friend with a confusing issue, stood up for him or her when someone had something bad to say, or kept a secret even though you didn't have to—that person is just an acquaintance you may or may not really value. In each of the centers, it's important for your students to recognize that the work they do, or application, is the proof that a concept is being mastered—

verification that a valuable connection has been made. Centers are the places where strategies ("getting to know you") and application ("now I understand you") converge.

For each of the centers provided, there is a "Taking It to the Next Level" component. Reading instruction requires a "next step," and struggling readers must learn how to take reading strategies to the next level by applying those strategies in a concrete format. The following two cross-indexes list strategies that can be used in the centers to enable your students to connect and form friendships with literature. Ten well-known and beloved strategies are split into two groups: **reading only** and **both reading and writing**. Each strategy includes an explanation and application ideas, as well as a list of centers where that strategy is best integrated.

## Cross-Index of Centers and Strategies: Reading Only

| Strategy | Explanation and Application Ideas | Centers |
|---|---|---|
| **Acronym Charts** | • Mnemonic devices used to help students remember lists, terms, etc. For instance, when they remember the eight parts of speech, they remember "Never Put Very Pretty Candles Around Any Infants"—Nouns, Pronouns, Verbs, Prepositions, Conjunctions, Adjectives, Adverbs, and Interjections. As students read a story, they record examples of each part of speech to show they can identify and contrast their use.<br>• Try to create words that are catchy and easy for kids to remember.<br>• This strategy works well with the story paper strategy. | • Skill Set VII: Fact and Opinion, Center 4: Analyzing Magazine Articles for Facts<br>• Skill Set VIII: Author's Purpose, Center 3: Persuasion<br>• Skill Set VIII: Author's Purpose, Center 4: Autobiographies<br>• Bonus Pre-Test Skill Set: Standardized Testing Must-Have Skills, Center 2: Inference |
| **RAFT** | • RAFT is an acronym for **R**ole, **A**udience, **F**ormat, **T**opic plus strong verb (Santa, 1988).<br>• Teachers choose a **role** for the students to assume, anything from another character to an inanimate object. The intended **audience** (who will be reading the writing) can vary as well. A **format** (advice column, journal entry, thank-you note, obituary, etc.) should be chosen to reflect a targeted skill. Decide on the structure of the writing by adding a strong verb (persuade, explain, sequence, compare and contrast, describe, etc.) to the **topic** (who or what the writing is about).<br>• Teachers and students can develop any number of possible RAFTs based on the same text because they can be adjusted for skill level and rigor.<br>• If you're not familiar with RAFT, I encourage you to seek CRISS (Creating Independence through Student-owned Strategies) training immediately! | • Skill Set V: Sequence of Events, Center 2: Sequence of Events in a Work of Fiction<br>• Skill Set VIII: Author's Purpose, Center 4: Autobiographies |

| | | |
|---|---|---|
| **Story Maps, Plot Lines, and Free-Form Mapping** | • Story maps and plot lines are used for structuring narrative text. Story maps require students to identify characters, settings, conflicts, and solutions, while plot lines provide students with a concrete framework for identifying the elements of plot (exposition, rising actions, climax, and resolution).<br>• Free-form mapping is a way of brainstorming, but it requires all ideas to be connected to the center or one another. This works with both fiction and nonfiction. You could direct your students to create a free-form map showing the main idea, conflicts, or character representations. Maps can be represented with words, phrases, quotations from the text, and illustrations. | • Skill Set V: Sequence of Events, Center 2: Sequence of Events in a Work of Fiction |
| **Vocabulary Maps** | • This is an effective strategy for learning new words and can be adapted to fit the needs of your students.<br>• In the middle of the map, place the central word or concept. At the top, write the denotation or literal translation of the word or concept. On the right-hand side, think of three "is" relationships: synonyms, examples, associations, or properties of the word. On the left-hand side, think of non-examples, what the word "is not": antonyms, opposite meanings, or non-descriptions. The bottom of the map can be a scene *showing* the word's meaning (I usually ask for five details in the drawing) that can be captioned with a sentence using the word correctly. | • Skill Set I: Main Ideas, Center 1: Topic Sentences<br>• Skill Set III: Compare and Contrast, Center 1: Comparing and Contrasting Personality Traits<br>• Skill Set III: Compare and Contrast, Center 4: Finding Contrasts<br>• Skill Set VI: Literature Terms, Center 3: Characterization<br>• Skill Set VII: Fact and Opinion, Center 1: Introduction to Bias<br>• Skill Set VII: Fact and Opinion, Center 2: Validity and Accuracy<br>• Skill Set VIII: Author's Purpose, Center 1: Tone Words<br>• Bonus Pre-Test Skill Set: Standardized Testing Must-Have Skills, Center 3: Test Words<br>• Bonus Pre-Test Skill Set: Standardized Testing Must-Have Skills, Center 4: Elaborations |

## Cross-Index of Centers and Strategies: Both Reading and Writing

<table>
<tr><th>Strategy</th><th>Explanation and Application Ideas</th><th>Centers</th></tr>
<tr><td>ABC Brainstorming</td><td><ul><li>Find examples, descriptions, or related words for each letter of the alphabet.<ul><li>Fiction<ul><li>words and phrases related to a specific character, friendship, or group (adjectives, a familiar phrase, names of friends and acquaintances, favorite places, action verbs, and so on)</li><li>words and phrases related to a concept, theme, or abstract noun from the story (divorce, justice, grief, love, etc.)</li></ul></li><li>Non-fiction<ul><li>words and phrases related to a period in history (WWII, Romans, Medieval Times, etc.)</li><li>geographic location (Brazil, Germany, Ethiopia, etc.)</li><li>almost any nonfiction topic (current event, drama, music, science, art, business, etc.)</li></ul></li></ul></li></ul></td><td><ul><li>Bonus Pre-Test Skill Set: Standardized Testing Must-Have Skills, Center 1: Brainstorming</li></ul></td></tr>
<tr><td>Framed Sentences</td><td>Framed sentences are fill-in-the-blank sentences that require students to use information they have read to draw conclusions, compare ideas, and make observations.</td><td><ul><li>Skill Set I: Main Ideas, Center 4: Predictions</li><li>Skill Set II: Cause and Effect, Center 3: Cause and Effect in Short Stories</li><li>Skill Set II: Cause and Effect, Center 4: Cause and Effect in Nursery Rhymes and Song Lyrics</li><li>Skill Set III: Compare and Contrast, Center 2: Comparing and Contrasting Headlines</li><li>Skill Set III: Compare and Contrast, Center 3: Focus on Comparisons</li><li>Skill Set III: Compare and Contrast, Center 4: Finding Contrasts</li><li>Skill Set VI: Literature Terms, Center 3: Characterization</li><li>Skill Set IX: Reference and Research, Center 2: Using a Variety of Reference Materials</li></ul></td></tr>
<tr><td>Bio Poem</td><td>Line 1: Your character's first name<br>Line 2: Four words that describe your character<br>Line 3: Brother or sister of...<br>Line 4: Lover of...(three ideas or people)<br>Line 5: Who feels...(three ideas)<br>Line 6: Who needs...(three ideas)<br>Line 7: Who gives...(three ideas)<br>Line 8: Who fears...(three ideas)<br>Line 9: Who would like to see...<br>Line 10: Resident of...<br>Line 11: His or her last name</td><td><ul><li>Skill Set VIII: Author's Purpose, Center 4: Autobiographies</li></ul></td></tr>
</table>

| | | |
|---|---|---|
| **Foldables** | Dinah Zike's "Foldables," or manipulatives, are a fabulous tool for helping students collect and organize information. I use the "Tri-fold," "Three-tab," "Accordion Book," "Bound Book," and "Vocabulary Book" formats most often. | • Skill Set II: Cause and Effect, Center 1: Cause and Effect in Encyclopedia Articles<br>• Skill Set II: Cause and Effect, Center 4: Cause and Effect in Nursery Rhymes and Song Lyrics<br>• Skill Set III: Compare and Contrast, Center 3: Focus on Comparisons<br>• Skill Set IV: Vocabulary, Center 2: Homonyms, Homographs, and Homophones<br>• Skill Set V: Sequence of Events, Center 1: Chronological Order and Order of Importance<br>• Skill Set VI: Literature Terms, Center 1: Literary Devices in Headlines<br>• Skill Set VI: Literature Terms, Center 3: Characterization<br>• Skill Set IX: Reference and Research, Center 1: Graphs<br>• Bonus Pre-Test Skill Set: Standardized Testing Must-Have Skills, Center 3: Test Words |
| **Story Paper** | • Story paper has a multitude of applications for middle-school teachers of all subjects and can be found in most educational supply stores.<br>• The paper has open space at the top for drawing and is primary-lined at the bottom; comes in two sizes: 12" x 9" and 18" x 12".<br>• Struggling readers lack the ability to break down a difficult concept. If they are able to locate an example of imagery, figurative language, or symbolism, they seem to grasp meaning better when they have an opportunity to draw.<br>• Frame the directions with an air of choice: "Find your favorite example of imagery from the story and draw a picture with at least five details that shows how important the imagery is to the story," or "Find the a line or group of lines from the story that best shows the mood of the story."<br>• Story paper works well with other reading and writing strategies: graphic organizers, RAFT, and vocabulary maps. | • Skill Set I: Main Ideas, Center 2: Details<br>• Skill Set III: Compare and Contrast, Center 1: Comparing and Contrasting Personality Traits<br>• Skill Set VI: Literature Terms, Center 2: Types of Conflict<br>• Skill Set VI: Literature Terms, Center 4: Imagery<br>• Skill Set VII: Fact and Opinion, Center 1: Introduction to Bias<br>• Skill Set VII: Fact and Opinion, Center 4: Analyzing Magazine Articles for Facts<br>• Skill Set VIII: Author's Purpose, Center 1: Tone Words<br>• Skill Set VIII: Author's Purpose, Center 3: Persuasion |
| **3-2-1 Strategy** | • This is another strategy that can be adapted to fit varying levels and abilities.<br>• Some teachers use this as a homework strategy to help students comprehend what they have read.<br>• For younger adolescents, the requirements can be simple: write down **3 things you did not know**, **2 interesting facts or details about the topic**, and **1 question you still have**.<br>• If you scaffold the strategy to help students increase comprehension, you might want to make the lesson a bit more challenging: **3 differences between two concepts, beliefs, or ideas**, **2 effects of a cause**, and **1 question**; or **3 ways something in the text was achieved**, **2 characteristics of a topic**, and **1 question**.<br>• When using 3-2-1 specifically with fiction, students can provide: **3 ways something changed**, **2 character descriptions**, and **1 way a problem was solved**. | • Skill Set II: Cause and Effect, Center 2: Cause and Effect in Newspaper Articles<br>• Skill Set V: Sequence of Events, Center 4: Using Magazines and Newspapers |

# Chapter Three
# Organizing, Managing, and Assessing the Centers: Frequently Asked Questions

## Organization

### Why literacy centers?

**Literacy centers can easily be built around your state's reading standards criteria.** The "Big Ten" skills I have used to create the forty centers in Chapter Four are, from my experience, the most commonly tested skills, but they are also the most needed skills. Some will argue that sounds too much like we are teaching the test, but using the standards as guidelines helps track areas you may not have previously covered as well. The goals of your literacy centers should correlate with your state's reading standards.

Along those same lines, we should be teaching kids about the standards and what they are required to know. During my planning period some months ago, I noticed that my neighbor, a science teacher named Cindy Jannazo, had one of the state's science standards projected on to a screen, and she asked a student to read the benchmark: "The eighth-grade student knows that the average kinetic energy of the atoms or molecules of different objects varies with their temperature." Cindy turned it into a reading lesson by asking a clarifying question: "What is it you should know after we learn this skill?"

Why had I not thought of this before? Cindy was setting the stage for the content she was about to teach. Before she took students through an experiment or guided them through complicated text, she wanted them to be thinking about what they should eventually understand. She was teaching them to take control of their own learning.

Include the standards (maybe a more student-friendly version) in the literacy centers goals and, when you are moving around the room, ask probing questions to determine the students' understanding of those objectives. It may seem like an unnecessary step, and honestly, I wasn't even sure if the kids noticed. But, one day I overheard a student say to another, "I don't think I know how to read informational text very well," and I had to smile.

### How many students should be in a center?

**Three to five students.** The April 2006 issue of the *Journal of Personality and Social Psychology* suggests that groups of three people are able to solve difficult problems better than pairs or individuals working alone. Many teachers are concerned with behavior and noise level in groups, but there is a time and a place for structured discussions. Centers still require order and regulation, but learning is never silent.

In my experience, even numbers do not work nearly as well as odd in middle-school settings because kids are more likely to have a one-on-one discussion in an even-numbered setting. In groups of three or five, there's always the "odd man" who can't quite hear the mumblings of personal conversation and messes up the flow of whispered gossip between friends—bad for teenage scandal and chit-chat, good for teachers who know what conversations should be taking place in a literacy center. Try not to create centers where more than five students are working together, however. Once you group six or more students together, you are compromising the benefits of the small-group setting. It's not realistic to expect a larger group to stay on task or interact effectively.

## How do I group students?

**Randomly seems to work best.** I number each center for organizational purposes and assign students to groups randomly. Try standing at the door when students enter the room, and hand each a slip of paper that coincides with the center numbers—each student takes one and reports to his or her desk. This eliminates unnecessary movement after class has started, and no one feels punished. If you know there are students who cannot work together effectively, make sure they do not get the same number.

## How should I lay out the room?

**Create intimate spaces.** Literacy centers are based on the idea that the whole class has to be broken down into smaller, manageable groups. Sometimes these groups work collaboratively, but for the most part, the small size has more to do with creating intimacy and closeness with the literature. The small-group setting encourages positive interaction, interdependence, social-skills training, and group processing.

Visualize how you can structure your classroom to promote positive interactions. Dr. Judith A. Langer, former director of the National Research Center on English Learning & Achievement (CELA), reported in *Beating the Odds: Teaching Middle and High School Students to Read and Write Well* (CELA, 2000), "In higher performing schools, students work in communicative groups, and teachers help students participate in thoughtful dialogue."

If groups are too close together, the integrity of the small settings will be breached; if groups are too far apart or isolated, you won't be able to adequately supervise and manage, and your students are more likely to get off topic when they sense you're not paying attention.

Provide spaces between the desks so that you can easily travel from one group to the next. Try carrying a small stool. Kids really focus when you pull up a chair to ask for updates and encourage progress. Make sure that book bags, purses, and other personal belongings are either set along an unused wall or tucked under desks. I cannot tell you how many times I have tripped over backpack straps and handbags as I was moving to speak with a group of students.

Modern desk construction is not always conducive to creating groups, but you want to turn the desks inward so students are facing each other. If you have tables, even better.

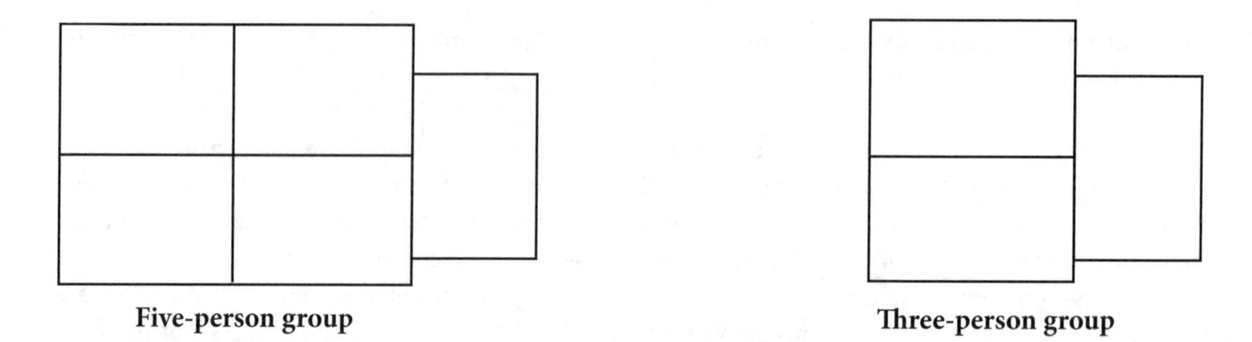

Five-person group

Three-person group

### What are the most common materials I need for the centers?

**Manila envelopes, manila paper, colored pencils, glue sticks, scissors, and rulers.** Manila envelopes are excellent for keeping instructions, materials, and student examples in one place. List all of the contents of the envelope on the outside of it, so students can quickly take inventory before they leave and get the center ready for the next class. All of the materials students need should be at the center when class begins so that they do not have to leave their seats to retrieve materials. At the end of the day, you can quickly collect the envelopes for easy storage.

Another good idea is to keep loaded caddies or plastic storage boxes ready for centers. Again, list all of the items included on the outside of the box. Laminate the instructions so you can use them for another school year.

## Management

### How often should students work in centers?

- **Option one: Use literacy centers as a culminating activity over the course of several days—once a grading period or after several skills and strategies have been taught.** Each center can have a set time limit, and students can rotate every twenty, twenty-five, or thirty minutes. Keep in mind that struggling readers may not be successful with activities that require an extended amount of attention, so design centers that require only one or two steps to completion. Try to be mindful of your students and their capabilities. Depending on the motivation and ability of your students, you could require them to complete the unfinished tasks as homework. I do not recommend sending literacy-center work home with struggling readers. They need your guidance, and they will pay more attention to detail and quality under your watchful eye. If it is not possible for your students to get to every center, you may want to provide a checklist and indicate the centers that must be completed.
- **Option two: Complete literacy centers over time—once a week or once every other week, with your goal being for students to complete each center over the course of an entire grading period.** Consider designing literacy centers that last an entire period, but break up the activity into smaller, manageable parts. If you are willing to circulate and keep the students on task, it is reasonable to expect students to complete two-, three-, and even four-step activities. Literacy-center work should be completed by the end of the period, so you may want to have other assignments, puzzles, or independent reading available if the students finish before the class ends. Provide a checklist of literacy centers, and have the students keep track of the date and which centers they have completed.
- **Option three: Make literacy centers a regular part of your curriculum done every day.** I recommend this for block-scheduled classes. The time limit and rotation should be routine, and work should be turned in every day. You may still want the students to keep track of which centers they have completed, but the goal is to move them through a variety of literacy center experiences.

## How many centers should I manage at a time?

**Consider class size, how well your students cooperate, and the number of assignments you can handle grading each week.**

- **Class size.** Groups should be made up of three to five students; however, you may need to finagle the number of students in each group to fit into a manageable number of centers.
- **Cooperation.** If your students work well in groups, plan to assign five people to one center. However, if behavior is an issue, create smaller groups and more centers.
- **Assignments.** A good way to prevent managing an overwhelming number of different centers and grading too many assignments is to simply repeat a center. For instance, if you teach eighteen challenging students, divide the class into six groups of three and repeat three of the centers. That way, you only have to grade or assess three different assignments, which might be a more realistic task for you.

## How long should students work at each center?

**Accommodate the time needs to the varying abilities of your students, and remember to be flexible.** The goal is not to get your students through every activity. The goal is to make each activity a meaningful learning experience. Try to make sure all of the centers are filled with activities that share an equitable expectation for completing the work. Would you expect students to complete each of the tasks in twenty minutes or in one class period?

## How can I prevent bad behavior in the centers?

- **Understand the adolescent.** Adolescents are loud, they don't want to sit still, and many do not know how to behave. In fact, a lot of adolescents have spent the better part of their lives figuring out ways to dodge good instruction. Statistics show that struggling readers come from lower socio-economic groups, and many of those kids do not have adults in their lives who have made reading a priority. They don't see the value in your instruction, and they may not be getting any support at home. That does not mean it's time to give up. Move forward and attempt out-of-the-box ideas to reach your students.
- **Don't take it personally.** What good behavior comes down to is cooperation, and most teachers who report misbehavior are really struggling with a lack of cooperation. This lack of cooperation is often interpreted as a personal strike—a deliberate action against the teacher. You have to remember that, when working with any group of adolescents, there's bound to be sarcasm, mischief, and often, disrespect. The very hardened will try to make you believe they are only behaving badly because you're not giving them any other option. That's manipulation, and a good teacher will recognize it immediately. If you are tenacious and willing to create an atmosphere that is conducive to learning, there is no reason centers cannot work in your classroom.
- **Be prepared.** Students who are engaged in learning are less apt to misbehave, so make sure centers are ready to go when students enter the room.
- **Put a classroom-management plan in place from day one.** If you are dealing with challenging kids, there are many resources that address all levels of misbehaviors—everything from level systems to a reward program. I suggest *Classroom Management for Middle and High School Teachers* by Edmund T. Emmer, Carolyn M. Everston, and Murray E. Worsham (Allyn & Bacon, 2005) and *Fred Jones Tools for Teaching* (Fredric H. Jones & Associates, 2000) by Fredric H. Jones. Stay connected to teachers who share the same vision as you. The last thing you want is to feel defeated by your own colleagues. Do your research and make a commitment to follow through.

- **Be firm but fair.** Firm is in the tone you use, the posture you take, and the eye contact you make. Your students should know by the tone of your voice (not voice level) what you are thinking. Do what you say you're going to do, and model the behaviors you expect from your students. Do not make empty threats at a high volume—you would not tolerate that from your students; why would they tolerate it from you?
- **Pay attention to proximity.** If you are monitoring your students, you are moving throughout the class, stopping to ask questions, skimming their work to give feedback, or just letting them know you are there. Sometimes it's as simple as standing next to someone who is misbehaving.
- **Understand that behavior management is as nonverbal as it is verbal.** My students say I have "The Eye." I think I was born with it. I know Mrs. Willifred, my eighth-grade English teacher, had the same "Eye." If she caught your gaze while you were talking or laughing during class, she could melt you with a death-ray-like stare. Yes, there's a certain humor attached to my nonverbal communication, but I'm serious: "I see what you're doing, and I'm hoping you'll fix it before I have to intervene." Though I'm far from calm and quiet, I like to think I exude an assertive, in-control energy. Running around yipping orders is counterproductive. Yelling simply becomes white noise to a middle schooler.
- **Low-profile interventions go a long way.** Tough kids put up thick walls. Often, they are accustomed to yelling and other combative behavior from authority figures. Catch them off guard. In the lunchroom, stop by the table of the kid who is *really* hard to handle. Speak low and with a positive voice: "Look, I know you were working hard today to hold still. It's a huge improvement, and I hope you'll keep working at it." If you have to redirect negative behavior, lean over and speak softly: "I want you to keep your voice down." Remember, bad behavior is often attention seeking, so take away the audience.
- **Know the difference between *assertive* and *mean*.** While I do think middle schoolers tend to fall back on "The teacher doesn't like me" when they aren't getting their way, I also think it's true that many teachers are not always aware of how mean-spirited their interactions are perceived. It's a struggle because the converse of that idea is the teacher who cares more about being a friend than an educator—which also doesn't work. I never said this was easy, but it's sure worth an internal talk: "Am I being callous or unkind?"
- **Praise good behavior and always say something positive.** You would be surprised how far this will take you. I taught a very troubled young man almost ten years ago. He was new to the school, and he openly carried a huge chip on his shoulder. One day, I took him aside and told him I appreciated his leadership but asked if he could help me get another (far less disruptive) boy to stay on task. I think he knew my game, but he smiled and gave me his word. We still had our run-ins, but for the most part, I could always appeal to his need for a "thank you" or "good job."
- **Set routines and be consistent.** This one is tough. Post class work and homework in the same place. Always begin class with a bell-ringer or similar attention-grabber. Make sure students know where passes, supplies, and turn-in boxes are located. Encourage them to use the bathroom and sharpen pencils before class. Students, especially low-performing ones, need structure, and sometimes school is the only part of the day that is even remotely predictable. You'll appreciate the time and energy that routines will save you as well.

## How should I address bad behavior in the centers if it does arise?

**Stay calm and do not allow the behavior to take control.** Before the centers begin, talk yourself through the worst-case scenarios. I often compare this with an athlete who visualizes his or her motions prior to the big game. If there is a student who has posed a challenge in the past, have a desk ready to separate him or her from the group. You may want to have an alternative assignment ready—anything to eliminate confrontation and distraction. Simply put, remove the disruption and try not to break stride.

Occasionally group work leads to a "group disagreement." Do not allow your students to engage in disrespectful behavior, and make sure they understand that you are a facilitator, not a mediator. Ignore comments and questions that require you to take sides, and redirect students to the tasks if you sense there is deviation from the assignments.

## Besides activity directions, what are some guidelines I'll need to explain to students?

- **What an acceptable noise level is.** A small metal bell works very well for noise control! If students hear the bell, they know to stop, look, and listen—I might be inviting them to look at a classmate's good work, making an announcement that pertains to everyone, or asking them to watch their noise level. You could have a "three strikes" rule; if you ring the bell three times to address noise level, the class returns to seat work.
- **How to ask a question.** To avoid students repeatedly getting out of their seats to ask you questions, try the stoplight flip ring. Simply laminate and assemble red, yellow, and green circles on metal book rings (up to 2" in diameter; usually 50 in a box), and make enough so that each center includes a complete set. While at the centers, groups will display the color on their desks that represents their level of need to the teacher. Green signals "We understand the directions, and we don't need help at this time." Yellow means "Someone has a question, but it's not an emergency." Red indicates "Stop! One or all of us is confused and we need help!" I've seen variations of the stoplight using hand shapes, so you can be creative with this management technique. Obviously, you would need to go over how to use the stoplight tool effectively by defining what really constitutes a red, etc.
- **Where to put completed work.** Putting completed work in a manila envelope with the center number and class period on the outside works great. Because middle-school teachers may have multiple classes, it's important to keep the work separated. Make sure students write their name on their work, especially if you rotate groups during the class period. Envelopes of completed work can be left at each center for you to collect or handed to you at the end of the period.
- **How to rotate.** Review the rotation pattern (center one goes to center two, center two to center three, . . .) before you allow students to move. Class timers can function as both the time keeper and the signal to clean up and prepare to leave or move to the next center. You will need a good, loud kitchen timer. It's easy to get wrapped up in the activities and lose track of time. The last thing you need is to finish off a successful literacy center day with chaos.
- **What to do when finished.** There's a lot of value in putting an active reading program in place. My students are pretty good about reading their personal novels if they are finished with their work, and I expect them each to have a book in their backpacks. If you just don't feel your students have that kind of discipline, you may want to consider "over-planning" the centers. This means you will embed tasks, worksheets, or puzzles into the centers that you have no intention of grading or assessing. Puzzlemaker.com is a great source for generating puzzles to fit the individual needs of a center, such as a word-find or crossword puzzle that includes related vocabulary words.

## How do I prevent total chaos during movement from one center to another?

**Be willing to move.** For literacy centers to work smoothly, you have to be willing to move. Students will have questions, require clarification, and most likely, need redirection. If your students are working and attentive to the task at hand, make sure you stop to give positive feedback. It is important for you to be as close to the largest number of students for the greatest amount of time, so put yourself in proximity to students who are showing signs of getting off task.

On the other hand, student movement should be limited. Once the students are in their centers, they should be expected to stay there. For students who are in the habit of popping out of their seats, try to keep them seated with nonverbal cues: eye contact, low-level gestures, standing behind their desk. Put your hand on his or her shoulder and ask questions related to the task. Often times, students who exhibit restless behaviors lack self-regulation. The occasional pat on the back or casual reminder to focus will make a difference.

# Interaction, Participation, and Assessment

## What are the barriers to making centers work?

- **You have preconceived notions.** Struggling readers do not always know they need help, so it seems almost silly to them to think of their teachers as benefactors. For the educator who has a predetermined idea of the teaching experience, it can be a real disillusionment to learn that their words are falling on deaf ears. It's tough to be realistic and determined at the same time, and the gap between what was expected and the reality of the classroom can produce a bitterness and indignation. Try to approach literacy centers with an open mind, but be aware that they won't immediately run perfectly.
- **You are unprepared for the kinds of behaviors that are present in the modern-day classroom.** Bullying, drugs, alcohol, and vandalism are all issues in middle school. With low-level kids especially, you have to understand that their world may be very different from your own. Educate yourself and learn as much as you can about behavior management. There are clear benefits to knowing and understanding your students, so take advantage of literature and workshops.
- **You are easily frustrated with your students' attention, attitude, and ability.** Even the most well-meaning, motivated teacher is going to run into indifference. But, if you step back and look at how a lack of attention negatively influences attitude, it's not difficult to see how a negative attitude will almost certainly affect ability. There's no limit to what I have tried to defeat this beast of an enemy: reasoning, raging, telling jokes, mocking, singing songs, pleading, disregarding, and even weeping. I could tell you to focus on the kids who really want your help, but I think we all know that it's nearly impossible to ignore a kid who just doesn't care. The bottom line—try it all, do it all, and in the end, be okay with the outcome.
- **You lack parental support.** Low-performing students are not always supported at home, for whatever reason, and teachers can feel like they are all alone. Many parents of struggling adolescent readers may not have felt success in their own educational experiences and consider learning a separate issue from being a supportive parent. This doesn't mean that parents don't care about their children. It just means that the way they care doesn't necessarily center around the development of learning goals. While frustrating and often infuriating, it's reality. Though it isn't always easy, we need to try to build good communication and relationships with parents—invite them to open house and orientations, keep them informed, and ask them for support regarding behavior and discipline. Call them to tell them the good things before you have to call and tell them about the bad.
- **You are reluctant or overeager to take an authoritative role.** No matter what your teaching style, it is a real battle to find that "happy place" where you are not blowing blood vessels or being blown off by adolescents who see you more as a pushover than an authority figure. Recently, I read through a great resource, *Reluctant Disciplinarian: Advice on Classroom Management From a Softy Who Became (Eventually) a Successful Teacher* (Cottonwood Press, 1999) by Gary Rubinstein. He went from a disastrous first few years of teaching math in an inner-city middle school to being voted Teacher of the Year. Rubinstein draws a lot of common-sense conclusions—how incremental, inconsistent discipline in an out-of-control classroom is like trying to slay a dragon with a fly swatter. A good teacher will make the effort to improve. To me, that's the key. Admit to yourself it's an issue and commit to finding resolution.

## How can I ensure productive discussions in the centers?

**Provide opportunities for students to process information and discuss their thoughts.** The success of literacy centers (or any effort to improve literacy, for that matter) is going to depend on how well you engage all of your students in meaningful, one-to-one discussions. It's not just the concrete, student-created products that should be assessed in a literacy center; it's also the verbal interaction between teacher and student and between student and student. Teachers should provide opportunities for students to process information, consider and analyze their peers' responses, and make judgments based on content, collaboration, and critical thinking.

For whatever reason—fear of embarrassing a child, a lack of confidence in their ability to respond, or an overall disinterest in pushing the issue—teachers do not teach the art of discussion. While the conversational "flow" might be better served by kids who are quick to answer, the real challenges are to pose a thought-provoking question to a student who has always struggled with comprehension, allow time for that student to process and respond, and *not* crush an answer that seems wrong or erroneous. I battled with this issue for a long time. At first I made a conscious effort to call on everyone, but I still didn't know what to do about the kids who struggled. I would pose a question, wait for the student to finally give an answer, and immediately begin correcting the shortcomings. Obviously, the result would be a student who would shut down or, worse, one who had learned to simply guess some irrelevant answer so that the teacher would be the one processing and relating the material, while the student said and learned nothing.

Once I figured out the "scam," I began to read and research methods of discussion that were more effective. The more profitable tactic for literacy-center interaction is to approach a group and identify a need for clarification or procedure by asking a question along those lines. The students are then cued to begin thinking independently and collaboratively to solve the problem using discussion tools and strategies. The teacher's role is to "coach" students through the process, constantly challenging them to look at the content and their responses from a variety of perspectives and alternative methods.

## How can I help less outgoing students feel more comfortable speaking in a literacy center?

- **Explain the need for processing.** In math, students are constantly reminded to show their work. Think of literacy centers as extended math problems. The final product is not always the most important part; it's the steps to get to that final product that make the biggest difference. My belief is that it is important to speak frankly and truthfully about this process: "If you do not know how to think about your thinking, you are not increasing your ability to comprehend."
- **Do not allow students to dodge questions.** One of the greatest successes I've felt with literacy centers is the ability to hold a student accountable for his or her answer and the pure joy a student shows when he or she figures out a viable, thoughtful solution to a question. Over and again, my students will try to wiggle out of the interaction. Many will say, "I don't know" (quite indignantly, I might add). At times, this can resemble a power play, but try to stay focused and calm. Say, "I know it feels like you don't know, but I am going to stand here and give you some time to figure out how you want to respond."
- **Use Socratic discussion starters.** Initially, you, as the facilitator, will make an arguable statement on a topic. After you have made the statement, you should not interfere with the conversation again. The group will then discuss this topic thoroughly. Each comment must begin with one of the stems, every person is allowed to speak once, and the topic does not change until everyone at the center has added to the conversation. This teaches students to use the appropriate words to reach an understanding and express their thoughts. If you would like to assess the discussion, you

can assign five points for stems 1, 2, and 3; ten points for stem 4; and one point for stem 5 (stem 5 can only be used once a day).

1. I agree and I'd like to add . . .
2. I disagree because . . .
3. I like what you said, but . . .
4. I have a question about . . .
5. I'd like to hear from . . .

- **Vary the types of questions you ask.** Carefully consider the difficulty of the question. You may want to begin the interaction with simple, straightforward questions that lay a foundation for success and then build up to the more complex questions. Adolescents will cooperate more if they sense they have achieved some success.

  *Low-level questions* are based on recall and knowledge, while *high-level questions* require evaluation and extended thinking. A *convergent question* involves a single right answer, making it risky to respond and requiring more time to organize a reply; however, a *divergent question* implies that there are a number of possible answers, making it safer to venture an opinion and allowing for a natural, spontaneous response.

  The structure of a question refers to whether it provides a framework or guidelines for preparing an answer. An *unstructured question* is wide open and forces a student to organize a good answer on their own (not easy). In contrast, a *structured question* leads the student to think about specific aspects of the information. This helps students narrow their focus and arrive at an answer more quickly.

- **Provide a fair amount of "wait time" for responses.** A lot of teachers will answer the question themselves, go on to ask other questions, or make further points rather than allow an adequate amount of time for students to respond. Good questions require lengthier wait times. We are programmed to believe that silence is an indication of failure, but if we don't allow for adequate time to think, kids tend to become incapable of discussing a topic effectively. The repeated use of short wait times tends to solidify little or no responses. We are creating reinforcement for not answering, and eventually a struggling reader will stop trying.

- **Teach the "healthy response."** Give your students some tools for thinking that might help eliminate those awkward silent moments. Talk about how "Huh?" and "What?" don't really ask for clarification and how we all want to learn how to be "smart talkers." My students will giggle at first, but believe me, they quickly realize that these strategies are good for "looking cool" while you're thinking.

  Well, . . .

  I'll need time to think about that.

  That's a very interesting question because . . .

  To be honest, I might have trouble with that.

  What do you mean by that?

  Well, that depends on what you mean . . .

  If you ask me, . . .

- **Always respond to student comments with a vision in mind.** A big reason my students weren't initially engaging in discussion was because they had not been taught how to go that step beyond simply answering a question to reasoning and responding effectively. When I circulate around my class, I am always thinking of this next step and how I can get students to take it. Just like it's important to create literacy centers that contain activities with a "next step," the verbal interactions you have with your students need to reflect a similar pattern. I want my students to feel my presence, not as a threat, but as a challenge. It's not enough to get an answer. There has to be an explanation.

### How do I make sure every student participates while in the centers?

**Address students by their names, and teach them to do the same.** Include everybody, and think of ways to force small discussions. You might want to carry a timer in your pocket to assure that you get to every group. Try to make the last question a culminating question that takes everything you've discussed with the group into consideration. A sample interaction might resemble this one, which involves students being asked to organize events from S.E. Hinton's *The Outsiders* (Dell, 1967) in chronological order.

**Teacher:** "Paula, tell me what your group has to do today."

**Paula:** "We have to organize the events in chronological order."

**Teacher:** "John, what does it mean to be in 'chronological order?'"

**John:** "That's the order they took place in time."

**Teacher:** "John, has it been easy to figure out the order of events?"

**John:** "No."

**Teacher:** "Explain why it hasn't been easy."

**John:** "Well, I guess it's because these events happened at all different times."

**Teacher:** "Nina, do you agree with John's statement?"

**Nina:** "I do."

**Teacher:** "Nina, what is it called when the author is reflecting on something that happened before?"

**Nina:** "What do you mean by that?"

**Teacher:** "The term I am looking for is a literature term that refers to a memory of something that happened before the present time in the story."

**Nina:** "Oh yeah, that's a flashback."

**Teacher:** "Excellent. As a group, can you find an example of a flashback in the story? Only raise your hand when everyone agrees on an answer."

*(Discussion, then hands go up)*

**Teacher:** "Marcus, why don't you show us where a flashback took place."

**Marcus:** "The guy is remembering when Johnny got beat up."

**Teacher:** "Great. So, Marcus, if a flashback took place as a memory, how would you organize 'Johnny getting beat up' in chronological order?"

**Marcus:** "I think it was an event that happened early."

**Teacher:** "But, Marcus, how would I know by looking at your paper that Johnny got beat up early? Is there a strategy or tool you could use to keep your information organized?"

**Marcus:** "Wait! I know this! A timeline!"

**Teacher:** "You're on a roll, Marcus, so I'm going to give you the opportunity to go big. I want you to think about plot lines—the way a plot is organized. If you're using a timeline to organize a flashback as one of the first events in chronological order, how will you know from a plot line when an event might be one of the last events to take place?"

**Marcus:** "One of the last events is going to take place in the falling action of the story!"

**Teacher:** "How do you know that?"

**Marcus:** "Falling actions are the last parts of a story. On a plot line, falling actions happen after the climax."

**Teacher:** "Great answer! But, group, can you look at your list of events from the story and find one event that took place in the falling action? Again, only raise your hands when everyone agrees."

*(Discussion, then hands go up)*

**Teacher:** "Paula, back to you. Tell me an event from the falling action."

**Paula:** "Ponyboy decides to write what happened for an assignment."

**Teacher:** "Excellent. Paula and John, I want you two to discuss everything we've just talked about for a second, but then finish this statement. You can write it down if you need to. *When I am thinking about chronological order, it's important to remember . . .*" *(Paula and John discuss, Paula raises her hand)*

**Paula:** "When I am thinking about chronological order, it's important to remember flashbacks and plot lines, and I might want to use a timeline!"

**Teacher:** "Oh my gosh! This group has done an amazing job! Class, I hope all of you can do as great a job as this group! They participated perfectly!"

A good rule to keep in mind is to make sure you broadcast the successes. Though it might seem unheard of in middle schools where students are determined to protect their privacy, I have really seen a big difference in my students' willingness to go the distance when I make a big deal about a kid who took an answer far above what I might have expected.

### How can I keep from getting frustrated if there is not immediate success?

**Recognize the gains and seek out support.** Focus on the conversation you were able to hold with the shy student who usually never says a word in a whole-class structure. Freeze the moment in your memory when the kid who always goofs around and seemingly never pays attention asks you for clarification in a sincere, genuine tone. Also, make sure you are collaborating with other colleagues who use literacy centers. Many of the same struggles you may be having could be handled more effectively with a little professional brainstorming. There are many websites designed for teachers who seek feedback—I highly recommend reading and posting questions and comments on the "Middle School Chatboard" on Teachers.net.

### What do I do if a center just stops being effective or running smoothly?

**Re-evaluate your goals often.** Literacy centers should be part of a well-rounded curriculum that involves whole-class, small-group, and individual learning experiences. Students should sense that the centers are goal-driven and have a purpose. You should feel as though progress is being made. If any of these factors are not addressed, it may be time to step back and re-evaluate. Anything less could lead to chaos.

### How can I assess the work that is being done at the centers?

**Be flexible.** The same flexibility that goes into designing literacy centers should apply to assessing the work that students produce. I truly believe this is a real opportunity to stress what is learned over the value of a letter grade. If you have worked with struggling readers, you probably have gotten the sense that grades may not be valued. In my experience, specific verbal and written feedback regarding individual abilities and efforts are far more valuable than letter grades to an adolescent who has not felt academic success. That doesn't mean they don't care about their grades, but often, they don't understand their grades. To a low-level reader, an "A" means "I am smart" and an "F" means "I am stupid." It's as simple as that.

Literacy centers require formative assessments, information gained from observations, discussion, and analysis of student work to guide teaching and learning. Try the following formative assessments to document and assess center behavior, discussion, and finished work.

- **Anecdotal records**. These are great for conferencing with students and parents because students feel successful, and they like to know you are monitoring their progress. Put together a one-inch binder for each class with one anecdotal worksheet for each student and sheets of address stickers. As you are observing and interacting with the students, write the date, name of the student, and observation on an address sticker, but keep the stickers on the sheet. Your goal is to record ten anecdotal records per student over the course of a school year. When you have time, move the stickers to the individual student's worksheet. You will notice who has and has not been observed over time, so it's a good method for alerting you to keep track of everyone. Try to begin your notation with a strong verb to describe a specific behavior related to literacy. Some suggestions:

| | | |
|---|---|---|
| Arranges | Determines | Recounts |
| Classifies | Distinguishes | Relates |
| Compares | Identifies | Responds |
| Concludes | Illustrates | Retells |
| Connects | Organizes | Selects |
| Contrasts | Provides | Summarizes |
| Decodes | Questions | Supports |
| Demonstrates | Recognizes | Uses |

- **Checklists**. I like checklists because I can visualize all of the goals I may have for a set of literacy centers and see whether my students are practicing the strategies. Moreover, I can recognize trends regarding comprehension. For example, a checklist to use with the four centers that focus on main idea (see Chapter 4) would list the following:

  _____ recognizes topic sentences

  _____ uses supporting sentences to show support for topic sentences

  _____ organizes paragraphs effectively

  _____ utilizes active reading strategies, such as selective highlighting or two-column notes to identify important information

- **Rubrics**. Rubrics have been my assessment of choice for literacy centers. Like it or not, students like to see grades. I always felt it was difficult to give a grade when the goals were subjective (as is often the case in literacy centers). However, rubrics help to designate a point value to a skill, and those points can easily be translated into letter grades. For each center, I create five areas of proficiency that should be mastered if the student were to show competency. Each of those skills or abilities could be rated on a scale of one to five. After each area is assessed, the total points (highest possible being twenty-five) are multiplied by four, and viola! No, it's not fool-proof, but it is specific, thoughtful, and definitely leads to discussions about what students have actually learned. I have included a rubric with each of the forty literacy centers.

# Chapter Four
# The Centers: Tackling the "Big Ten"

## Hitting the Hard-to-Reach Skills

It's becoming increasingly clear that teachers are being held accountable for student progress, and sadly, teachers sense that test scores are a reflection of the effort they make to improve their students' achievement. That's a lot of pressure, but logistically, it's very difficult to document what has and has not been taught—especially with reading. The skills overlap one another, and it's difficult to say what your students can and cannot accomplish with regards to comprehension.

The way I look at this, we have to approach the issue of documentation from a simplistic point of view. Narrow the scope to the most needed skills, and hammer them again and again. You will find that the most needed skills are also the most tested skills. As I mentioned earlier, I call these the "Big Ten": main idea, cause and effect, compare and contrast, vocabulary in context, sequence of events, literary devices, fact and opinion, reference and research, author's purpose, and summarizing.

I purposely give them this exaggerated, larger-than-life title because I want my lowest functioning learners to learn the terms, attach meaning to their names, and recognize when we are covering each of these skills. If a student is troubled by one or all of the Big Ten by the middle-school years, there's a sense of urgency in the effort. Covering the Big Ten is the equivalent of learning plays for a football game. This is our game, and here are our strategies for winning. My students love sports analogies, and I cannot stress enough how hard it would be to play baseball or basketball well if you didn't drill the basics.

For remedial or low-level readers, it may be beneficial to provide repetitive practice that focuses on the same skill using a variety of literary texts. In other words, throughout the calendar year (depending on when your state's tests are administered), you want to make sure your students have participated in a set of literacy centers focused around each particular Big Ten skill. If a student were to rotate through centers that dealt with the same focused skill, he would gain a more comprehensive understanding of the concepts and related ideas. This is the benefit of managing a variety of centers at the same time.

I have provided four literacy centers for each skill. The goal is to connect kids with literature and offer a variety of textual experiences. Remember to be flexible. It may be necessary to adjust the expectations and performance criteria to fit the needs of your students.

You shouldn't feel like your students are never going to get through all of this; moreover, you should be thinking how you could integrate some or all of the ideas to work in your classroom. A colleague of mine recently captured the essence of my meaning perfectly: "Think of it as a tasting party rather than an all-you-can-eat buffet." Take what works for you and use what works best for your students.

# The Centers

Each of the centers includes teacher directions, student directions, and worksheets. The targeted goals for students, preparation needed, and a list of suggested materials are included on the teacher directions, as well as any special considerations to note for that center. The student directions are divided into three sections: "Focus on the Skill" (a warm-up exercise), "Practice the Skill," and "Take It to the Next Level," all of which are included on the teacher directions as well. Students will also see a rubric on their directions sheet so that the exact requirements for each center are made clear. The worksheets follow the same format as the student directions and include "Focus on the Skill," "Practice the Skill," and "Take It to the Next Level."

# Teacher Directions: Examining Topic Sentences and Main Idea in a Paragraph

## Goals for Student

1. Analyze word relationships.
2. Determine a text's major ideas and how those ideas are supported with details.
3. Use increasingly complex reading texts and assignments to find main ideas, supporting details, and practice summarizing skills.

## Preparation

1. Your class should have enough background knowledge to recognize and use the term "topic sentence." They should begin to see that topic sentences are supported by details and elaborations.
2. Find three to five paragraphs about a person or group who does something (wins an award, goes on a journey, loses a game, etc.), both from fiction and non-fiction sources. Separate each topic sentence from each paragraph, and place them into a small envelope.
3. If you are working with an average to advanced group, you may want to separate all of the sentences in the paragraph.

## Materials

- "Examining Topic Sentences and Main Idea in a Paragraph" worksheet
- Envelope with topic sentences and supporting sentences separated
- Glue stick
- Manila drawing paper
- Pen or pencil

## Focus on the Skill

1. The students will first create a vocabulary map of the term "topic sentence" on the "Examining Topic Sentences and Main Ideas in a Paragraph" worksheet.
2. They will determine words, phrases, and concepts that are related (to go on the "is" lines), as well as words, phrases, and concepts that are the opposite or not related (the "is not" lines). Then they will create a small sketch with a caption that shows they understand the meaning of a topic sentence in the box below the map.

## Practice the Skill

1. The students must empty the contents of the envelope and reorganize the paragraphs to their original format.
2. They will use a glue stick to paste their paragraphs onto 9" x 12" manila drawing paper to show they understand which details support each topic sentence.
3. They will underline the topic sentence.
4. Then, under each paragraph, they should list each supporting detail, not complete sentences. Their lists should show they get the gist of details being used as support. For example, if the following were a supporting sentence, the detail from that sentence would be short and to the point.

| Whole Sentence | Detail from the Sentence |
|---|---|
| The lost cougar seemed hungry and exhausted. | *hungry and exhausted* |

# Teacher Directions: Examining Topic Sentences and Main Idea in a Paragraph (continued)

## Take It to the Next Level

1. Have the students choose one paragraph to analyze for main idea. The paragraph should be about a person or a group who is doing something, so they can evaluate the paragraph using a *who does what to whom or what, when, how, and why* format to summarize the information.
2. Students will use the chart on the "Examining Topic Sentences and Main Ideas in a Paragraph" worksheet.

## Special Considerations

For low-performing students, you must locate examples that vary in difficulty. A middle-school textbook will provide simple examples, while newspapers and magazine publications will provide more complicated examples. Also, keep in mind the width of the articles. Many times students will pay attention to the spatial clues when reorganizing paragraphs more than contextual clues. You may want to get your paragraphs from an Internet source or retype them on the computer so the width of each paragraph is uniform or can be adjusted to be uniform.

# Student Directions: Examining Topic Sentences and Main Idea in a Paragraph

## Focus on the Skill

1. First, create a vocabulary map of the term "topic sentence" on the "Examining Topic Sentences and Main Ideas in a Paragraph" worksheet.
2. Determine words, phrases, and concepts that are related on the "is" side, and then find words, phrases, and concepts that are the opposite or not related for the "is not" side. Next, in the box below the map, create a small sketch with a caption using the term "topic sentence" that shows you understand the meaning.

## Practice the Skill

1. Empty the contents of the envelope and reorganize the paragraphs to their original format.
2. Use a glue stick to paste the paragraphs to 9" x 12" manila drawing paper to show you understand which details support each topic sentence.
3. Underline the topic sentence.
4. Then, under each paragraph, list each supporting detail, not complete sentences. Your lists should show you get the idea of details being used as support. For example, if the following were a supporting sentence, the detail from that sentence would be short and to the point.

| Whole Sentence | Detail from the Sentence |
|---|---|
| The lost cougar seemed hungry and exhausted. | *hungry and exhausted* |

## Take It to the Next Level

1. Choose one paragraph to analyze for main idea. The paragraph should be about a person or a group who is doing something, so you can evaluate the paragraph using a *who does what to whom or what, when, how, and why* format to summarize the information.
2. You will use the chart on the "Examining Topic Sentences and Main Ideas in a Paragraph" worksheet to determine the main idea of the paragraph.

## How You Will Be Graded

| | 1 little or no evidence | 2 below average | 3 adequate evidence | 4 better than average | 5 superior evidence | TOTAL |
|---|---|---|---|---|---|---|
| Attention to neatness and presentation | | | | | | |
| Able to map the term "topic sentence" effectively | | | | | | |
| Able to organize the paragraphs to match topic sentences with supporting details | | | | | | |
| Able to identify supporting details in each paragraph | | | | | | |
| Used the chart effectively to summarize a paragraph for main idea | | | | | | |
| **Total points multiplied by four** | | | | | | |
| **Final grade** | | | | | | |

# Worksheet: Examining Topic Sentences and Main Idea in a Paragraph

## Focus on the Skill

**Vocabulary Map of Topic Sentence.** Determine words, phrases, and concepts that are related on the "is" side, and then determine words, phrases, and concepts that are the opposite or not related on the "is not" side. Next, in the box below the map, create a small sketch with a caption using the term "topic sentence" that shows you understand the meaning. The definition has been provided.

<u>**Definition**</u> - a sentence that captures the meaning of an entire paragraph. It tells what the passage is about.

IS NOT

IS NOT

IS NOT

Topic Sentence

IS

IS

IS

## Take It to the Next Level

Choose one of the paragraphs you reconstructed. Write the topic sentence for the paragraph you selected. Use the chart to collect information and summarize the main idea of that paragraph.

Topic sentence of the paragraph ______________________________

______________________________

| | |
|---|---|
| Who? (Person or group) | |
| Does what (use a strong action verb)? | |
| To whom or what? | |
| When? | |
| How? | |
| Why? | |
| Summarize all of the details into one sentence (no less than eight words) that shows you understand the main idea of the paragraph. | |

# Teacher Directions: Examining Supporting Details in "Help Wanted" and "For Sale" Ads

## Goals for Student

1. Use multiple sources to locate relevant information.
2. Record and summarize information using organizational tools.
3. Determine a text's major ideas and how those ideas are supported with details.

## Preparation

1. Your class should have a basic understanding of supporting details. They should begin to recognize that facts, examples, statistics, and elaborations are all types of details.
2. Collect several "help wanted" ads and "for sale" ads that feature cars, boats, and homes that are for sale in the newspaper. Make copies (one set for each student) and place in a small envelope.

## Materials

- "Examining Supporting Details" worksheet
- Envelope with "help wanted" and "for sale" ads from the newspaper classifieds
- Two highlighters (different colors)
- Glue stick
- Manila drawing paper
- White story paper
- Colored pencils

## Focus on the Skill

To activate prior knowledge about supporting details, students will begin by brainstorming the details of common nouns: a fireman, hospital, bird, and car. This helps them pay attention to details and see that everything is made up of smaller parts.

## Practice the Skill

1. Require the students to highlight the main idea of the ad in one color and all of the supporting details in the other.
2. They then paste the articles onto a piece of manila paper.
3. Using the "Supporting Details" chart on the "Supporting Details" worksheet, they will chart the topic and list all of the details from the ad.
4. They will then create a one-sentence summary (no less than eight words) that captures the main idea of the ad.

## Take It to the Next Level

1. Students will transfer their main idea sentence to the bottom lines of a piece of story paper.
2. In the space above the lines, they will draw a picture or diagram that reflects the sentence with all of the details from the original ad. For example, if they are working with a "home for sale" ad, the one-sentence summary may be, "Luxury home with lots of space and plenty of land available today!" The drawing (or diagram) should reflect the details of the home's amenities—attic, basement, home theatre, fire place, walk-in pantry, and built-in pool.

## Special Considerations

Try to find ads that may refer to unfamiliar terms. For instance, many boat ads will refer to "skid plates," "payload," or "hull." You may want to provide a list of definitions for the unfamiliar terms and have the students rewrite the ads using the new information in common terms without the jargon.

# Student Directions: Examining Supporting Details in "Help Wanted" and "For Sale" Ads

## Focus on the Skill

To activate prior knowledge about supporting details, begin by brainstorming the details of common nouns: a fireman, hospital, bird, and car. Make sure you include good, specific details.

## Practice the Skill

1. Read each ad.
2. Highlight the main idea of the ad in one color and all of the supporting details in the other.
3. Then, paste the articles onto a piece of manila paper.
4. Choose one of the ads.
5. Using the "Supporting Details" chart on the "Supporting Details" worksheet to chart the topic and list all of the details from the ad.
6. Then, in the last row of the chart, create a one-sentence summary (no less than eight words) that captures the main idea of the ad.

## Take It to the Next Level

1. Transfer your main idea sentence to the bottom lines of a piece of story paper.
2. In the space above the lines, draw a picture or diagram that reflects the sentence with all of the details from the original ad. Add color and make sure the picture is detailed.

## How You Will Be Graded

| | 1<br>little or no evidence | 2<br>below average | 3<br>adequate evidence | 4<br>better than average | 5<br>superior evidence | TOTAL |
|---|---|---|---|---|---|---|
| Attention to neatness and presentation | | | | | | |
| Able to brainstorm supporting details for common nouns | | | | | | |
| Able to differentiate the main idea from the supporting details | | | | | | |
| Able to use the chart to create an effective summarizing sentence that captures the tone of the ad | | | | | | |
| Re-creates the tone of the ad on story paper with details from the ad | | | | | | |
| **Total points multiplied by four** | | | | | | |
| **Final grade** | | | | | | |

# Worksheet: Examining Supporting Details in "Help Wanted" and "For Sale" Ads

## Focus on the Skill

Begin by brainstorming the details of common nouns: a fireman, hospital, bird, and car. Make sure you include good, specific details.

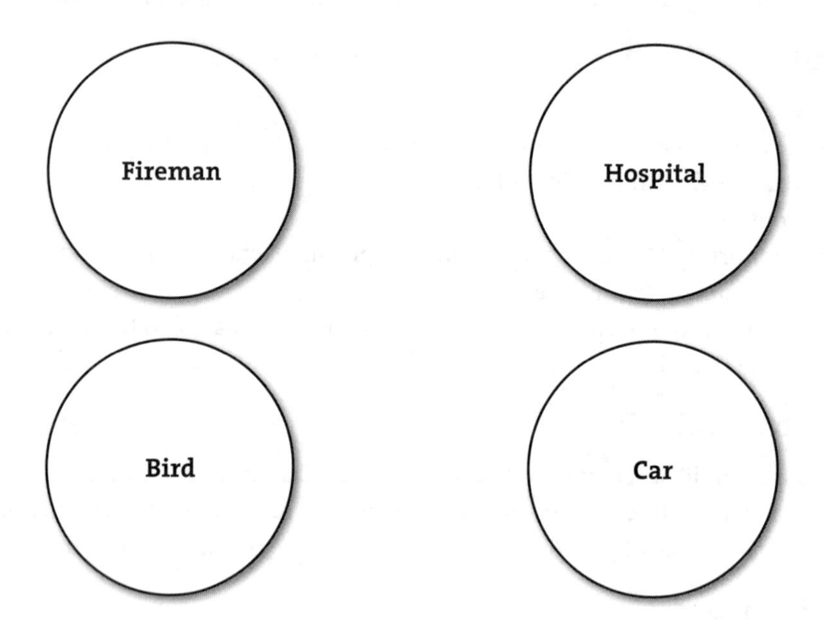


## Practice the Skill

Choose one of the ads. Using the "Supporting Details" chart, chart the topic and list all of the details from the ad. Then, in the last row of the chart, create a one-sentence summary (no less than eight words) that captures the main idea of the ad.

**Supporting Details**

| | |
|---|---|
| Topic | |
| Detail 1 | |
| Detail 2 | |
| Detail 3 | |
| Detail 4 | |
| Detail 5 | |
| Use the topic and details to create a one-sentence summary of the ad (no less than eight words. | |

# Teacher Directions: Recognizing Inferences

## Goals for Student

1. Examine text to clarify meaning.
2. Make inferences and generalizations about what is read.
3. Paraphrase text to draw meaning.

## Preparation

1. Your class should be familiar with the term "inference."
2. Make copies of the "Inference Matching" worksheet for each student (an answer key is included). The students will cut the paper up into strips, so provide a paper clip for the students to keep the strips together.
3. Provide a variety of elementary-level joke books.

## Materials

- "Inference Matching" worksheet (student copy)
- "Recognizing Inferences" worksheet
- Glue stick
- Manila drawing paper
- ***Charlotte's Web*** (E. B. White), *Island of the Blue Dolphins* (Scott O'Dell), *A Christmas Carol* (Charles Dickens), and *Holes* (Louis Sachar)

## Focus on the Skill

To begin, have the students complete the "Common Sense Inferences" section of the "Recognizing Inferences" worksheet.

## Practice the Skill

1. Have the students cut the "Inference Matching" worksheet into individual strips. There are a total of twenty strips.
2. Next, the students will match the types of inference with the example that best represents the inference description. They will glue their matches down on a piece of manila paper.
3. The types of inference will go on the left and the examples of those inferences will go on the right.
4. Next, have the students choose one of the bumper sticker slogans on the "Recognizing Inferences" worksheet.
5. Using the "Understanding Humor Chart," the students must list all facts, opinions, ideas, inferences, and related real-life situations that come to mind. In the end, they must explain what it is that makes the bumper sticker funny.

## Take It to the Next Level

1. Allow the students to locate a joke of their own in one of the joke books.
2. They will turn the "Recognizing Inferences" worksheet over and draw a comic strip that illustrates the joke. Underneath, they must explain what makes the joke funny.

## Special Considerations

For students that get overwhelmed with finding matches, make sure they know that each is labeled with either "Type of Inference" or "Example." If you want to challenge your students, use correction fluid to cover these identifying terms before you make copies of the list.

# Student Directions: Recognizing Inferences

## Focus on the Skill

To begin, complete the "Common Sense Inferences" section of the "Recognizing Inferences" worksheet.

## Practice the Skill

1. Now, cut the "Types of Inference" worksheet into individual strips. There are a total of twenty strips.
2. Match the types of inference with the example that best represents the inference description. Glue your matches down on a piece of manila paper. The types of inference will go on the left and examples of those inferences will go on the right.
3. Next, choose one of the bumper sticker slogans on the "Recognizing Inferences" worksheet.
4. Transfer the bumper sticker to the first column of the "Understanding Humor" chart. In the second column, rephrase the bumper sticker slogan in ordinary language. What is it REALLY saying?
5. In the third column, write every observation you can think of about the bumper sticker—the way words are organized, sarcasm, exaggeration, author's purpose, etc.
6. Finally, in the last column, explain why the bumper sticker is funny.

## Take It to the Next Level

1. Locate a joke of your own in one of the joke books.
2. Turn the "Recognizing Inferences" worksheet over and write the joke as a comic strip. Underneath the comic strip must explain what makes the joke funny.

## How You Will Be Graded

| | 1 little or no evidence | 2 below average | 3 adequate evidence | 4 better than average | 5 superior evidence | TOTAL |
|---|---|---|---|---|---|---|
| Attention to neatness and presentation | | | | | | |
| Able to determine the commonalities in a category | | | | | | |
| Able to match types of inference with examples of inference | | | | | | |
| Uses details and examples to find meaning in humor | | | | | | |
| Drawing reflects the meaning of a humorous bumper sticker slogan | | | | | | |
| **Total points multiplied by four** | | | | | | |
| **Final grade** | | | | | | |

# Worksheet: Types of Inference—Key

| | |
|---|---|
| Type of inference: Figure out the grammatical function of an unknown word | Example: In the following sentence, what **part of speech** will the missing word be?<br><br>*He drove a __________ car to work every day.* |
| Type of inference: Figure out the meaning of unknown words from context clues | Example: Guess the meaning of the boldfaced word.<br><br>*The liquid is **flammable**, so do not smoke by it.* |
| Type of inference: Identify characters' beliefs, personalities, and motivations | Example: Based on the description of the rat, Templeton, from *Charlotte's Web*, which detail supports the idea that he loves to eat? |
| Type of inference: Offer conclusions from facts presented in the text | Example: The food was described as round, flat, and covered in sauce. Obviously, the food is pizza. |
| Type of inference: Provide details about the setting | Example: The San Nicholas Island (the inspiration for *Island of the Blue Dolphins*), off the California coast, is covered in volcanic rock, coyote brush, and a few trees. |
| Type of inference: Provide explanations for events or ideas that are presented in the text | Example: Scrooge (in *A Christmas Carol*) may have decided to send a turkey to his employee, Bob Cratchit, because he realized that he had been wrong for being miserly and needed to be kind. |
| Type of inference: Recognize the antecedents for pronouns | Example: Who is it the word "her" refers to in the following sentence?<br><br>*Sara lost her keys again.* |
| Type of inference: Recognize the author's biases | Example: *I don't choose girls to be on my kickball team, because they are not very strong and they don't try as hard as the boys.* |
| Type of inference: Understand characters' relationships to one another | Example: *Because the Hardy boys are so close in age, the two brothers are dedicated to one another and never hesitate to help one another in a crisis.* |
| Type of inference: Understand the tone of characters' words | Example: Think about how the warden from *Holes* responds to Stanley's discovery when she says, *"Stanley, won't you just open it? Just let me see what's inside it, please!"* |

## Worksheet: Types of Inference—Student Copy

| | |
|---|---|
| Type of inference: Understand characters' relationships to one another | Example: In the following sentence, what part of speech will the missing word be?<br><br>*He drove a __________ car to work every day.* |
| Type of inference: Identify characters' beliefs, personalities, and motivations | Example: Guess the meaning of the boldfaced word.<br><br>*The liquid is* ***flammable****, so do not smoke by it.* |
| Type of inference: Figure out the grammatical function of an unknown word | Example: Based on the description of the rat, Templeton, from *Charlotte's Web*, which detail supports the idea that he loves to eat? |
| Type of inference: Figure out the meaning of unknown words from context clues | Example: The food was described as round, flat, and covered in sauce. Obviously, the food is pizza. |
| Type of inference: Offer conclusions from facts presented in the text | Example: The San Nicholas Island (the inspiration for *Island of the Blue Dolphins*), off the California coast, is covered in volcanic rock, coyote brush, and a few trees. |
| Type of inference: Recognize the antecedents for pronouns | Example: Scrooge (from *A Christmas Carol*) may have decided to send a turkey to Bob Cratchit, because he realized that he had been wrong for being miserly and needed to be kind. |
| Type of inference: Provide explanations for events or ideas that are presented in the text | Example: Who is it the word "her" refers to in the following sentence?<br><br>*Sara lost her keys again.* |
| Type of inference: Understand the tone of characters' words | Example: *I don't choose girls to be on my kickball team, because they are not very strong and they don't try as hard as the boys.* |
| Type of inference: Provide details about the setting | Example: *Because the Hardy boys are so close in age, the two brothers are dedicated to one another and never hesitate to help one another in a crisis.* |
| Type of inference: Recognize the author's biases | Example: Think about how the warden from *Holes* responds to Stanley's discovery when she says, *"Stanley, won't you just open it? Just let me see what's inside it, please!"* |

# Worksheet: Recognizing Inferences

## Focus on the Skill

**Common Sense Inferences.** Examine each list and determine what each list has in common. BE SPECIFIC! (Hint: The first group is not JUST a group of cars.)

| *Category 1* | *Category 2* | *Category 3* |
|---|---|---|
| Ferrari Enzo Coupe | New York, New York - 8,143,197 | Simba |
| Porsche GT2 | Los Angeles, California - 3,844,829 | King Mufasa |
| BMW Z8 | Chicago, Illinois - 2,842,518 | Scar |
| Mercedes-Benz CL 600 | Houston, Texas - 2,016,582 | Timon |
| Jaguar XK 100 Convertible | Philadelphia, Pennsylvania - 1,463,281 | Pumbaa |
| These are all ___________ | These are all ___________________ | These are all ____________ |

## Practice the Skill

Choose one of the following bumper sticker slogans. Use the "Understanding Humor" chart to figure out what makes the sticker funny.

***Change is inevitable, except from a vending machine.***

***I souport publik edekasion***

***I thought I was indecisive; now I'm not so sure.***

***It's been Monday all week.***

***Just say NO to negativity***

***If you can read this, I've lost the trailer!***

**Understanding Humor**

| The bumper sticker I choose to analyze | Rephrased in my own words, the sticker is saying . . . | Every observation I can make about the joke . . . (look for sarcasm, the way the words are organized, author's purpose, exaggerations, etc.) | From all of the information I have gathered, the sticker is funny because . . . |
|---|---|---|---|
| | | | |

# Teacher Directions: Making Predictions

## Goals for Student

1. Read and predict from graphic representations (illustrations, diagrams, graphs, maps).
2. Synthesize collected information using a matrix or other graphic organizer.
3. Predict ideas or events that may take place in the text, give rationale for predictions, and confirm and discuss predictions as the story progresses.

## Preparation

1. Your class should be used to making predictions as part of their active reading habits.
2. Label three brown bags with the numbers 1, 2, and 3. In one bag, place three marbles. In the second, place three marshmallows, and in the third, place three ping pong balls.
3. Provide a picture book with illustrations; a narrative song with lyrics (and illustrations, if possible); an article from a magazine with pictures, captions, a map, and subheadings; and/or a newspaper article that contains a graph or chart.

## Materials

- Picture book, song, and/or article
- "Making Predictions" worksheet
- Three brown bags with mystery contents
- 9" x 12" manila drawing paper

## Focus on the Skill

1. The students DO NOT look in the bags.
2. They will make a prediction (using their senses—except for taste) about what's in each bag, what the items could be used for, and what all of the contents of all three bags have in common. They will log their predictions on the "Making Predictions" worksheet.
3. Then, they may look in the bag (leaving the contents in the bag so other students do not see—try to make a big deal about secrecy) and determine if the predictions matched the contents.
4. On the "Making Predictions" worksheet, they will complete the "After You Look Inside the Bag" section to explain how their predictions matched what was really in the bags.

## Practice the Skill

1. The students will select one of the pieces of literature that has been provided.
2. Instruct the students NOT to read the text. Instead, they should consider the title, illustrations, and all other non-print stimuli to create a prediction on the "Learning to Predict" chart of the "Making Predictions" worksheet. They should consider what the article is going to be about and how they know.

## Take It to the Next Level

Have the students create a picture-notes summary of the text on the back side of the worksheet. They can use pictures, sketches, diagrams, graphs, and words (as captions) to express their ideas. This is a free-form activity, and the students should capture as many main ideas as possible from the text.

## Special Considerations

If it seems overwhelming to put different types of literature out for the students to choose, supply the same picture book, song lyrics, magazine article, or newspaper article to the whole group. Make sure they understand this is a PREDICTION activity—the point is to consider clues beyond the body of text and determine if their guesses about the text were correct.

# Student Directions: Making Predictions

## Focus on the Skill

1. DO NOT look in the bags.
2. Taking one bag at a time, make a prediction (using your senses) about what's in each bag, what the items could be used for, and what all of the contents of all three bags have in common.
3. Log your predictions on the "Making Predictions" worksheet.
4. Then, you may look in each bag (leaving the contents in the bag so other students do not see) and determine if your predictions matched the contents.
5. On the "Making Predictions" worksheet, you will complete the "After You Look Inside the Bag" section to explain how your predictions matched what was really in the bags.

## Practice the Skill

1. Select one of the pieces of literature (picture book, song lyrics, or article) that has been provided.
2. DO NOT to read the text. Instead, consider the title, illustrations, and all other non-print stimuli to create predictions on the "Learning to Predict" chart of the "Making Predictions" worksheet.
3. Read the text.
4. When you are done, complete the "Learning to Predict" chart. Make sure you summarize the article by considering text and non-text details.

## Take It to the Next Level

Using the same piece of literature, create a picture-notes summary of the text on the back side of the worksheet. You can use pictures, sketches, diagrams, graphs, and words (as captions) to express your ideas. This is a free-form activity, and you should capture as many main ideas as possible from the text.

## How You Will Be Graded

| | 1 little or no evidence | 2 below average | 3 adequate evidence | 4 better than average | 5 superior evidence | TOTAL |
|---|---|---|---|---|---|---|
| Attention to neatness and presentation | | | | | | |
| Able to make a prediction, consider uses, and draw conclusions using senses | | | | | | |
| Uses the title, illustrations, captions, charts, graphs, and other non-print clues to make a prediction about the story | | | | | | |
| Reviews and confirms predictions | | | | | | |
| Picture-notes summary uses details effectively to show the main ideas from the text | | | | | | |
| **Total points multiplied by four** | | | | | | |
| **Final grade** | | | | | | |

# Worksheet: Making Predictions

## Focus on the Skill

What's in the bag? Evaluate each bag and log your predictions in the chart below.

### Bag One

| Consider | Observation |
|---|---|
| Smells? | |
| Feels? | |
| Sounds? | |
| Looks? | |
| How could the contents be used? | |

### Bag Two

| Consider | Observation |
|---|---|
| Smells? | |
| Feels? | |
| Sounds? | |
| Looks? | |
| How could the contents be used? | |

### Bag Three

| Consider | Observation |
|---|---|
| Smells? | |
| Feels? | |
| Sounds? | |
| Looks? | |
| How could the contents be used? | |

**BEFORE YOU LOOK INSIDE THE BAG,** predict what the contents of the bags have in common.

______________________________________________

______________________________________________

______________________________________________

**AFTER YOU LOOK INSIDE THE BAG,** explain how your predictions matched what was really in the bags.

______________________________________________

______________________________________________

______________________________________________

## Practice the Skill

1. Make predictions without reading the text provided in this center. Complete the first row of the "Learning to Predict" chart.
2. Then, read the text and complete the framed sentence in the second row.
3. Write a summary in the third row.

## Worksheet: Making Predictions (continued)

### Learning to Predict

| Guided Directions | My Observations |
|---|---|
| 1. Before reading: Consider the cover, title, illustrations, pictures, captions, map, subheadings, graphs, and chart (non-text details) to finish the sentences in the right column.<br><br>DO NOT READ THE TEXT UNTIL YOU HAVE FINISHED WRITING THE SENTENCES.<br><br>Make sure your sentences are complete. Be specific, and use the non-text details to support your answer. | I think . . .<br><br>I wonder if . . .<br><br>I predict . . . |
| 2. Now, read the text and determine if your prediction is confirmed. Finish the sentence in the column to the right. | After reading the text, I have determined that my prediction was ______________________ because ______________________________________________ ______________________________________________ ______________________________________________. |
| 3. Write a summary of the story, song, or article using both the text and non-text details. | |

# Teacher Directions: Cause and Effect in Encyclopedia Articles

## Goals for Student

1. Restate text by note-making or summarizing.
2. Examine sources to clarify meaning (for example, encyclopedia, web site, or expert).
3. Analyze ways writers organize and present ideas of cause and effect.

## Preparation

1. Your class should be aware of the purpose of encyclopedias. They should begin to recognize titles, headings, pictures, and captions as important features of text.
2. Find encyclopedia articles about how a liquid becomes a solid, how fossils are formed, how the dinosaurs disappeared, how clouds form, how volcanoes erupt, and how tornadoes are formed. The Internet is a great source.

## Materials

- Encyclopedia articles
- "Cause and Effect in Encyclopedia Articles" worksheet
- 9" x 12" manila drawing paper
- Colored pencils

## Focus on the Skill

First, students will consider real-life cause-and-effect relationships in their own routines: brushing their teeth, wearing sunglasses, wearing shoes, putting their name on their paper, and using a spoon. They will complete the chart on the "Cause and Effect in Encyclopedia Articles" worksheet, explaining why we do these things and what the results are.

## Practice the Skill

Students will choose three of the nonfiction topics, and using the same format as the chart below, students determine causes and effects related to each topic from encyclopedia articles.

| Topic | What causes this to happen? | What happens after this? |
|---|---|---|
| Clouds forming | Water vapor is cooled. | Lots of shapes are formed—mostly Cirrus, Cumulus, and Stratus |

## Take It to the Next Level

To take this lesson to the next level, have the students choose one topic and draw a series of sketches that shows the process (try the "Three-Tab Foldable" from Dinah Zike's website at www.dinah.com). For instance, if they choose to draw how a cloud is formed, their drawings may include the following steps: 1. air containing water vapor is cooled; 2. water vapor condenses; 3. condensation becomes tiny water droplets floating in the sky. It may be beneficial for you to draw a well-detailed sample (using another topic, such as how pollution becomes a problem) to model the quality you would expect from your students.

## Special Considerations

If your students have trouble with this, they may need to use a close-reading technique. While they are reading the article, they should underline any information that has to do with the cause of the topic and put a star beside effects. If you happen to have hardback versions of encyclopedias, use them. Middle-school-aged students lack experience with indexes and alphabetized information. The extra step would be beneficial to all levels of this age group.

# Student Directions: Cause and Effect in Encyclopedia Articles

## Focus on the Skill

First, consider real-life cause-and-effect relationships in your own routines: brushing your teeth, wearing sunglasses, wearing shoes, putting your name on your paper, and using a spoon. Complete the chart on the "Cause and Effect in Encyclopedia Articles" worksheet. Why do we do these things, and what is the result?

## Practice the Skill

1. Choose three of the non-fiction topics from the '"Cause and Effect with Encyclopedia Articles" worksheet and, using the same format as the chart below, determine causes and effects related to each topic.
2. If there are multiple causes (more than one), number your answers in the chart.

| Topic | What causes this to happen? | What happens after this? |
|---|---|---|
| Clouds forming | Water vapor is cooled. | Lots of shapes are formed—mostly Cirrus, Cumulus, and Stratus |

## Take It to the Next Level

Choose one of the topics and draw a series of sketches that shows the process. For example, to draw how a cloud is formed, your drawing may include the following steps: 1. air containing water vapor is cooled; 2. water vapor condenses; 3. condensation becomes tiny water droplets floating in the sky.

## How You Will Be Graded

| | 1 little or no evidence | 2 below average | 3 adequate evidence | 4 better than average | 5 superior evidence | TOTAL |
|---|---|---|---|---|---|---|
| Attention to neatness and presentation | | | | | | |
| Able to recognize cause and effect in personal, everyday routines | | | | | | |
| Recognizes how a process occurs and the results of those processes | | | | | | |
| Effectively shows one process in a series of sketches | | | | | | |
| Uses details and captions to communicate meaning in sketches | | | | | | |
| **Total points multiplied by four** | | | | | | |
| **Final grade** | | | | | | |

# Worksheet: Cause and Effect in Encyclopedia Articles

## Focus on the Skill

**My Routines.** Fill in the chart below. In the left column are the routines. In the right column are the reasons for those routines.

| Routine | Outcome of the Routine |
|---|---|
| I brush my teeth because . . . | |
| | to protect my eyes from ultraviolet rays |
| I wear shoes because . . . | |
| | so my teacher knows whose paper it is |
| I use a spoon because . . . | |

## Practice the Skill

**Understanding a Process.** Choose three of the topics below. Write the topics in the column labeled 'Topic.' Read the articles for each topic. In the second column, list as many causes as you can for the topic. In the third column, make a list of the outcomes that occur because of those causes. An example has been done for you.

How a liquid becomes a solid
How fossils are formed
How the dinosaurs disappeared
How clouds form
How volcanoes erupt
How a tornado forms

| Topic | What causes this to happen? | What happens after this? |
|---|---|---|
| How pollution becomes a problem | 1. People throw trash on the ground<br>2. People dump chemicals into the water<br>3. Not recycling<br>4. Smoke and exhaust from cars is released into the atmosphere<br>5. Factories release gases and chemicals | 1. Communities look dirty.<br>2. The water is not safe to drink.<br>3. People are wasteful.<br>4. The air smells bad<br>5. Smog |
| | | |
| | | |
| | | |

# Teacher Directions: Cause and Effect in Newspaper Articles

## Goals for Student

1. Use a timeline to clarify the order of events in a text.
2. Identify and examine the influence of personal values.
3. Analyze ways writers organize and present ideas of cause and effect.

## Preparation

1. Your class should have experience reading newspaper ads. They should use information from titles, photos, and captions to find meaning.
2. Collect newspaper articles about a person who has made a bad choice. Perhaps it is a bank robber or a car thief. The article must have a description of what the person did and the consequences for his/her action (sentenced to jail, fined, etc.). Make a copy for every student so they can write on the article.

## Materials

- Newspaper article
- "Cause and Effect in Newspaper Articles" worksheet
- 9" x 12" manila drawing paper
- Colored pencils

## Focus on the Skill

Students will begin by analyzing their own experiences. They will choose an example of a bad choice and process the experience using the 3-2-1 strategy on the "Cause and Effect in Newspaper Articles" worksheet.

## Practice the Skill

1. Next, students will read an article about someone who made a bad choice (cause) and what happened as a result of that choice (effect).
2. On manila paper, the students must create a timeline of events. The timeline must be illustrated with three to five drawings showing what happened in the article.
3. The students must circle the point on the timeline where the person made an irreversible, bad choice—the point where they knew the consequences would be bad.

## Take It to the Next Level

To take this lesson to the next level, have the students use the chart on the "Cause and Effect in Newspaper Articles" worksheet to process the events of the article. Then, they should write an alternate ending to the story as if the person made a good choice. You should encourage creativity and even exaggeration.

## Special Considerations

There are many, many articles about criminals who made bad choices. Some are very funny and even entertaining. Keep in mind the length of the article and, obviously, the maturity of the subject matter.

# Student Directions: Cause and Effect in Newspaper Articles

## Focus on the Skill

Begin by analyzing your own experiences. Choose an example of a bad choice and process the experience using the 3-2-1 strategy on the "Cause and Effect in Newspaper Articles" worksheet.

## Practice the Skill

1. Next, read an article about someone who made a bad choice (cause), and what happened as a result of that choice (effect).
2. On manila paper, create a timeline of events from the article. The timeline must be illustrated with three to five drawings showing what happened.
3. Circle the point on the timeline where the person made an irreversible, bad choice—the point where they knew the consequences would be bad.

## Take It to the Next Level

Use the chart on the "Cause and Effect in Newspaper Articles" worksheet to process the events of the article. Then, write an alternate ending to the story as if the person made a good choice. Think creativity and even exaggeration.

## How You Will Be Graded

| | 1 little or no evidence | 2 below average | 3 adequate evidence | 4 better than average | 5 superior evidence | TOTAL |
|---|---|---|---|---|---|---|
| Attention to neatness and presentation | | | | | | |
| Able to process a personal bad choice | | | | | | |
| Creates a timeline that accurately reflects events from the article | | | | | | |
| Timeline is illustrated with three to five details from the article | | | | | | |
| Creates an alternate ending that considers effects of a better choice by the person in the article | | | | | | |
| **Total points multiplied by four** | | | | | | |
| **Final grade** | | | | | | |

# Worksheet: Cause and Effect in Newspaper Articles

## Focus on the Skill

**My Bad Choice.** Think about a time when you made a bad choice. Perhaps it was related to schoolwork, or maybe you chose to ignore a parent's command. First, write the bad choice on the line below, and then use the 3-2-1 strategy to process that choice. Make sure you really think about the experience, and use good details and examples for your response!

**My Bad Choice was** ______________________________

| 3 Reasons I Made the Bad Choice | 2 Consequences for the Bad Choice | 1 Lesson I Learned from the Experience |
|---|---|---|
| | | |

## Take It to the Next Level

| Guided Directions | Information from the Article |
|---|---|
| Write the headline of the story | |
| Summarize the cause(s) and effect(s) (consequences) of the choice made in the article. | Causes of the bad choice (if available):<br><br>Effects of the bad choice: |
| Describe the point in the story where the person could have made a better choice and changed the outcome of the story (i.e., the bank robber decided not to put the mask on his head). | |
| Now, rewrite the ending by changing that point in the story. Since you have changed the cause or causes, the effects are going to be different as well. Be creative! | |

# Teacher Directions: Cause and Effect in Short Stories

## Goals for Student

1. Monitor personal comprehension and make modifications when understanding breakdowns by rereading a portion aloud or silently.
2. Know the primary conflicts in a short story and explain their resolutions.
3. Analyze ways writers organize and present ideas of cause and effect.

## Preparation

1. Your class should have experience reading short stories. They should recognize basic literary terms like character, setting, and plot.
2. Find a short story that can be read in the time period allotted for the literacy center. Make sure it is grade- and ability-appropriate for the group you teach. I recommend "The Strap Box Flyer." You can find it (as well as other fun-to-read stories) in *Unreal!* by Paul Jennings.

## Materials

- Short story
- "Cause and Effect in Short Stories" worksheet

## Focus on the Skill

On the back of the "Cause and Effect in Short Stories" worksheet, the students will write the title of three of their favorite children's stories. Underneath each title, they will complete a framed sentence about the events of the story:

*Because* ______________________________, *the* ______________________________."

## Practice the Skill

1. Next, students will use close reading to annotate the story provided. They should circle unfamiliar words, underline important events, and put a question mark in the margins next to incidents that seem unusual or difficult to understand. Make sure they understand that their annotations are graded!
2. Students should look back and find five events that they underlined.
3. Using the "Analyzing the Events" chart on the worksheet, they will place the five most important events in the left column. In the right column, they will consider the event and finish the sentence, "As a result, . . ."

## Take It to the Next Level

To take this lesson to the next level, have the students record the climax of the story on the worksheet. Then, have them create an acrostic poem using the word "CAUSE." Each line of the poem should describe important events that led to the climax of the story and begin with the letter on that line (for example, lines can begin with strong verbs, adjectives, or nouns). Students will then record the resolution, or falling action of the story, under the poem.

## Special Considerations

Close reading and annotating are skills that can be adjusted to fit the needs of your students. Model this skill, and guide them through a variety of literature using the strategy. You may want to show an example of the acrostic poem activity. Use a story that your class has already read, and model the quality and details you would want to see in this assignment.

# Student Directions: Cause and Effect in Short Stories

## Focus on the Skill

On the back of the "Cause and Effect in Short Stories" worksheet, write the titles of three of your favorite children's stories. Underneath each title, complete a framed sentence about the events of the story: *Because* ______________________________, *the* ______________________________."

Example for *The Three Little Pigs: Because the wolf was so greedy, the pigs had to defend themselves by tricking him into a pot of boiling water.*

## Practice the Skill

1. Now choose one of the short stories provided. Use close reading to annotate the story. You should **circle unfamiliar words, underline important events,** and **put a question mark in the margins next to incidents that seem unusual or difficult to understand**. Make sure you understand that your annotations are graded—your active reading skills should shine!
2. When you are done reading, look back and <u>find five of the most important events</u> that you underlined.
3. Using the "Analyzing the Events" chart on the worksheet, you will place the five important events in the left column. In the right column, you will consider the event and finish the sentence, "As a result, . . ."

## Take It to the Next Level

1. Finally, record the climax (the highest point of the story) on the worksheet. Then, create an acrostic poem using the word "CAUSE." Each line of the poem should describe important events that led to the climax of the story. Make sure each line begins with the letter on that line (example for *The Three Little Pigs*: *Courageous pigs hide from a determined wolf.*).
2. When you have finished the acrostic poem, record the resolution, or falling action, of the story on the lines provided.

## How You Will Be Graded

| | 1 little or no evidence | 2 below average | 3 adequate evidence | 4 better than average | 5 superior evidence | TOTAL |
|---|---|---|---|---|---|---|
| Attention to neatness and presentation | | | | | | |
| Uses good active reading skills like circling unfamiliar words and underlining important events in the story | | | | | | |
| Identifies 5 important events in the story | | | | | | |
| Identified results of five important events in the story | | | | | | |
| Recognized the climax and falling action in the story; successfully created an acrostic poem made up of rising actions from the story | | | | | | |
| **Total points multiplied by four** | | | | | | |
| **Final grade** | | | | | | |

# Worksheet: Cause and Effect in Short Stories

## Practice the Skill

Choose one of the children's stories and select five important events to list in the left column of the chart below. Think about the event and complete the sentence, "As a result…" in the right column of the chart.

**Analyzing the Events**

| Cause | Effect |
|---|---|
| Event #1: | As a result, . . . |
| Event # 2: | As a result, . . . |
| Event #3: | As a result, . . . |
| Event #4: | As a result, . . . |
| Event #5: | As a result, . . . |

## Take It to the Next Level

**Acrostic Poem.** First, write the event from the story that was the climax (highest point in the story) on the first line. Now, think of all of the rising actions that led to the climax in the story. Create an acrostic poem using the letters from the word "CAUSE" to document five of those causes (be creative and flexible with your thinking). Finally, determine the resolution (events after the climax) of this story.

What event is the climax in this story? ______________________________

**C**

**A**

**U**

**S**

**E**

What was the resolution in this story? ______________________________

# Teacher Directions: Cause and Effect in Nursery Rhymes and Song Lyrics

## Goals for Student

1. Use plot elements from various texts.
2. Understand ways cause-and-effect relationships affect the development of a plot.
3. Analyze ways writers organize and present ideas of cause and effect.

## Preparation

1. Your students should understand that nursery rhymes and song lyrics are forms of prose that often have catchy words and rhythms. What they may not know is that nursery rhymes and songs may also have a plot; therefore, they are great for studying cause/effect relationships.
2. Find the lyrics for "Big Bad John," written by Jimmy Dean; if you can get a copy of the song (performed by Johnny Cash), even better. You might want to edit the curse word if that's the version you find—change it to "lies one *heck* of a guy!"

## Materials

- Short story
- "Cause and Effect in Nursery Rhymes and Song Lyrics" worksheet
- Story paper
- Colored pencils
- Lyrics to "Big Bad John"

## Focus on the Skill

To begin, the students will read the nursery rhymes on the "Cause and Effect in Nursery Rhymes and Song Lyrics" worksheet. They should complete the framed sentences to show they understand the cause/effect relationships. You may want them to blend inference and details (example for *Little Miss Muffet*: *The spider sat beside her, and little girls are usually afraid of spiders.*).

## Practice the Skill

1. Next, students will read (or listen to) "Big Bad John." The goal is to follow the plot and pay attention to cause/effect relationships. Students should try to adhere to the "Rule of Three"—there are usually at least three good details in the answer. (Example: *John is unpredictable, he's very large, and it's rumored he killed a man is a solid list of causes for why "You don't talk back to Big John."*)
2. Have the students use the lyrics to fill in the chart on the worksheet. If you find another song that follows the same kind of cause/effect pattern, just change the events in the chart.

## Take It to the Next Level

To take this lesson to the next level, have the students create a cartoon using one of the nursery rhymes or song lyrics that shows the most important events in order. Their cartoon should reflect details that show they understand cause/effect relationships. Try the "Accordion Book Foldable" from Dinah Zike's website at www.dinah.com.

## Special Considerations

Your students may or may not have much experience with nursery rhymes. If they get hung up on the terms (*curds, whey*, etc.), you may want to provide a glossary. A good homework assignment may be for them to locate other nursery rhymes that contain cause/effect relationships.

# Student Directions: Cause and Effect in Nursery Rhymes and Song Lyrics

## Focus on the Skill

To begin, read the nursery rhymes on the "Cause and Effect in Nursery Rhymes and Song Lyrics" worksheet. You should complete the framed sentences to show you understand the cause/effect relationships. Try to blend inference and details to show that you are a top notch reader! (Example for *Little Miss Muffet*: *The spider sat beside her, and little girls are usually afraid of spiders.*)

## Practice the Skill

1. Next, read (and/or listen to) "Big Bad John," written by Jimmy Dean and sung by Johnny Cash. The goal is to follow the plot and pay attention to cause/effect relationships.
2. Use the lyrics to fill in the chart on the worksheet. Make sure you try to locate two to three details to support your answers.

## Take It to the Next Level

Finally, create a cartoon using one of the nursery rhymes or song lyrics that shows the most important events in order. Your cartoon should reflect details that show you understand cause/effect relationships.

## How You Will Be Graded

| | 1 little or no evidence | 2 below average | 3 adequate evidence | 4 better than average | 5 superior evidence | TOTAL |
|---|---|---|---|---|---|---|
| Attention to neatness and presentation | | | | | | |
| Able to complete framed sentences correctly | | | | | | |
| Identifies cause/effect relationships in a song | | | | | | |
| Cartoon accurately reflects plot in the correct order | | | | | | |
| Uses details in cartoon to show most important events | | | | | | |
| **Total points multiplied by four** | | | | | | |
| **Final grade** | | | | | | |

# Worksheet: Cause and Effect in Nursery Rhymes and Song Lyrics

## Focus on the Skill

**Popular Nursery Rhymes.** *Interesting Story: Humpty Dumpty was allegedly a canon that fell off the wall of a church tower in England in 1649. All of the king's horses (the cavalry) and all the king's men (the infantry) could not put him back together.*

Read each of the nursery rhymes and finish the sentences to explain what happens.

### Little Miss Muffet

*Little Miss Muffet sat on a tuffet,*
*Eating her curds and whey;*
*Along came a spider,*
*Who sat down beside her,*
*And frightened Miss Muffet away.*

Miss Muffet was frightened because ______________________________________________.

### Humpty Dumpty

*Humpty Dumpty sat on a wall.*
*Humpty Dumpty had a great fall.*
*All the king's horses and all the king's men*
*Couldn't put Humpty together again!*

When Humpty Dumpty fell off the wall, ______________________________________________.

### The Eensy Weensy Spider

*Eensy Weensy spider*
*Crawled up the water spout.*
*Down came the rain*
*And washed the spider out.*
*Out came the sun*
*And dried up all the rain;*
*And the Eensy Weensy spider*
*Crawled up the spout again.*

Because of the rain, ______________________________________________.

## Practice the Skill

Use the lyrics from "Big Bad John" to fill in the chart below. Make sure you try to locate two to three details to support your answers (some may be inferred).

| This is the Cause | This is the Effect |
|---|---|
| | You don't talk back to Big John. |
| Big John hit someone over a girl. | |
| | Men started crying in the mine. |
| Big John held up a falling support beam. | |
| | The miners took jacks and hammers to get back into the mine. |
| A rumble was heard. | |
| | The mine was never reopened. |

# Teacher Directions: Comparing and Contrasting Personality Traits

## Goals for Student

1. Compare and contrast characters from various texts.
2. Synthesize collected information using a graphic organizer.
3. Study word meanings consistently.

## Preparation

1. Your class should be familiar with the terms "personality trait" and "characterization."
2. Collect different kinds of sunglasses, hats, belts, shoes, gloves, socks, purses, and other accessories (great finds at garage sales and thrift stores) that represent a lot of different kinds of personalities. Have fun with this!
3. Also, collect well-known children's story books—*Goldilocks and the Three Bears, Little Red Riding Hood, Hansel and Gretel,* etc.

## Materials

- "What Are Personality Traits?" worksheet
- "Comparing and Contrasting Characterizations" worksheet
- Sunglasses, hats, belts, shoes, gloves, socks, purses, and other unique accessories
- Story paper

## Focus on the Skill

1. Have the students complete a vocabulary map for the term "personality trait" on the "What Are Personality Traits?" worksheet.
2. Then, have the students choose one of the unique accessories and complete a "Personality Inventory of Someone Who Accessorizes" chart on the "What Are Personality Traits?" worksheet.

## Practice the Skill

1. Have the students circle two personality traits from the list on the "Comparing and Contrasting Characterizations" worksheet and look both words up in the dictionary. They will write both definitions on the lines provided and think about both meanings.
2. The students will use a Venn diagram to compare and contrast the two personality traits they defined. They should consider **likes, dislikes, habits, fears, hopes, beliefs, and other related thoughts**. They should think of other words that might describe a person with this personality trait.
3. Next, have the students choose one of the personality traits. Have them think of a time (a situation) when THEY demonstrated this trait. On a piece of story paper, they will draw a detailed picture of themselves displaying this personality trait. A sentence that describes the picture with the personality trait should be written under the picture.

## Take It to the Next Level

After the students have compared personality traits and thought about how they may possess these traits, they will read a well-known children's story. They then need to choose a main character from the story and, on the back of their story paper, create a web about that character. They should brainstorm as many of the personality traits that might apply to this character as possible and sketch drawings for the web.

## Special Considerations

Characterizations can be difficult. A lot of this has to do with personal experience. Many standardized tests are using very complicated words in relation to characterization, and though this may be a complex task, it is worth going over these terms with your students to clarify their understanding.

# Student Directions: Comparing and Contrasting Personality Traits

## Focus on the Skill

1. You will complete a vocabulary map for the term "personality trait" on the "What Are Personality Traits?" worksheet.
2. Next, choose one of the unique accessories and complete a "Personality Inventory of Someone Who Accessorizes" on the "What Are Personality Traits?" worksheet.

## Practice the Skill

1. Circle two personality traits from the list on the "Comparing and Contrasting Characterizations" worksheet and look both words up in the dictionary. Write both definitions on the lines provided and think about both meanings.
2. Now, use a Venn diagram to compare and contrast the two personality traits you defined. You should consider **likes, dislikes, habits, fears, hopes, beliefs, and other related thoughts**. Think of other words that might describe a person with this personality trait.
3. Next, choose one of the personality traits you defined. Think of a situation when YOU demonstrated this trait. On a piece of story paper, draw a detailed picture of yourself displaying this personality trait. Write a sentence that describes the picture with the personality trait under the picture.

## Take It to the Next Level

After you have compared personality traits and thought about how you might possess these traits, you will read a well-known children's story. Choose a main character from the story and, on the back of your story paper, create a web about that character. Brainstorm as many of the personality traits that might apply to this character as possible. Sketch drawings for your brainstorming web.

## How You Will Be Graded

| | 1 little or no evidence | 2 below average | 3 adequate evidence | 4 better than average | 5 superior evidence | TOTAL |
|---|---|---|---|---|---|---|
| Attention to neatness and presentation | | | | | | |
| Created a vocabulary map that shows understanding for the term "personality trait," and uses divergent thinking to complete the "Personality Inventory" | | | | | | |
| Able to define both personality traits; definition is clear and understood | | | | | | |
| Venn diagram reflects an understanding of the two personality traits; details support the characterizations | | | | | | |
| Able to apply personality trait to personal experience AND to the character of a popular children's story | | | | | | |
| **Total points multiplied by four** | | | | | | |
| **Final grade** | | | | | | |

# Worksheet: What Are Personality Traits?

## Focus on the Skill

The definition for "personality trait" is provided. On the right side of the web, think of examples and related words to better explain the term. On the left side of the web, think of a personality trait that describes you. Draw a sketch that shows you understand the meaning of the trait you have selected. Be creative and try to be unique.

**a distinguishing feature, as of a person's character**

**PERSONALITY TRAIT**

**IS**

**IS**

**IS**

One personality trait of mine that I am proud of is that I am ______________________.

**Personality Inventory of Someone Who Accessorizes**

| The person who wears ______________ (the item you selected) | Personality trait |
|---|---|
| likes to . . . | |
| dislikes . . . | |
| hopes for . . . | |
| has these habits . . . | |
| worries about . . . | |

# Worksheet: Comparing and Contrasting Characterizations

## Practice the Skill

Circle two of the personality traits from the list below. Look both words up in the dictionary. Write both definitions on the lines provided and think about both meanings.

| | | | |
|---|---|---|---|
| Affectionate | Dainty | Impetuous | Secretive |
| Agitated | Dominant | Nervous | Solitary |
| Ailing | Energetic | Obnoxious | Stern |
| Alert | Fearful | Persistent | Timid |
| Annoyed | Gloomy | Pessimistic | Tranquil |
| Bland | Gossipy | Procrastinating | Trustworthy |
| Considerate | Guarded | Raucous | Whiney |

Personality trait #1: ______________________________
Definition: ______________________________________________________________________________
______________________________________________________________________________________

Personality trait #2: ______________________________
Definition: ______________________________________________________________________________
______________________________________________________________________________________

Now, use a Venn diagram to compare and contrast the two personality traits you defined. You should consider **likes, dislikes, habits, fears, hopes, beliefs, and other related thoughts**. It might help you to number your ideas in each circle. **Be specific.**

**Personality trait #1** ________________________

**Personality trait #2** ________________________

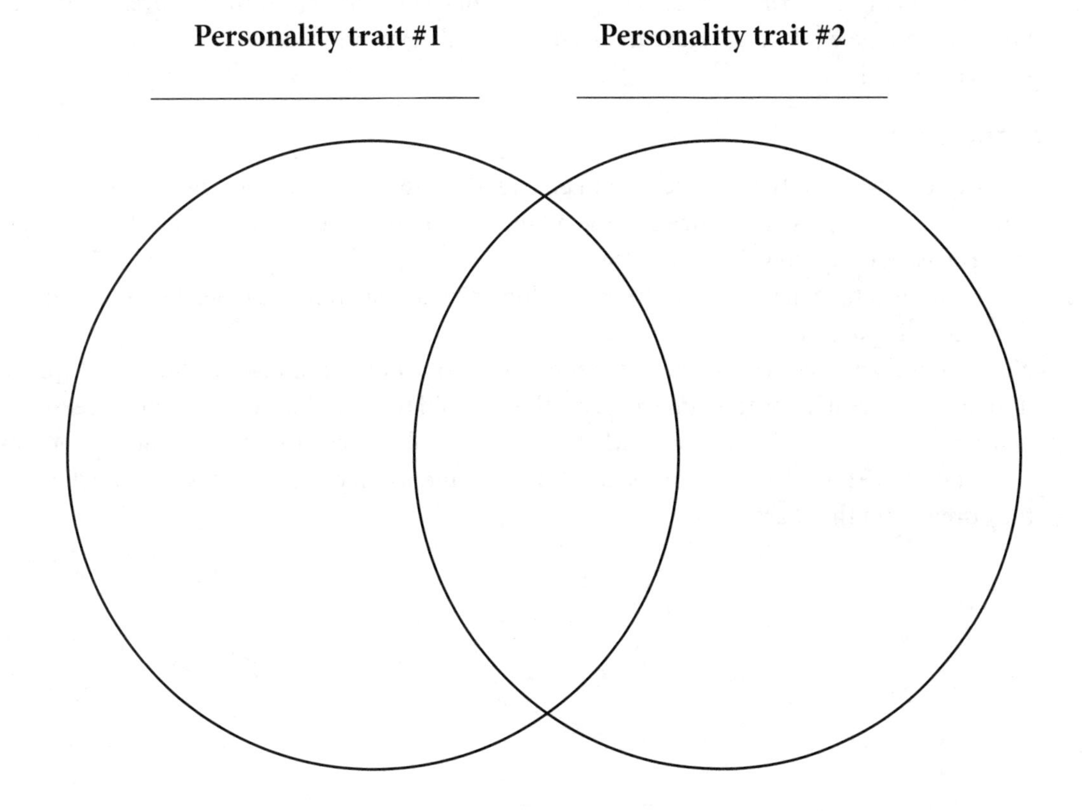

# Teacher Directions: Comparing and Contrasting Headlines

## Goals for Student

1. Use context and word structure clues to interpret words and ideas in text.
2. Make inferences and generalizations about what is read.
3. Compare and contrast ideas from various texts.

## Preparation

1. Your class should be able to interpret headlines and informational text.
2. Collect articles from the local or national newspaper. Photocopy the articles and cut off the headlines.
3. Put the articles in one envelope labeled #1 and the headlines in another envelop labeled #2. Try to find articles that are interesting, short, and concise.

## Materials

- "Comparing and Contrasting Newspaper Headlines" worksheet
- Envelope #1 with newspaper articles
- Envelope #2 with matching headlines
- 9" x 18" manila paper
- Glue stick

## Focus on the Skill

1. The students will begin the center activity by considering headlines on the "Comparing and Contrasting Newspaper Headlines" worksheet. These actual headlines have double meanings, and the students must determine which meaning was intended by the author.
2. After practicing analyzing for meaning, the students will then determine the events for four headlines on the worksheet. Have the students briefly explain what events occurred based on the headlines alone.

## Practice the Skill

1. The students will empty envelope #1 and consider the content, purpose, and tone of each article. They will paste the articles to the manila paper and write a unique headline for each of the articles that captures the main idea.
2. Then, they will take the headlines from envelope #2 and match the real headlines to their corresponding articles.
3. Now, the real analysis begins when students choose one of the original headlines and compare it to one they created for the same article. They should use the chart on the worksheet to determine if each headline explains what the article is about, catches your attention, and has a lot of detail. Then, they will complete a framed sentence that summarizes two conclusions they drew from the chart.

# Teacher Directions: Comparing and Contrasting Headlines (continued)

## Take It to the Next Level

1. The students should choose one of the original headlines from the worksheet. They will write the headline at the top of a piece of manila paper (or type a large-font version of the article and paste it to the top of the manila paper).
2. Then, the students will write their own version of the article. They should pay attention to the who, what, where, when, why, and how of their fictitious events.

## Special Considerations

I have yet to see a released test where there was not a question like "If this article was renamed, which would be the best headline?" My students struggle so much with the context of the question, and I realized it wasn't always because they didn't understand the original work; they did not recognize the headlines as text that required interpretation. Also, they had no experience creating information to fit the structure of an article—they lacked the ability to invent! This center helps students tackle this important skill.

# Student Directions: Comparing and Contrasting Headlines

## Focus on the Skill

1. Consider the headlines on the "Comparing and Contrasting Newspaper Headlines" worksheet. These actual headlines have double meanings, and you must determine which meaning was intended.
2. After practicing analyzing for meaning, determine the events for four headlines on the worksheet. Briefly explain what events occurred based on the headlines alone.

## Practice the Skill

1. Empty envelope #1, and consider the content, purpose, and tone of each article. Paste the articles to the manila paper, and write a unique headline for each article that captures the main idea.
2. Take the headlines from envelope #2, and match the real headlines to their corresponding articles.
3. Choose one of the original headlines and compare it to one you created for the same article. Use the chart on the worksheet to determine if each headline explains what the article is about, catches your attention, and has a lot of detail. Then, complete a framed sentence that summarizes two conclusions you drew from the chart.

## Take It to the Next Level

1. Choose one of the original headlines from the worksheet. You will write the headline at the top of a piece of manila paper (or type a large-font version of the article and paste it to the top of the manila paper).
2. Write your own version of the article. Pay attention to the who, what, where, when, why, and how of your fictitious events.

## How You Will Be Graded

| | 1 little or no evidence | 2 below average | 3 adequate evidence | 4 better than average | 5 superior evidence | TOTAL |
|---|---|---|---|---|---|---|
| Attention to neatness and presentation | | | | | | |
| Determines the meanings of newspaper headlines | | | | | | |
| Able to match headlines with actual articles | | | | | | |
| Creates headlines that capture the meaning of the articles | | | | | | |
| Compares original headline with headline he/she created | | | | | | |
| **Total points multiplied by four** | | | | | | |
| **Final grade** | | | | | | |

# Worksheet: Comparing and Contrasting Newspaper Headlines

## Focus on the Skill

**Analyze these real-life articles and determine what is really happening.**

1. *Enraged Cow Injures Farmer with Ax*

a) A mad cow hurt a farmer who was holding an ax.

b) A mad cow with an ax hurt a farmer.

2. *Miners Refuse to Work after Death*

a) Miners refused to work after they died.

b) Miners refused to work after another worker died in the mine.

3. *Two Soviet Ships Collide—One Dies*

a) Two Soviet ships ran into each other and one person died.

b) Two Soviet ships ran into each other and one of the ships died.

4. *Milk Drinkers are Turning to Powder*

a) People who drink milk turn to powder.

b) People who drink milk are drinking more powdered milk.

5. *Quarter of a Million Chinese Live on Water*

a) In China, a quarter of a million people drink only water.

b) In China, a quarter of a million people live on a lake, river, or ocean.

6. *Local high school dropouts cut in half*

a) Fewer students are dropping out of local high schools.

b) High school dropouts in local high schools are being cut in half.

(Permission from Paco Hope, editor, "The Funny Pages," http://funnies.paco.to/)

## Worksheet: Comparing and Contrasting Newspaper Headlines (continued)

**Now, describe the events that occurred in the articles for these headlines. In short, what happened?**

*Difficult Times Ahead*

______________________________
______________________________
______________________________

*Passerby Sees Woman Jump*

______________________________
______________________________
______________________________

*Man Killed in Accident*

______________________________
______________________________
______________________________

*Workers Protest Pay Cuts*

______________________________
______________________________
______________________________

### Practice the Skill

| The original headline for the article: | Yes or no | Why or why not? | My headline for the article: | Yes or no | Why or why not? |
|---|---|---|---|---|---|
| Explains what the article is about | | | Explains what the article is about | | |
| Catches your attention | | | Catches your attention | | |
| Has a lot of detail | | | Has a lot of detail | | |

When I compare my headline with the original, two things I notice are:

______________________________
______________________________

and ______________________________
______________________________.

# Teacher Directions: Focus on Comparisons

## Goals for Student

1. Read and interpret graphic representations.
2. Separate collected information into useful components using a variety of techniques.
3. Compare ideas from various texts.

## Preparation

1. Your class should be familiar with comparisons. They should know to look for details that can be compared and stretch their minds to imagine how two seemingly unrelated items or ideas can be similar.
2. For this activity, provide ten common items to be compared: fork, straw, eraser, napkin, rubber band, paper clip, highlighter, colored pencil, index card, and sticky notes.

## Materials

- "Focus on Comparisons" worksheet
- "Comparing State Information" worksheet
- Fork, straw, eraser, napkin, rubber band, paper clip, highlighter, colored pencil, index card, and sticky notes

## Focus on the Skill

To begin, students will use the chart on the "Focus on Comparisons" worksheet to compare the specific features of apples and oranges and clocks and watches. They will use the information they collect to write detailed sentences explaining how the items are the same.

## Practice the Skill

1. Then, on the "Focus on Comparisons" worksheet, the students will compare the common items using the signal words. They should use complete sentences, and all items should be used at least once.
2. The students will then consider the information about six states on the "Comparing State Information" worksheet. They will choose two states and compare their features using the framed sentences. They can consider the state mottos, flags, shapes, sizes, and even spellings. After they have completed the sentences, ask the students to go back through the sentences and circle words that signal a comparison is being made.

## Take It to the Next Level

1. The students will create similes to compare information about different states. Provide an almanac or encyclopedia with information about different states: state song, motto, bird, flower, etc. You may also want to provide informational articles with historical background, facts, and elaborative details about the songs, mottos, birds, etc.
2. On a piece of manila paper, they will create three similes and draw sketches to show their interpretations. (Example: *The Florida Mockingbird is like a bully on the street corner.*) Try the "Tri-fold Foldable" from Dinah Zike's website at www.dinah.com.

# Teacher Directions: Focus on Comparisons (continued)

## Special Considerations

You might think it's strange to break the compare and contrast skills apart, but remember that struggling readers miss the details because they don't recognize details as being important. Help kids understand that they need to look for ways that people, places, events, or ideas are the same. Struggling readers need to think about use, color, size, and shape, or other similar characteristics, and they have to learn how to ask themselves questions about two or more objects, people, places, or ideas. A helpful strategy is to recognize words and phrases that signal that a comparison is going to be made (*at the same time, both, equally, in comparison, in the same manner, in the same way, like, likewise, similarly*, etc.).

# Student Directions: Focus on Comparisons

## Focus on the Skill

Use the chart on the "Focus on Comparisons" worksheet to compare the specific features of 1) apples and oranges and 2) clocks and watches. Use the information you collect to write detailed sentences explaining how the items are the same.

## Practice the Skill

1. Then, on the "Focus on Comparisons" worksheet, compare the common items using the signal words. You are expected to use complete sentences, and all items should be used at least once.
2. Consider the information about six states on the "Comparing State Information" worksheet. Choose two states and compare their features using the framed sentences. You can consider the state mottos, flags, shapes, sizes, and even spellings.
3. After you have completed the sentences, go back through the sentences and circle words that signal a comparison is being made.

## Take It to the Next Level

1. You will create similes to compare information about different states (use "like" or "as" to make comparisons). Look in an almanac or encyclopedia, and choose what you would like to compare: state song, motto, bird, flower, etc. Try to find historical background, facts, and elaborative details about the songs, mottos, birds, etc.
2. On a piece of manila paper, you will write three similes and draw sketches to show your interpretations. (Example: *The Florida Mockingbird is like a bully on the street corner.*)

## How You Will Be Graded

| | 1 little or no evidence | 2 below average | 3 adequate evidence | 4 better than average | 5 superior evidence | TOTAL |
|---|---|---|---|---|---|---|
| Attention to neatness and presentation | | | | | | |
| Able to collect information and write about similarities | | | | | | |
| Uses complete sentences to describe comparisons of common items | | | | | | |
| Identifies a variety of features of the states being compared and identifies signal words in sentences that show a comparison is being made | | | | | | |
| Creates similes that make accurate, thoughtful comparisons | | | | | | |
| **Total points multiplied by four** | | | | | | |
| **Final grade** | | | | | | |

# Worksheet: Focus on Comparisons

## Focus on the Skill

When you compare, you are looking for similarities. Consider specific features and fill in the chart below. Use the information to complete the two sentences.

| Features to be Compared | Apples and Oranges | Clocks and Watches |
|---|---|---|
| Shape | | |
| Size | | |
| Use | | |
| Similar details | | |
| What the pair is used together for | | |
| Textures | | |
| Anything else they have in common | | |

Apples and oranges share a lot in common, such as ______________________________

________________________________________________________________________

________________________________________________________________________.

Clocks and watches are a lot alike as well because ______________________________

________________________________________________________________________

________________________________________________________________________.

## Practice the Skill

### Comparison Signal Words

| | | |
|---|---|---|
| *at the same time* | *in comparison* | *like* |
| *both* | *in the same manner* | *likewise* |
| *equally* | *in the same way* | *similarly* |

Consider the features of all ten items provided in the center, and determine what items have in common. The first comparison has been done for you, so begin by finding two new items to compare. Use the signal words to connect each comparison, and use each item only once.

*A fork and a straw are both found in restaurants.*

________________________________________________________________________

________________________________________________________________________

________________________________________________________________________

________________________________________________________________________

________________________________________________________________________

## Worksheet: Comparing State Information

Analyze the **features** of the boxes below. Use the information about each state to make comparisons in the framed sentences. Try to use each state at least once.

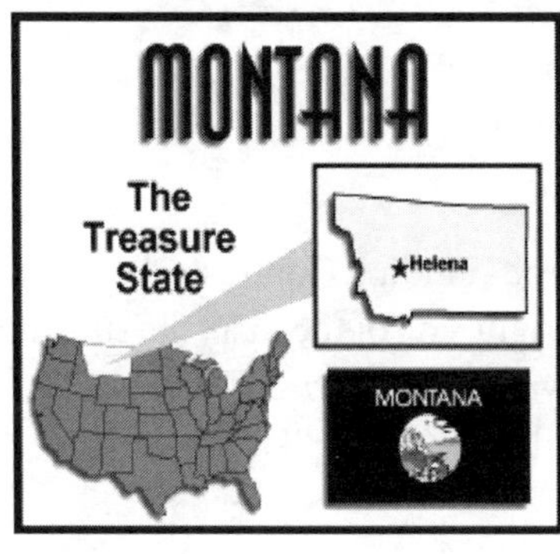

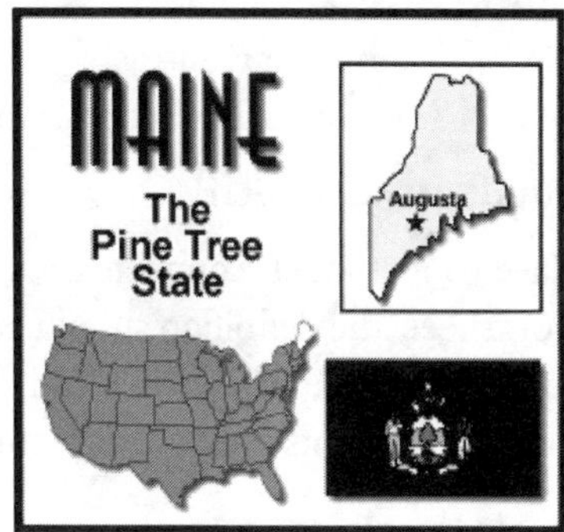


(reprinted with permission from http://www.graphicmaps.com)

1. The state of ____________________ resembles the state of ____________________ because ________________________________________________________________________________
________________________________________________________________________________.

2. Two flags that share something in common are the flag of ____________________ and the flag of ____________________ because ______________________________________________
________________________________________________________________________________.

3. The state of ________________ and the state of ________________ equally remind me of ________________________________________________________________________ because
________________________________________________________________________________.

4. The state of ________________'s ________________ and the state of ________________'s ______________________ both ________________________________________________.

5. The location of both ____________________ and ____________________ could be compared because they are ________________________________________________________________
________________________________________________________________________________.

# Teacher Directions: Finding Contrasts

## Goals for Student

1. Compare and contrast plot elements from various texts.
2. Study word meanings consistently.
3. Use a graphic organizer to clarify meaning of text.

## Preparation

1. Your students should be familiar with the term "contrast." They should know how to look for details that can be contrasted and stretch their minds to see how two seemingly related items, ideas, or stories differ.
2. Collect fables or folktales. Aesop's fables, like the ones on the "Contrasting Fables" worksheet, work well.

## Materials

- "Finding Contrasts" worksheet
- "Contrasting Fables" worksheet
- Manila paper
- Colored pencil

## Focus on the Skill

Have your students complete a vocabulary map for the word "contrast" on the "Finding Contrasts" worksheet (the definition should be located at the top of the map). On the right side of the map, the students will write synonyms for the word. On the left side, they will think of antonyms for the term. Under the map, the students must think of three examples of contrasting ideas (example: "on" is not like "off").

## Practice the Skill

1. Students will consider "non-examples" on the "Finding Contrasts" worksheet. They must consider the category in the box and think of specific non-examples for each category.
2. Next, the students will read and analyze the fables, "The Wolf and the Crane" and "The Lion and the Mouse," on the "Contrasting Fables" worksheet for contrasts—elements of characterization, setting, or plot that are different.
3. The students will read the five sentences that follow the fables on the "Contrasting Fables" worksheet. They will read and complete each sentence.
4. They should read the "points to consider" for each sentence. That will help them determine what element of the story should be contrasted. Their answers should be detailed and show a full understanding of the contrasts in the story.

## Take It to the Next Level

Have the students create an illustrated Venn diagram to compare the two fables. Instead of using words, they use pictures with captions and even thought bubbles to show the comparisons and contrasts. They should use a sheet of manila paper large enough for two circles to hold a variety of pictures and drawings.

## Special Considerations

Just as it is important for struggling readers to recognize that comparisons are very specific, they also need to see how contrasts (finding differences) can be cued by signal words. They must learn that people, events, and ideas are different, and they need to consider why and how. Students have to learn how to ask themselves questions to help them identify obvious and inferred differences. This center directs struggling readers to focus on specific issues.

# Student Directions: Finding Contrasts

## Focus on the Skill

Complete a vocabulary map of the word "contrast" on the "Finding Contrasts" worksheet (the definition should be located at the top of the map). On the right side of the map, write synonyms for the word. On the left side, think of and write antonyms for the term. Under the map, you must think of three examples of contrasting ideas (example: "on" is not like "off").

## Practice the Skill

1. Consider "non-examples" on the "Finding Contrasts" worksheet. Look at the category in the box and think of specific "non-examples" for each category. You may use words or drawings to show your ideas.
2. Read and analyze the fables, "The Wolf and the Crane" and "The Lion and the Mouse," on the "Contrasting Fables" worksheet. You should be looking for contrasts—elements of characterization, setting, or plot that are different.
3. Read the five framed sentences that follow the fables on the "Contrasting Fables" worksheet. Complete each sentence.
4. Read the "points to consider" for each sentence. Determine what element of the story should be contrasted. Your answers should be detailed and show a full understanding of the contrasts in the story.

## Take It to the Next Level

Create an illustrated Venn diagram to compare the two fables. This just means that instead of using words, you will use pictures with captions and even thought bubbles to show the comparisons and contrasts. Use manila paper that is large enough for the two circles to hold a variety of pictures and drawings.

## How You Will Be Graded

| | 1 little or no evidence | 2 below average | 3 adequate evidence | 4 better than average | 5 superior evidence | TOTAL |
|---|---|---|---|---|---|---|
| Attention to neatness and presentation | | | | | | |
| Able to effectively map the word "contrast" | | | | | | |
| Provides details to show understanding of "non-examples" | | | | | | |
| Sentences show ability to contrast specific information in text | | | | | | |
| Creates an effective, illustrated Venn diagram that shows detail and support | | | | | | |
| **Total points multiplied by four** | | | | | | |
| **Final grade** | | | | | | |

## Worksheet: Finding Contrasts

### Focus on the Skill

(v) to show or emphasize differences

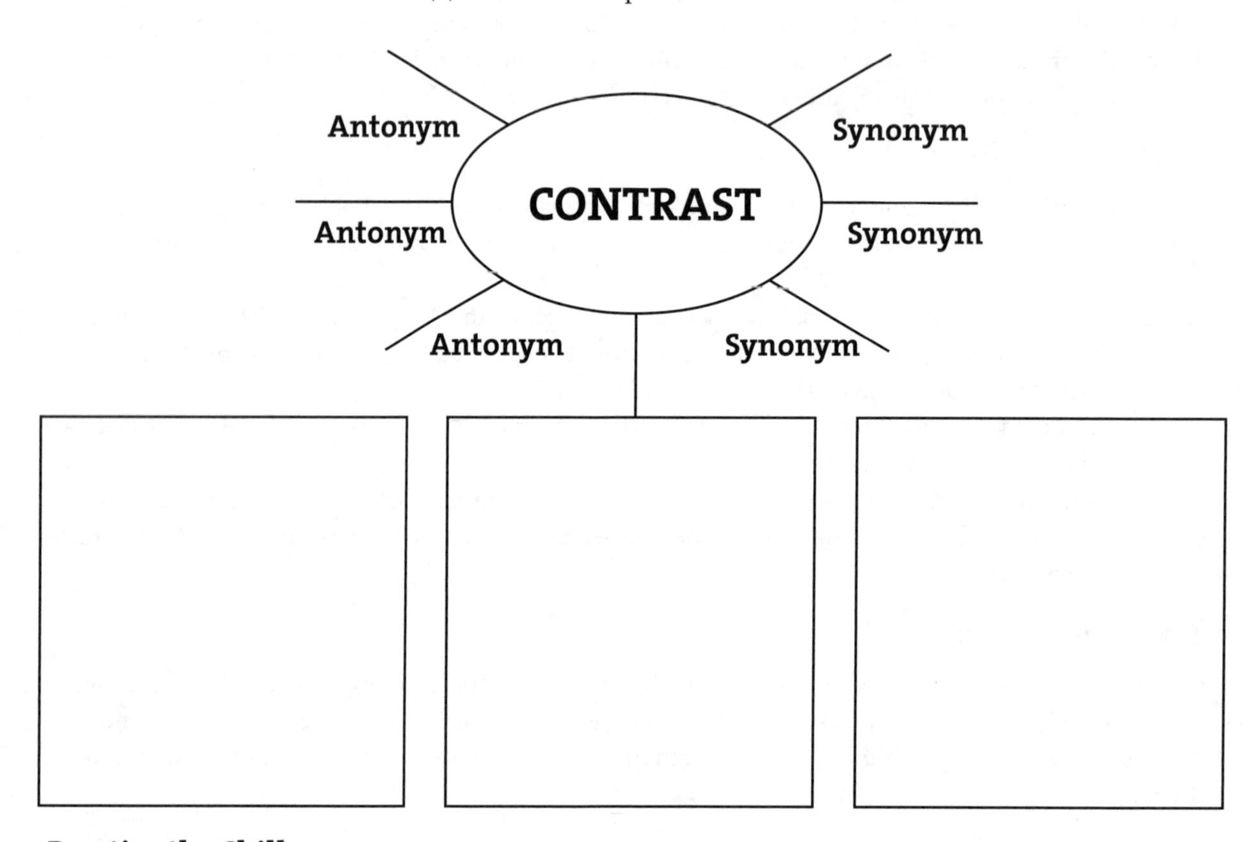


### Practice the Skill

**Non-examples.** Sometimes to understand what something IS, you have to figure out what it IS NOT. These are called non-examples. When you think of contrasts and differences, it helps to look for non-examples.

| Non-examples of lazy men | Non-examples of a person who hates dancing |
|---|---|
| | |
| **Non-examples of sports that are played as a team** | **Non-examples of jobs that require uniforms:** |
| | |
| **Non-examples of a fancy restaurant** | **Non-examples of verbs that show action** |
| | |

# Worksheet: Contrasting Fables

## "The Wolf and the Crane"

A Wolf had been gorging on an animal he had killed when suddenly a small bone in the meat stuck in his throat and he could not swallow it. He soon felt terrible pain in his throat and ran up and down groaning and groaning and seeking something to relieve the pain. He tried to induce every one he met to remove the bone. "I would give anything," said he, "if you would take it out." At last the Crane agreed to try and told the Wolf to lie on his side and open his jaws as wide as he could. Then the Crane put its long neck down the Wolf's throat and, with its beak, loosened the bone till at last it got it out.

"Will you kindly give me the reward you promised?" asked the Crane.

The Wolf grinned and showed his teeth and said: "Be content. You have put your head inside a wolf's mouth and taken it out again in safety; that ought to be reward enough for you."

**THEME: Gratitude and greed go not together.**

## "The Lion and the Mouse"

Once when a Lion was asleep, a little Mouse began running up and down upon him; this soon wakened the Lion, who placed his huge paw upon him and opened his big jaws to swallow him.

"Pardon, O King," cried the little Mouse. "Forgive me this time; I shall never forget it. Who knows but what I may be able to do you a turn some of these days?" The Lion was so tickled at the idea of the Mouse being able to help him that he lifted up his paw and let him go. Some time after, the Lion was caught in a trap, and the hunters who desired to carry him alive to the King tied him to a tree while they went in search of a wagon to carry him on. Just then, the little Mouse happened to pass by and, seeing the sad plight in which the Lion was, went up to him and soon gnawed away the ropes that bound the King of the Beasts. "Was I not right?" asked the little Mouse.

**THEME: Little friends may prove great friends.**

(Points to consider: crane and mouse)

1. Both stories are about large, predatory animals who found themselves in trouble, **but** __________

______________________________________________.

(Points to consider: wolf and lion)

2. The crane and the mouse are both small animals. **In contrast,** __________

______________________________________________.

(Point to consider: wolf's reaction)

3. The lion returned the favor to the mouse. **Nevertheless,** the wolf __________

______________________________________________.

(Points to consider: themes of both stories)

4. The main ideas of both stories are very similar. **On the other hand**, the themes are different because

______________________________________________

(Point to consider: the mouse's request)

5. **Rather** than ask for a reward like the crane, the mouse __________

______________________________________________.

# Teacher Directions: Morphemes

## Goals for Student

1. Use word origins as a strategy for understanding historical influences on word meanings.
2. Examine other sources (a dictionary) to clarify meaning.
3. Identify word parts, such as prefixes, suffixes, and root words.

## Preparation

Your class should understand morphemes, the smallest meaningful unit in grammar. Encourage students to study morphemes as a strategy for decoding word meanings.

## Materials

- "Morphemes" worksheet
- Manila paper
- Colored pencils

## Focus on the Skill

The students will begin by going through ten sentences at the top of the "Morphemes" worksheet and determining the meaning of each underlined word. The sentences do not contain context clues; however, some of the words may be known or already understood. A definition is still required.

## Practice the Skill

1. Instruct the students to look over the "Studying Prefixes, Root Words, and Suffixes" portion of the worksheet. In your discussions, you might want to ask if there are words they recognize and examples of other words they already know that might contain the same morphemes.
2. The students will then construct a complete definition for the words from the ten sentences in the chart. They will write the prefix and its definition, the root word and its definition, and the suffix and its definition for each of the terms from the sentences.
3. After they have created new definitions, it's important for them to compare their guesses with the new findings (validating information). Have students then look up each word in the dictionary and write the definitions on the back of the worksheet. A side lesson might be for them to compare and contrast their definitions with the dictionary definitions.

## Take It to the Next Level

Have the students select one of the original ten sentences (one with a word they could not figure out) from the "Morphemes" worksheet. They will rewrite the sentence on manila paper in large writing at the bottom of the paper. At the top of the paper, they will write the word and its meaning broken down by prefix, root word, and suffix. In the center of the paper, they will draw a picture that reflects the meaning of the sentence using the definition. The picture should be detailed enough to show they understand the implied meaning of the sentence.

## Special Considerations

Students who do not understand word origins and morphemes are unable to recognize patterns in word meanings. After students have defined all word parts, they should create the complete definition starting from the root meaning. For example, the word "affection" comes from the prefix "af" (toward), the root "fect" (to make), and the suffix "ion" (the result of). The literal combined definition is "the result of making toward," so you would need to help your students infer and fill in the gaps.

# Student Directions: Morphemes

## Focus on the Skill

Begin by going through the ten sentences at the top of the "Morphemes" worksheet and determining the meaning of each underlined word. The sentences do no possess context clues; however, you might already know or understand some of the words. A definition is still required.

## Practice the Skill

1. Look over the "Studying Prefixes, Root Words, and Suffixes" portion of the worksheet. Are there words you recognize and examples of other words you know that might contain those morphemes?
2. Construct a complete definition for each of the words from the ten sentences in the chart. Write the prefix and its definition, the root word and its definition, and the suffix and its definition for each of the terms from the sentences. You should start from the suffix and create a smooth definition with the prefix and root meanings.
3. After you have created new definitions, it's important for you to compare your guesses with the new findings (validating information). Then, look up the words in the dictionary and write the definitions on the back of the worksheet. A side lesson might be for you to compare and contrast your definitions with the dictionary definitions.

## Take It to the Next Level

Select one of the original ten sentences (one with a word you could not figure out) from the worksheet. Rewrite the sentence on manila paper in large writing at the bottom of the paper. At the top of the paper, write the word and its meaning broken down by prefix, root word, and suffix. In the center of the paper, draw a picture that reflects the meaning of the sentence using the definition. The picture should be detailed enough to show you understand the implied meaning of the sentence.

## How You Will Be Graded

| | 1 little or no evidence | 2 below average | 3 adequate evidence | 4 better than average | 5 superior evidence | TOTAL |
|---|---|---|---|---|---|---|
| Attention to neatness and presentation | | | | | | |
| Made a guess for the meaning of a word based on the context of the sentences | | | | | | |
| Completed the prefix, root word, and suffix chart successfully | | | | | | |
| Able to construct a good definition using the clues from the morphemes | | | | | | |
| Illustrated one of the ten sentences to reflect the meaning using details that show real understanding | | | | | | |
| **Total points multiplied by four** | | | | | | |
| **Final grade** | | | | | | |

# Worksheet: Morphemes

## Focus on the Skill

Figuring out word meanings without context clues can be difficult. Determine the meaning of each underlined word based on your experiences and the topic of the sentence, and write your answer on the line.

Her story seemed contradictory. ____________________
The bay is a compartment on a ship. ____________________
Diabetics must carry hypodermic needles. ____________________
The friends must coordinate their plans. ____________________
Child abduction is a crime. ____________________
Joe is a credible witness. ____________________
An endoscopic tool can locate the clog in the pipe. ____________________
The paramedic is a hero in the community. ____________________
The soldier should write an autobiography. ____________________
A revision has to be made to the paper. ____________________

## Practice the Skill

**Studying Prefixes, Root Words, and Suffixes**

| Prefix | Root | Suffix |
|---|---|---|
| ab – away | bio – life | ate – to become associated with |
| auto – self | cred – believe | ible – capable of being |
| co – together | derm – skin | ic – having the nature of |
| com – with | dict – to say | ion – the result of |
| contra – against | duct – to lead | ize – to become |
| endo – within | fect – to make | ment – state of |
| hypo – under | graph – write | ory – a place for |
| in – not | medic – physician | tion – the result of |
| para – beside | ordin – order | y – a version of |
| re – again | part – piece or portion | |
| | scop – to see | |
| | vis – to look | |
| | vital – full of life | |

Now, take each word apart. Consider the prefix, root, and suffix meaning of each word to create a new definition that shows a real understanding of the word. An example has been done for you.

| Word | Prefix and Definition | Root and Definition | Suffix and Definition | Complete Definition |
|---|---|---|---|---|
| revitalize | *re – again* | *vital – full of life* | *ize – to become* | *to become full of life again* |
| contradictory | | | | |
| compartment | | | | |
| hypodermic | | | | |
| coordinate | | | | |
| abduction | | | | |
| credible | | | | |
| endoscopic | | | | |
| paramedic | | | | |
| autobiography | | | | |
| revision | | | | |

# Teacher Directions: Homonyms, Homographs, and Homophones

## Goals for Student

1. Study word meanings consistently.
2. Select appropriate meaning for a word according to context.
3. Analyze word relationships.

## Preparation

1. Your class should have some knowledge of homonyms, homographs, and homophones. They should know all three fall under the category of "commonly confused words" and begin to recognize why those misconceptions occur.
2. Provide your students with a picture book that contains a good number of homonyms (*Cloudy with a Chance of Meatballs* by Judi Barrett and *The King Who Rained* by Fred Gwynne are just a couple of examples). The goal is for your students to find examples of homonyms and recognize each version of the word as a term that may have two meanings.

## Materials

- Picture Book with Homophones
- "Homonyms, Homographs, and Homophones" worksheet
- Colored copy paper
- Colored pencils

## Focus on the Skill

1. To begin, have your students read the picture book you have provided and make a list of words that are easily confused in the story.
2. Have students review the definitions and examples of homonyms, homographs, and homophones. On the back of the worksheet, they should write their list of confused words and determine what best describes the pair: homonyms, homographs, or homophones.
3. Students should then go back to the "Homonyms, Homographs, and Homophones" worksheet and place the pairs of words in the "Categorizing Commonly Confused Words" chart under the correct category—homonym, homograph, or homophone.

### Answer Key

colon/colon – homonyms
invalid/invalid – homographs
knot/knot – homonyms
lean/lean – homonyms
produce/produce – homographs
record/record – homographs
ring/wring – homophones
stare/stair – homophones
sundae/ Sunday – homophones

# Teacher Directions: Homonyms, Homographs, and Homophones (continued)

## Practice the Skill

1. Using colored copy paper, students should create a four-page "Commonly Confused Words Review Book" with that title on the front. Try the "Bound Book Foldable" from Dinah Zike's website at www.dinah.com.
2. On the left side of the first page, they should write a definition of "homonym" and an example from the homonym list on the "Homonyms, Homographs, and Homophones" worksheet. On the right side of the first page, the students will draw two captioned pictures—each with details and a sentence that shows the pair of words used correctly.
3. On the left side of the second page, they should write a definition of "homograph" and an example from the homograph list on the "Homonyms, Homographs, and Homophones" worksheet. On the right side of the second page, the students will draw two captioned pictures—each with details and a sentence that shows the pair of words used correctly.
4. On the left side of the third page, they should write a definition of "homophone" and an example from the homophone list on the "Homonyms, Homographs, and Homophones" worksheet. On the right side of the first page, the students will draw two captioned pictures—each with details and a sentence that shows the pair of words used correctly.

## Take It to the Next Level

Have the students write a short story using a pair of homophones, homographs, and homonyms. If you feel your students are capable, require the story to include exposition, rising action, climax, and falling action.

## Special Considerations

Don't be terribly disappointed if students are confused by the terms "homonyms," "homographs," and "homophones." There are many *teachers* who use the terms interchangeably. However, you want your struggling readers to understand why these words are so confusing and to pay attention to pronunciation, spelling, and meaning. Education World has a cumulative online list (second grade through high school) in a lesson called "Create Your Own Homophone Worksheets" at http://www.educationworld.com. You can create PowerPoint quizzes, game questions, or an endless number of fun plans from this list alone.

# Student Directions: Homonyms, Homographs, and Homophones

## Focus on the Skill

1. Read the picture book provided and make a list of words that are easily confused in the story on the back of the "Homonyms, Homographs, and Homophones" worksheet.
2. Review the definitions and examples of homonyms, homographs, and homophones. Turn the worksheet over and write your list of confused words from the story. Determine which best describes the pairs: homophones, homographs, or homonyms.
3. Then, go back to the worksheet and place the pairs of words in the "Categorizing Commonly Confused Words" chart under the correct category—homonym, homograph, or homophone.

## Practice the Skill

1. Using colored copy paper, create a four-page "Commonly Confused Words Review Book" with that title on the front.
2. On the left side of the first page, write a definition of "homonym" and an example from the homonym list on the "Homonyms, Homographs, and Homophones" worksheet. On the right side of the first page, draw two captioned pictures—each with details and a sentence that shows the pair of words used correctly.
3. On the left side of the second page, write a definition of "homograph" and an example from the homograph list on the "Homonyms, Homographs, and Homophones" worksheet. On the right side of the second page, draw two captioned pictures—each with details and a sentence that shows the pair of words used correctly.
4. On the left side of the third page, write a definition of "homophone" and an example from the homophone list on the "Homonyms, Homographs, and Homophones" worksheet. On the right side of the first page, draw two captioned pictures—each with details and a sentence that shows the pair of words used correctly.

## Take It to the Next Level

Finally, write a short story using a pair of homophones, homographs, and homonyms.

## How You Will Be Graded

| | 1 little or no evidence | 2 below average | 3 adequate evidence | 4 better than average | 5 superior evidence | TOTAL |
|---|---|---|---|---|---|---|
| Attention to neatness and presentation | | | | | | |
| Reflects understanding of homonyms with sentences and detailed drawings | | | | | | |
| Reflects understanding of homographs with sentences and detailed drawings | | | | | | |
| Reflects understanding of homophones with sentences and detailed drawings | | | | | | |
| Effectively categorizes homonyms, homophones, and homographs | | | | | | |
| **Total points multiplied by four** | | | | | | |
| **Final grade** | | | | | | |

## Worksheet: Homonyms, Homographs, and Homophones

**Homonyms: same sound, same spelling, different meanings**

angle – where two lines meet
angle – to fish

ball – round object
ball – a dance

bank – side of a river
bank – place for money

bowl – a dish
bowl – to throw a ball

long – great length
long – hope

race – group of people
race – run in a competition

season – time of year
season – add flavor to food

tip – a point
tip – to push over

yard – a measurement
yard – a back garden

**Homographs: same spelling, different sounds, different meanings**

address – speech or written statement
address – place where a person or organization is located

resume – written account of qualifications
resume – to continue

tear – water from the eye
tear – to pull apart

**Homophones: same sound, different meanings, different spellings**

farrow – a litter of pigs
pharaoh – ancient Egyptian king

cannon – mounted gun
canon – a general rule

bald – little or no hair on the scalp
bawled – to cry or sob loudly

alter – to change or modify
altar – elevated platform for worship

discussed – to speak with others
disgust – a strong dislike

sighed – exhaled a long breath
side – one surface that forms a boundary

route – course or passageway
root – downward anchors for plants

complement – something that completes or makes perfect
compliment – expression of praise

tract – expanse of land
tracked – to follow

**Categorizing Commonly Confused Words.** Study the word pairs below. Based on the definitions and examples from above, decide which category each pair falls under. Write each pair of words under the correct column in the chart below.

| Homonyms | Homographs | Homophones |
|---|---|---|
| | | |
| | | |
| | | |

colon – punctuation mark
colon – part of the large intestine

ring – jewelry for a finger
wring – to twist forcibly

invalid – sickly person
invalid – untrue; weak argument

knot – speed of a boat
knot – twisted string

stair – one in a series of steps
stare – to gaze intently

lean – thin or slender
lean – bend forward

sundae – ice cream dessert
Sunday – day of the week

produce – vegetables and fruit
produce – to make or manufacture

record – to copy
record – a document in writing

# Teacher Directions: Multiple Meanings

## Goals for Student

1. Understand ways figurative language can contribute to mood or meaning.
2. Understand ways the author's word choice contributes to the meaning of a text.
3. Distinguish denotative and connotative meanings of words.

## Preparation

1. Your class should understand the difference between "denotation" and connotation."
2. You will need to gather *Amelia Bedelia* books, which are full of idioms that are silly and easy to discuss.

## Materials

- "Multiple Meanings" worksheet
- Manila paper
- *Amelia Bedelia* books
- Colored pencils

## Focus on the Skill

The students should begin by completing the "Denotation and Connotation" section of the "Multiple Meanings" worksheet. They will read the sentence in the left column and look up the dictionary definition (denotation) for the word that is bolded and underlined. Then, they will read the sentence again and write the connotation, or figurative meaning for the word, in the last column.

## Practice the Skill

1. Have the students read the first book of the *Amelia Bedelia* series. On the "Multiple Meanings" worksheet, they will write three phrases from the story that Amelia gets confused. Explain that Amelia has taken the instructions literally and that she is looking at the denotation of every phrase. The students will analyze each idiom from the story to determine the connotation of each phrase and write their answer next to the idioms they found.
2. In the "More Practice with Idioms" section of the worksheet, students will analyze the listed idioms and determine their figurative meaning (connotation). They should write a definition for each idiom on the lines provided.

## Take It to the Next Level

Have the students select one of the idioms from the "More Practice with Idioms" section of the worksheet. They should write the idiom across the middle of a sheet of manila paper (lengthwise). They then fold the paper in half (hamburger fold turned sideways). On the left side, have them write "Denotation" across the top and draw a picture that reflects the literal meaning of the phrase. These will be humorous, and most kids will realize the absurdity of the phrase as a literal translation very quickly. On the right side of the paper, they should write "Connotation" and draw a picture that shows the figurative or implied meaning.

## Special Considerations

The terms "denotation" and "connotation" are very important. These are words that will transcend middle and high school, and it's crucial that students USE THE TERMS. Idioms are really a small part of the multiple meanings topic, but they're a good place to start with kids who really do not see shades of meaning.

# Student Directions: Multiple Meanings

## Focus on the Skill

Begin by completing the "Denotation and Connotation" section of the "Multiple Meanings" worksheet. Read the sentence in the left column and look up the dictionary definition (denotation) for the word that is bolded and underlined. Then, read the sentence again and write the connotation, or figurative meaning for the word, in the last column.

## Practice the Skill

1. Read the first book of the *Amelia Bedelia* series. On the "Multiple Meanings" worksheet, write three phrases from the story that Amelia gets confused because she has taken the instructions literally and is looking at the denotation of every phrase. Analyze each idiom from the story and determine the connotation of each phrase. Write your answers next to the idioms you found.
2. In the "More Practice with Idioms" section of the worksheet, analyze the idioms and determine their figurative meaning (connotation). Write a definition for each idiom on the lines provided.

## Take It to the Next Level

Select one of the idioms from the "More Practice with Idioms" section of the worksheet. Write the idiom across the middle of a sheet of manila paper (lengthwise). Fold the paper in half (hamburger fold turned sideways). On the left side, write "Denotation" across the top, and draw a picture that reflects the literal meaning of the phrase. On the right side of the paper, write "Connotation" across the top, and draw a picture that shows the figurative or implied meaning.

## How You Will Be Graded

| | 1 little or no evidence | 2 below average | 3 adequate evidence | 4 better than average | 5 superior evidence | TOTAL |
|---|---|---|---|---|---|---|
| Attention to neatness and presentation | | | | | | |
| Accurately reported the denotation and connotation meanings of common words | | | | | | |
| Identified three idioms from *Amelia Bedelia* | | | | | | |
| Analyzed common idioms and determined the connotative meaning of each | | | | | | |
| Illustrated the denotation and connotation of common idiom phrases | | | | | | |
| **Total points multiplied by four** | | | | | | |
| **Final grade** | | | | | | |

# Worksheet: Multiple Meanings

## Focus on the Skill

**Denotation and Connotation.** To understand multiple meanings, you have to understand that words sometimes have a dictionary definition (denotation) and a figurative meaning (connotation). Look at the sentences in the left column below. Read the sentence, and look up the dictionary definition for the word that is bolded and underlined. Decide the connotation of the word as it is used in the sentence. The first one has been done for you.

| | **Denotation** (strict dictionary meaning) | **Connotation** (emotional and figurative meaning) |
|---|---|---|
| *Stephanie's feelings about saving the environment are very* ***deep****.* | *deep – (adj.) far down below the surface* | *deep – Stephanie cares a lot about the environment* |
| Carlos's jumping, blocking, and passing skills were great, so he thought he could easily **bag** a spot on the team. | | |
| Kim practiced her speech over and over at home. She did not want to **choke** when she spoke in front of the audience. | | |
| Joe's parents always say, "Just be **straight** with us about how you're doing in school." | | |
| You need to go to sleep early because we're going to **roll** out of here around 4:30 in the morning. | | |

***Amelia Bedelia*** **Idioms.** Idioms are expressions. Read *Amelia Bedelia*, and find three examples of idioms where Amelia heard the literal meaning (denotation) instead of the figurative meaning (connotation). In the left column, write three of these idioms. In the right column, write the intended meaning of the phrase.

| ***Amelia Bedelia*** **Phrases** | **Connotation (What the phrase really means)** |
|---|---|
| Example: "dress the turkey" | prepare the turkey to be eaten |
| 1. ________________ | ________________ |
| 2. ________________ | ________________ |
| 3. ________________ | ________________ |

# Worksheet: Multiple Meanings (continued)

## Practice the Skill

**More Practice with Idioms.** Analyze the idioms and determine their figurative meaning (connotation). Write a definition for each idiom on the lines provided.

1. see eye to eye

 ______________________________________________

2. under the weather

 ______________________________________________

3. on pins and needles

 ______________________________________________

4. born yesterday

 ______________________________________________

5. feel like a million dollars

 ______________________________________________

6. hold your horses

 ______________________________________________

7. going bananas

 ______________________________________________

8. bury the hatchet

 ______________________________________________

# Teacher Directions: Context Clues

## Goals for Student

1. Select appropriate meaning for a word according to context.
2. Examine other sources (such as a dictionary) to clarify meaning.
3. Use context and word structure clues to interpret words and ideas in text.

## Preparation

Your class should have some understanding of the term "words in context." They should have a lot of experience (through discussion and class work) decoding word meaning using sentence clues.

## Materials

- "Contextual Vocabulary" worksheet
- Manila paper
- Colored pencils

## Focus on the Skill

1. Have the students read about the different types of context clues on the "Contextual Vocabulary" worksheet. They will read the ten sentences at the bottom of the worksheet and decide what kind of context clue was used in each by placing the letter of the matching clue type next to each sentence.
2. You may want them to look up the words in the dictionary and validate their guesses. It's important that they understand the definitions of each word.

## Practice the Skill

Have the students choose one of the ten sentences. At the bottom of a piece of manila paper, they will write the sentence in large writing and underline the parts of the sentence that served as clues. At the top of the paper, they will write the kind of context clue that was used with that sentence. In their own words, the students should explain how clues are used in sentences written like this (using the notes from the worksheet). In the middle of the paper, the students will draw a scene that reflects the meaning of the sentence. Details are important.

## Take It to the Next Level

Have the students find a sentence in the newspaper with vocabulary words that are difficult to understand paste it on the back of the manila paper. First, they will determine if there are context clues in the sentence using the notes from the "Contextual Vocabulary" worksheet. If so, they will underline the parts of the sentence that made the meaning clear and tell what type of context clue is being used. If a context clue is NOT present, they will look up the word or words that are difficult to understand. Using the definition that they find, they will rewrite the sentence and include context clues in the revision. They can use more than one sentence if needed, but the idea is to have them create context clues as well as locate them.

## Special Considerations

Struggling readers do not always recognize context clues, so be prepared to redirect and focus students verbally towards the answer. The focus of this lesson is for students to recognize patterns that are associated with context clues. You want your students to recognize the patterns as well as the clues themselves. After this lesson, make sure you ask specific questions about the type of context clues that are provided in sentences students are reading ("Is that a definition clue, a synonym clue, an antonym clue, or an inference clue?"). It's definitely a skill worth practicing.

# Student Directions: Context Clues

## Focus on the Skill

1. Read about the different types of context clues on the "Contextual Vocabulary" worksheet. Read the ten sentences at the bottom of the worksheet and decide what kind of context clue was used in each. Place the letter of the matching clue next to each sentence.
2. Look up the words in the dictionary to validate your guesses. It's important that you understand the definitions of each word.

## Practice the Skill

Choose one of the ten sentences. At the bottom of a piece of manila paper, write the sentence in large writing and underline the parts of the sentence that served as clues. At the top of the paper, write the kind of context clue that was used with that sentence. In your own words, you should explain how clues are used in sentences written like this (using the notes from the worksheet). In the middle of the paper, draw a scene that reflects the meaning of the sentence. Details are important.

## Take It to the Next Level

Find a sentence in the newspaper with vocabulary words that are difficult to understand, and paste it on the back of the manila paper. First, determine if there are context clues in the sentence using the notes from the "Contextual Vocabulary" worksheet. If so, underline the parts of the sentence that made the meaning clear and tell what type of context clue is being used. If a context clue is NOT present, look up the word or words that are difficult to understand in the dictionary. Using the definition that you find, rewrite the sentence and include context clues in the revision. You can use more than one sentence if needed, but the idea is to create context clues as well as locate them.

## How You Will Be Graded

| | 1<br>little or no evidence | 2<br>below average | 3<br>adequate evidence | 4<br>better than average | 5<br>superior evidence | TOTAL |
|---|---|---|---|---|---|---|
| Attention to neatness and presentation | | | | | | |
| Correctly identifies types of context clues used in sentences with difficult vocabulary | | | | | | |
| Determines the meanings of words using context clues | | | | | | |
| Validates and confirms guesses about word meanings | | | | | | |
| Illustrates one of the ten sentences to reflect the meaning using details that show real understanding | | | | | | |
| **Total points multiplied by four** | | | | | | |
| **Final grade** | | | | | | |

## Worksheet: Contextual Vocabulary

There are four good ways to think about context clues. Read over each description.

a. **Appositive or Definition Clues.** Writers define words and phrases immediately after they've been used. Writers will often use an appositive, where the definition or explanation is set off by commas.

Example: Johnny's canine, a miniature Dachshund who yips at the door, is annoying.

"Canine" might not be a word you know, but you can certainly tell by the explanation that a canine is a dog.

b. **Restatement or Synonym Clues.** Writers often like to clarify a word by restating it or providing a similar word or phrase (synonym).

Example: As the weather deteriorates and grows worse, we realize we're not going to the beach today.

"Deteriorates" means the same as "grows worse."

c. **Contrast or Antonym Clues.** Writers use signal words like "but" or "however" to create contrasts (differences), and the definition of a word can be better understood if you recognize the meaning of the contrasted information or antonyms (words with opposite meanings).

Example: At first, I was perplexed by the directions, but once I read them again, I realized they weren't that confusing.

"Perplexed" has the opposite meaning of "weren't that confusing."

d. **Inference Clues.** Writers will give clues to the meaning of a word in the sentence before or after the sentence that contains the difficult word.

Grandmother was always fastidious about our appearance. She never let us go out to play without making certain our faces were clean and our outfits were matching.

You have to think about what "making certain our faces were clean" and "outfits were matching" implies. If you were to consider both, the conclusion might be that Grandmother is "picky," which is a synonym for "fastidious."

## Worksheet: Contextual Vocabulary (continued)

**Decide which type of context clue is used in each sentence. Write the letter of the matching clue type on the line in front of each sentence. Then, determine the meaning of each underlined word and write the definition.**

1. ______ I have noticed a lot of people use diminutive forms, or shorter versions, of their real names. For instance, "Elizabeth" likes to be called "Liz."

   Definition of "diminutive" ______________________ ______________________

2. ______ The nefarious king was known for locking prisoners in the dungeon without food or water; however, the king decided later that he should be more kindhearted if he wanted his subjects to like him.

   Definition of "nefarious" ______________________ ______________________

3. ______ Children on the playground are known to ostracize, or ignore, other kids just to be mean.

   Definition of "ostracize" ______________________ ______________________

4. ______ She felt a lot of trepidation about the decision. Her heart was beating fast, and her palms began to sweat.

   Definition of "trepidation" ______________________ ______________________

5. ______ All of Sarah's friends felt so sorry for her when her dog died. When Sarah cried, they all went to her house to commiserate with her.

   Definition of "commiserate" ______________________ ______________________

6. ______ When the bank robber was found not guilty, everyone in the courthouse said a travesty, or a joke, of justice took place.

   Definition of "travesty" ______________________ ______________________

7. ______ Our cafeteria was serving the same boring, mundane, predictable menu as yesterday.

   Definition of "mundane" ______________________ ______________________

8. ______ Dozens of nurses and doctors tried to mollify the patient, but he was too frantic and distressed about his injuries.

   Definition of "mollify" ______________________ ______________________

9. ______ The general wanted the information to be passed on precisely and accurately. He felt orders to the soldiers should be repeated verbatim.

   Definition of "verbatim" ______________________ ______________________

10. ______ Scathing, sarcastic, and hurtful remarks were made about the captain of the cheerleaders.

    Definition of "scathing" ______________________ ______________________

# Teacher Directions: Chronological Order and Order of Importance

## Goals for Student

1. Analyze ways writers organize and present ideas through chronology.
2. Use context and word structure clues to interpret words and ideas in text.
3. Explain or demonstrate how phrases, sentences, or passages relate to personal life.

## Preparation

1. Your class should be comfortable using the terms "chronological order" and "order of importance." They should have practice identifying important events in a story and putting those events into chronological order as they happened. They also should have experience organizing information using paragraphs with topic sentences and transition words.
2. For this lesson, you will need page 81 of *The Trial* by Jen Bryant, entitled "Boxcars."

## Materials

- Page 81 of *The Trial* by Jen Bryant
- "Chronological Order and Order of Importance" worksheet
- Manila paper
- Colored pencils

## Focus on the Skill

On the back of the "Chronological Order and Order of Importance" worksheet, the students will list their morning routine, first in chronological order and then in order of importance.

## Practice the Skill

1. On the "Chronological Order and Order of Importance" worksheet, the students will find two paragraphs with sentences that are out of order.
2. Students will cut apart sentences for each paragraph. The first paragraph should be reorganized chronologically and the second by order of importance.
3. Have the students glue the sentences down in the correct order on a piece of manila paper.
4. When they are done reorganizing the paragraphs, have them read the newly structured paragraphs and determine how they knew to put the paragraph in order. Were there clues?
5. They will go back and circle the signal words (transition words) that served as clues in the activity.

## Take It to the Next Level

1. Next, students will divide the opposite side of the paper into three even sections (lines running vertically; try the "Tri-fold Foldable" from Dinah Zike's website at www.dinah.com). They will analyze the excerpt, "Boxcars" (page 81 of *The Trial* by Jen Bryant) and organize how the boxcars in the passage changed according to **three chronological events**.
2. They will draw a picture in each section that represents each event and what the trains have transported in the order they were mentioned. Below each picture, the students should write the line from the novel that best describes each picture. The pictures should have at least five details from the novel that shows the mood of the descriptions. Details can include items mentioned in the passage, characters and thought bubbles, or scenery. If they do this correctly, each box should reflect a deterioration of mood, from a plentiful time to a more desperate era.

## Special Considerations

Bryant takes a unique, first-person approach to revealing the events of the Lindbergh trial through verse. As students interact with fiction and non-fiction, discuss how information is organized in each.

# Student Directions: Chronological Order and Order of Importance

## Focus on the Skill

On the back of the "Chronological Order and Order of Importance" worksheet, you will list your morning routine, first in chronological order and then in order of importance.

## Practice the Skill

1. On the "Chronological Order and Order of Importance" worksheet, you will find two paragraphs that are out of order.
2. Cut apart the sentences for each paragraph. The first should be reorganized according to chronological order, and the second paragraph should be reorganized according to order of importance. Glue the sentences down in the correct order on a piece of manila paper.
3. When you are done reorganizing the paragraphs, read the newly structured paragraphs and determine how you knew to put the paragraph in order. Were there clues?
4. Go back and circle the signal words (transition words) that served as clues in the activity.

## Take It to the Next Level

1. Next, divide the opposite side of the manila paper into three even sections (lines running vertically). You will analyze the excerpt, "Boxcars," from *The Trial* by Jen Bryant and organize how the boxcars in the passage changed according to three chronological events.
2. You will draw a picture in each section that represents each event and what the trains have transported in the order they were mentioned. Below each picture, you should write the line from the novel that best describes each picture. The pictures should have at least five details from the novel that shows the mood of the descriptions. Details can include items mentioned in the passage, characters and thought bubbles, or scenery.

## How You Will Be Graded

| | 1 little or no evidence | 2 below average | 3 adequate evidence | 4 better than average | 5 superior evidence | TOTAL |
|---|---|---|---|---|---|---|
| Attention to neatness and presentation | | | | | | |
| Correctly reorganizes a paragraph according to chronological order | | | | | | |
| Correctly reorganizes a paragraph according to order of importance | | | | | | |
| Identifies signal words that serve as clues for ordering events | | | | | | |
| Illustration of excerpt from *The Trial* details the chronological order of the passage | | | | | | |
| **Total points multiplied by four** | | | | | | |
| **Final grade** | | | | | | |

# Worksheet: Chronological Order and Order of Importance

## Chronological Order

(1) As soon as Lindbergh discovered the baby was gone, he searched the grounds and called the state police.

(2) Unknown to all, the body of little Charles Jr., dead of a skull fracture, lay on the road, a few miles from the Lindberghs' home.

(3) The kidnapping and murder of the son of world-famous aviator Charles Lindbergh has become known as "The Crime of the Century."

(4) In the days and nights that followed, thousands of sympathy letters, ransom demands, and even death threats arrived at Lindberghs' home.

(5) Some time on the night of March 1, 1932, the child was taken from his second-floor nursery.

(6) In addition to the ransom note, investigators found a homemade ladder and a chisel near the house.

(7) The kidnapper left no fingerprints but did leave a note demanding $50,000 in ransom.

(8) On May 12, 1932, a truck driver discovered his tiny remains, and Americans demanded justice.

(9) Police and reporters rushed to the scene, destroying what might have been left of a kidnapper's footprints in the mud and snow.

(10) A desperate Lindbergh would pay the ransom, but the child was never returned.

## Order of Importance

(1) During a search of Hauptmann's house and garage, nearly $15,000 of the Lindbergh ransom money was found.

(2) First, a $10 gold certificate, with a license plate number written on it, was discovered at a local bank.

(3) Based on this evidence, Hauptmann was convicted and put to death on April 3, 1936.

(4) Additionally, prosecution experts testified that the ladder used in the kidnapping had been made from wood found in Hauptmann's attic and that Hauptmann's handwriting matched that found on the ransom notes.

(5) While there is some speculation about his guilt, the evidence suggests Bruno Richard Hauptmann kidnapped Charles Lindbergh's baby.

(6) Most important, however, eyewitnesses testified that it was Hauptmann who had spent some of the Lindbergh gold certificates and that he had been seen in the area of the Hopewell estate on the day of the kidnapping.

(7) The certificate was determined to have come from the Lindbergh ransom money, and the license plate belonged to Bruno Richard Hauptmann.

# Teacher Directions: Sequence of Events in a Work of Fiction

## Goals for Student

1. Read and discuss literature with differing viewpoints to enhance perspective.
2. Analyze and describe a situation related to the central conflict in a literary work from various points of view.
3. Understand plot events related to the central conflict.

## Preparation

1. Your class should have some understanding of the term "words in context." They should have a lot of experience (through discussion and class work) decoding word meaning using sentence clues.
2. Find a fictional picture book that has a clear plot structure: exposition, rising actions, climax, and falling actions. You should have enough copies for each student at the center.

## Materials

- "Story Map" worksheet
- Picture books

## Focus on the Skill

Have the students read their picture book and focus on the plot of the story.

## Practice the Skill

The students will complete the story map on the "Story Map" worksheet. They should illustrate each box to show the characters, setting, and plot (conflict, two events from the story, and the resolution).

## Take It to the Next Level

Using the RAFT (**R**ole, **A**udience, **F**ormat, and **T**opic plus a strong verb) strategy, students will take on the role of a newspaper reporter writing an article about the events for readers. Their article should tell the story in its entirety with details from the book to show they understood the order of events. Example for *The True Story of the Three Little Pigs* by Jon Scieszka:

**BIG BAD WOLF ARRESTED**

*Alexander T. Wolf was jailed yesterday after being charged with stalking and first-degree murder. Though he maintains his innocence, Mr. Wolf was found attempting to break down the door of respected businessman Mr. Pig Three.*

*"He knows his crimes!" said an emotional Mr. Three in response to the arrest. "I warned him to get away from my door. Both my brothers lost their lives to his evil ways."*

*Mr. Wolf, allegedly seeking a cup of sugar to make a cake for his dear Granny, has been linked to the killings of Mr. Pig One and Mr. Pig Two. Both resided near their brother in the Straw and Sticks sections of town.*

*If convicted, Mr. Wolf will be facing a maximum 99-year prison sentence. Now known as the "Huff and Puff Killer," he remains locked in the county penitentiary until his trial.*

## Special Considerations

Choose short picture books for this center, such as *Click, Clack, Moo: Cows That Type* by Doreen Cronin and Betsy Lewin, *The Story of Ferdinand* by Munro Leaf, *Where the Wild Things Are* by Maurice Sendak, and other books kids love!

# Student Directions: Sequence of Events in a Work of Fiction

## Focus on the Skill

Read a picture book and focus on the plot of the story.

## Practice the Skill

Complete the story map on the "Story Map" worksheet. You should illustrate and color each box to show the characters, setting, and plot (conflict, two events from the story, and the resolution).

## Take It to the Next Level

Using the RAFT (Role, Audience, Format, and Topic plus a strong verb) strategy, you will take on the role of a newspaper reporter. The audience is the newspaper's reading audience. You will write an article detailing the events from the picture book as if you had been sent to the scene to make the report. Your article should tell the story in its entirety and reflect details from the picture book to show you understood the order of events. Example for *The True Story of the Three Little Pigs* by Jon Scieszka:

**BIG BAD WOLF ARRESTED**

*Alexander T. Wolf was jailed yesterday after being charged with stalking and first-degree murder. Though he maintains his innocence, Mr. Wolf was found attempting to break down the door of respected businessman Mr. Pig Three.*

*"He knows his crimes!" said an emotional Mr. Three in response to the arrest. "I warned him to get away from my door. Both my brothers lost their lives to his evil ways."*

*Mr. Wolf, allegedly seeking a cup of sugar to make a cake for his dear Granny, has been linked to the killings of Mr. Pig One and Mr. Pig Two. Both resided near their brother in the Straw and Sticks sections of town.*

*If convicted, Mr. Wolf will be facing a maximum 99-year prison sentence. Now known as the "Huff and Puff Killer," he remains locked in the county penitentiary until his trial.*

## How You Will Be Graded

| | 1 little or no evidence | 2 below average | 3 adequate evidence | 4 better than average | 5 superior evidence | TOTAL |
|---|---|---|---|---|---|---|
| Attention to neatness and presentation | | | | | | |
| Recognizes characters and setting in a picture book | | | | | | |
| Identifies important events in a work of fiction | | | | | | |
| Identifies the major conflict and resolution in a work of fiction | | | | | | |
| Creates a newspaper article that reflects details from the original picture book | | | | | | |
| **Total points multiplied by four** | | | | | | |
| **Final grade** | | | | | | |

## Worksheet: Story Map

**Title of Story:** ______________________________

| CHARACTERS | SETTING |
| --- | --- |
| | |

| CONFLICT OF STORY |
| --- |
| |

| PLOT EVENT #1 | PLOT EVENT #2 |
| --- | --- |
| | |

| SOLUTION / RESOLUTION |
| --- |
| |

# Teacher Directions: Using Comic Strips and Photographs

## Goals for Student

1. Use a graphic organizer to clarify meaning.
2. Examine and interpret a graphic representation from differing viewpoints to enhance perspective.
3. Recognize chronological events in a variety of graphic representations.

## Preparation

1. Your class should have a lot of practice considering the way text is organized. They should begin to understand chronology and order of importance.
2. Find five comic strips from the newspaper.
3. Make copies so that each student will have all five comics.
4. Cut up all of the comics by their frames and put all of the frames into an envelope (one for each student).
5. Next, find a photo where something sad or happy has obviously occurred (a child's birthday party, a family standing in front of a burned house, a wedding, etc.). You may want to find a humorous or emotional photograph—depending on the tone you would like your students to recognize. Make a copy for each student.

## Materials

- "Using Comic Strips and Photographs" worksheet
- Manila paper
- Photograph
- Five cut-up cartoons in an envelope
- Glue stick

## Focus on the Skill

1. The students will begin by reassembling the comics to their original format and gluing the boxes in order on a sheet of manila paper.
2. They will choose one of the comics and fill in the "Chain of Events" table on the "Using Comic Strips and Photographs" worksheet. They will think about the details from each frame and show how one event led to another. In the "As a result" box, they should explain the outcome of the events or what made the comic funny.

## Practice the Skill

1. Students will paste the photo on the back of the manila paper in the center.
2. On the "Using Comic Strips and Photographs" worksheet, students will write down all of the details from the photograph in the column labeled "The photo—what is happening?" You may want to teach your students to break the photo into quadrants and, beginning at the top of the right-hand side, write every detail. They then move clockwise around the photo, studying each quadrant before considering the photo as a whole.
3. Then, students will brainstorm causes, or events that led to that picture, in the left-hand column and outcomes, or events that occurred after the picture was taken, in the right-hand column.

# Teacher Directions: Using Comic Strips and Photographs (continued)

## Take It to the Next Level

1. After they have brainstormed ideas, students will assume the role of one of the people or characters in the photo (other choices might include pets, onlookers, or other people who were at the scene but not present in the photo).
2. Students will write a one-paragraph description of the day's events from morning to night under the photo on the manila paper. They should use their notes from the chart and pay attention to tone and voice.

## Special Considerations

It's very important that struggling readers consider the order of events from many perspectives. By analyzing a comic and organizing a narrative, they are considering chronology—recognizing it in text as well as creating their own. They need these skills to build good reading habits.

# Student Directions: Using Comic Strips and Photographs

## Focus on the Skill

1. Begin by reassembling the comic strips to their original format and gluing the boxes in order on a sheet of manila paper.
2. Choose one of the comics and fill in the "Chain of Events" table on the "Using Comic Strips and Photographs" worksheet. You should think about the details from each frame and show how one event led to another. In the "As a result" box, you should explain the outcome of the events or what made the comic funny.

## Practice the Skill

1. Paste the photograph on the back of the manila paper in the center.
2. On the "Using Comic Strips and Photographs" worksheet, write down all of the details from the photograph under the column labeled "The photo—what is happening?" You may want to break the photo into quadrants and, beginning at the top of the right-hand side, write every detail. Move clockwise around the photo, studying each quadrant before considering the photo as a whole.
3. Then, brainstorm causes, or events that led to that picture, in the left-hand column and outcomes, or events that occurred after the picture was taken, in the right-hand column.

## Take It to the Next Level

1. Finally, assume the role of one of the people or characters in the photo (other choices might include pets, onlookers, or other people who are at the scene but not present in the photo).
2. Write a one-paragraph description of the day's events from morning to night under the photo on the manila paper. You may use your notes from the chart and pay attention to tone and voice.

## How You Will Be Graded

| | 1 little or no evidence | 2 below average | 3 adequate evidence | 4 better than average | 5 superior evidence | TOTAL |
|---|---|---|---|---|---|---|
| Attention to neatness and presentation | | | | | | |
| Correctly assembles comic strip frames in order | | | | | | |
| Identifies the chain of events of a comic strip; recognizes the outcome | | | | | | |
| Analyzes a photograph for details to determine meaning; considers events before and after photo was taken | | | | | | |
| Creates a detailed narrative that shows recognition of events in a day; understands a photo is only part of a chain of events | | | | | | |
| **Total points multiplied by four** | | | | | | |
| **Final grade** | | | | | | |

# Worksheet: Using Comic Strips and Photographs

## Focus on the Skill

**Analyzing a Comic Strip.** Choose one of the correctly ordered comics. Study the words and actions in each box. In the chart, write down all of the details that show you understand the "chain of events" or events in order. Think about the details from each frame, and show how one event led to another. In the "As a result" box, you should explain the outcome of the events or what made the comic funny.

**Chain of Events**

| First | And then | And then | And then | As a result |
|---|---|---|---|---|
| | | | | |

## Practice the Skill

**Analyzing a Photo**

| Before the photo was taken (brainstorm ideas of what happened) | The photo—what is happening? (analyze each section of the photo for details) | After the photo was taken (brainstorm ideas of what will happen) |
|---|---|---|
| | Top right quadrant:<br><br>Bottom right quadrant:<br><br>Bottom left quadrant:<br><br>Top left quadrant:<br><br>The photo as a whole: | |

# Teacher Directions: Using Magazines and Newspapers

## Goals for Student

1. Synthesize collected information using a matrix or other graphic organizer.
2. Separate collected information into useful components using a variety of techniques.
3. Recognize chronological events in non-fiction articles.

## Preparation

1. Your class should have some understanding of the term "words in context." They should have a lot of experience (through discussion and class work) decoding word meaning using sentence clues.
2. Find a magazine article that includes the complete recounting of a non-fiction story. Take into consideration the reading level of your students. You do not want to use an article that is too long or complicated. Make a copy of the article for each student—they will need it to take notes.
3. Provide newspapers that can be taken apart and cut.

## Materials

- "Using Magazines and Newspapers" worksheet
- Magazine article
- Newspaper
- Scissors
- Highlighters
- Glue stick
- Colored pencils

## Focus on the Skill

1. To begin, the students will read the magazine article. As they read, they should highlight main ideas and major events in the story. They may want to number the events as well. They will use the article to complete a timeline.
2. Have the students look back over their notes and choose FIVE major events from the article that tell the story.
3. The students will plot each event on the timeline on the "Using Magazines and Newspapers" worksheet. In each event box, they will write the main idea of the event (example: Event #1—Boy is caught in a tree; Event #2—Flood waters rise; Event # 3—A helicopter arrived on the scene, etc.). They will then create illustrations to detail each event.

## Practice the Skill

1. Students will select an article from the newspaper. The article should cover an event that is detailed and tells a complete story.
2. The students will cut the article out and glue it to the back of their "Using Magazines and Newspapers" worksheet.
3. Again, they will record the most important events from the article, this time using the "Chain of Events" table on the worksheet.

## Teacher Directions: Using Magazines and Newspapers (continued)

### Take It to the Next Level

Using the 3-2-1 strategy, have the students use the "Newspaper Article at a Glance" section of the worksheet to summarize the events of the article. They should list three major events, two characters from the article, and one sentence that shows they understand the main idea of the article.

### Special Considerations

Struggling readers may not be comfortable working with non-fiction. Newspapers and magazine articles are full of distracting information that is confusing and difficult to understand. The only way to help a middle-school-aged reader improve in this area is to provide lots of interaction with non-fiction structures. Newspaper scavenger hunts are tremendously popular—ask students to locate everything from classified ad information to the scheduled television shows.

# Student Directions: Using Magazines and Newspapers

## Focus on the Skill

1. Read the magazine article. As you read, highlight main ideas and major events in the story. You may want to number the events as well.
2. Look back over your notes and choose FIVE major events from the article that tell the story.
3. Plot each event on the timeline on the "Using Magazines and Newspapers" worksheet. In each event box, write the main idea of the event (example: Event #1—Boy is caught in a tree; Event #2—Flood waters rise; Event #3—A helicopter arrived on the scene, etc.).
4. Then create illustrations to detail each event.

## Practice the Skill

1. Next, you will select an article from the newspaper. The article should cover an event that is detailed and tells a complete story.
2. Cut the article out and glue it to the back of the "Using Magazines and Newspapers" worksheet.
3. Again, record the most important events from the article, this time using the "Chain of Events" table on the worksheet.

## Take It to the Next Level

Using the 3-2-1 strategy, fill in the "Newspaper Article at a Glance" section of the worksheet to summarize the events of the article. You should list <u>three</u> major events, <u>two</u> characters from the article (with short descriptions), and <u>one</u> sentence that shows you understand the main idea of the article.

## How You Will Be Graded

| | 1 little or no evidence | 2 below average | 3 adequate evidence | 4 better than average | 5 superior evidence | TOTAL |
|---|---|---|---|---|---|---|
| Attention to neatness and presentation | | | | | | |
| Uses active reading skills to highlight and make margin notes | | | | | | |
| Recognizes order of events in a magazine and newspaper article | | | | | | |
| Creates drawings that are detailed and show understanding of specific information | | | | | | |
| Uses 3-2-1 strategy effectively to show understanding of events, characters, and main idea of a newspaper story | | | | | | |
| **Total points multiplied by four** | | | | | | |
| **Final grade** | | | | | | |

# Worksheet: Using Magazines and Newspapers

## Focus on the Skill

**Timeline of a Magazine Article**

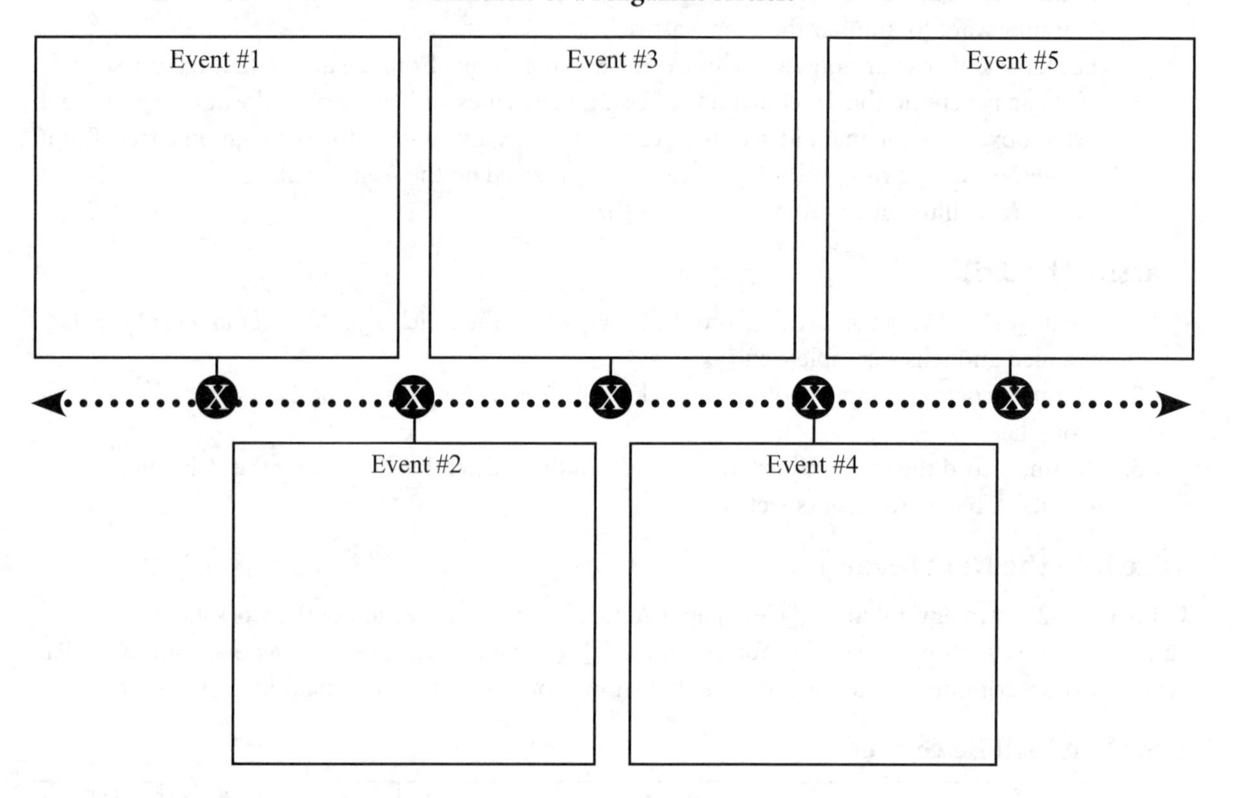


## Practice the Skill

**Chain of Events**

| First | And then | And then | And then | As a result |
|---|---|---|---|---|
| | | | | |

## Take It to the Next Level

**The Newspaper Article at a Glance**

**3** events from the article

**2** main characters from the article (with descriptions)

**1** sentence that explains the main idea of the article

# Teacher Directions: Literary Devices in Headlines

## Goals for Student

1. Understand different literary devices that are used in the study of literature.
2. Understand the impact on the reader of specific word choices (for example, multiple meanings, invented words, concrete or abstract terms, figurative language).
3. Identify literary devices.

## Preparation

1. Your class should begin to discuss literary devices used in mainstream prose like newspapers, periodicals, advertisements, etc.
2. Create a memory game with the definitions and literary devices used in this activity. Take twelve 3" x 5" note cards. Write the literary terms covered in this center on six of the cards: allusion, alliteration, cliché, colloquialism, euphemism, and pun. On six other cards, write the definitions. Leave a complete list of terms with definitions out for the students to use as a guide.

## Materials

- Literary devices memory game/answer key (one set per student or group)
- "Literary Devices in Headlines" worksheet
- Colored paper for a flip chart
- Colored pencils

## Focus on the Skill

The students should play the literary devices memory game to familiarize themselves with the terms and definitions.

## Practice the Skill

1. Students will complete the six sections of the "Literary Devices in Headlines" worksheet. In each section, there is a literary device and definition with three to four headlines that are examples of that device. The students must analyze the headline and follow the directions in each section.
2. At the bottom of the worksheet, there are six headlines that use literary devices. The students must match the definition of the device with the headline that is the best example of that device.

## Take It to the Next Level

Have the students create a flip book of literary devices. Try the "Bound Book Foldable" from Dinah Zike's website at www.dinah.com. On each page, they write the literary device, its device, a headline that uses that device (a higher skill would be for them to find their own examples in the newspaper), and a drawing with details that show comprehension of how the literary device is being used (example: "Clippers Will Cool Down Heat" could refer to temperatures or the basketball teams).

## Special Considerations

Recognize that this is not a center where mastery is the goal. Literary devices are often difficult for middle schoolers (struggling and otherwise); however, if you provide them with experiences that are guiding and interesting, they tend to pay more attention.

# Student Directions: Literary Devices in Headlines

## Focus on the Skill

Play the literary devices memory game to familiarize yourself with the terms and definitions.

## Practice the Skill

1. Complete the six sections of the "Literary Devices in Headlines" worksheet. In each section, there is a definition with three to four headlines that are examples of that literary device. You must analyze the headlines and follow the directions in each section.
2. At the bottom of the worksheet, there are six headlines that use literary devices. You must match the definition of the device with the headline that is the best example of that device.

## Take It to the Next Level

Finally, create a flip book of literary devices. On each page, write the literary device, its definition, a headline that uses that device (a higher skill would be for you to find your own examples in the newspaper), and a drawing with details that show comprehension of how the literary device is being used (example: "Clippers Will Cool Down Heat" could refer to temperatures or the basketball teams).

## How You Will Be Graded

| | 1 little or no evidence | 2 below average | 3 adequate evidence | 4 better than average | 5 superior evidence | TOTAL |
|---|---|---|---|---|---|---|
| Attention to neatness and presentation | | | | | | |
| Works independently to learn six literary devices through the use of memory card game | | | | | | |
| Accurately identifies parts of headlines that show the six featured literary devices | | | | | | |
| Accurately provides words that were euphemized and explains clichés effectively | | | | | | |
| Creates a flip book with terms, definitions, examples, and illustrations that is colorful and detailed | | | | | | |
| **Total points multiplied by four** | | | | | | |
| **Final grade** | | | | | | |

# Worksheet: Literary Devices in Headlines

## Part 1

**I. Alliteration.** The repetition of the same sounds or of the same kinds of sounds at the beginning of words or stressed syllables.

Directions: Read each headline below and underline the words in the headline that use **alliteration**.

"Generation Gap is Root of Flap Over Flip-Flops"

"Canes Want to Help Ousted Coach Coker Walk Away a Winner"

"New Democratic Day Dawns in Congress"

"Shopping Season Sees Strong Sales"

**II. Allusion.** A reference to a mythological, literary, or historical person, place, or thing.

Directions: Read each headline below. Decide what the **allusion** is referring to. Is it a famous character, a well-known saying, or a favorite children's story?

"The Little Grocery that Could"

______________________________

"The Diet Detective Advises: Eat, Drink, and Be Active"

______________________________

"Don't Let Scrooges Ruin Your Holiday"

______________________________

**III. Cliché.** A trite, overused expression or idea.

Directions: Read each headline below and explain what each cliché means.

"On Thin Ice"

______________________________

______________________________

"Politics May Clip the Wings of the Once-Energetic Airbus"

______________________________

______________________________

"Under the Gun on US 331"

______________________________

______________________________

"Reach for the Sky"

______________________________

______________________________

**IV. Colloquialism.** An expression not used in formal speech; usually slang and usually used within a limited geographic area.

Directions: Read each headline below and underline the part of the headline that is a colloquialism.

"Teachers Find Toys Mondo Gross"

"Peace, Order, and Good Government, Eh?"

"Why Not Get Some Fixins' Tonight?"

"Hawaii Bids Wagner Aloha as Coach"

## Worksheet: Literary Devices in Headlines (continued)

**V. Euphemism.** An agreeable expression used to avoid a more offensive expression.

Directions: Read each headline below and underline the part of the headline that is a euphemism. On the line, tell what the harsher, more realistic words might be.

"Fighting in Fallujah Sees Heavy Casualties"

______________________________________

"Former NASCAR Champion, Benny Parsons, Passes Away"

______________________________________

"Big Bird's Boo Boo"

______________________________________

"Washington Redskins Linebacker Coach Let Go"

______________________________________

**VI. Pun.** A humorous play on words; words are deliberately being used in a funny way.

Directions: Read each headline below and underline the part of the headline that is a pun. On the line, explain why the headline might be funny.

"Clippers Cool Down Heat"

______________________________________

"Will Aviation Development Fly?"

______________________________________

"The Rise of Fall"

______________________________________

"Who's in the Right About the Left Lane?"

______________________________________

### Part 2

Directions: Match the letter of the literary device with the headline that models that device.

___ "Debate Deepens the Divide"
___ "Mural, Mural on the Wall"
___ "A Picture Says a Thousand Words"
___ "Do People Still Play Bingo? You Betcha!"
___ "Ford Laid to Rest in Michigan"
___ "Science Friction: The growing—and dangerous—divide between scientists and the GOP."

a. pun
b. cliché
c. allusion
d. colloquialism
e. euphemism
f. alliteration

# Teacher Directions: Types of Conflict

## Goals for Student

1. Form and revise questions, and predict ideas or events that may take place in the text.
2. Categorize collected information using a chart.
3. Understand the primary conflicts in a variety of text types and the difference between internal and external conflicts.

## Preparation

1. Your class should understand types of conflicts (man vs. man, man vs. nature, man vs. society, and man vs. himself) and the difference between internal and external conflicts. As they read, they should begin to see how conflicts affect plot, characterization, and theme.
2. Collect short, picture-book biographies that can be read in a short period of time (about forty pages) and that have different types of conflicts. The following titles work well: *39 Apartments of Ludwig Van Beethoven* by Jonah Winter; *John Henry* by Julius Lester; *The Man Who Walked Between the Towers* by Mordicai Gerstein; and *Marvelous Mattie: How Margaret E. Knight Became and Inventor* by Emily Arnold McCully. They are each forty pages or less and good material for even reluctant readers.

## Materials

- "Types of Conflict" worksheet
- Story paper
- Colored pencils
- Picture-book biography

## Focus on the Skill

Have the students turn the "Types of Conflict" worksheet over and brainstorm types of conflicts they have experienced in the last twenty-four hours. They should think of a conflict to fit each of the following categories: man vs. man, man vs. nature, man vs. society, and man vs. himself.

## Practice the Skill

1. The students will read the picture-book biography in a group with each student reading two pages at a time.
2. Students should select a "reader leader" for the group. This is the person who will keep time and keep track of where the group is in the story.
3. The person to the right of the reader leader will read two pages of the story. After two pages have been read, the person to the right of the person who just read will comment about the selection. They can refer to the "Discuss While You Read" section of the "Types of Conflict" worksheet to prompt discussion ideas.

## Take It to the Next Level

Have the students choose one of the conflicts. They will write the type of conflict on the top of a sheet of story paper. Under the type, they should write whether the conflict was internal or external. Then, they will draw a picture of the scene where the conflict occurred. In the space below the scene, they should write the lines of text that *shows* the scene.

## Special Considerations

Dependent upon time, it is not always important that your lower-level readers finish the biography. If they are motivated, they will ask you if they can borrow the book to finish, and if not, the point of the exercise was to help them recognize conflicts during the reading they finished.

# Student Directions: Types of Conflict

## Focus on the Skill

Turn the "Types of Conflict" worksheet over and brainstorm types of conflicts you have experienced in the last twenty-four hours. Think of a conflict to fit each of the following categories: man vs. man, man vs. nature, man vs. society, and man vs. himself.

## Practice the Skill

1. You will read a picture book biography in a group with each person reading two pages at a time.
2. Select a "reader leader" for the group. This is the person who will keep time and keep track of where the group is in the story.
3. The person to the right of the reader leader will read two pages of the story. After two pages have been read, the person to the right of the person who just read will comment about the selection. You can refer to the "Discuss While You Read" section of the "Types of Conflict" worksheet to prompt discussion ideas.
4. Every time a conflict occurs, agree as a group to write it down on the worksheet under the correct column.
5. Continue this process until you have completed the story.

## Take It to the Next Level

Choose one of the conflicts. Write the type of conflict on the top of a sheet of story paper. Under the type, write whether the conflict was internal or external. Then, draw a picture of the scene where the conflict occurred. In the space below the scene, write the lines of text that *shows* the scene.

## How You Will Be Graded

| | 1 little or no evidence | 2 below average | 3 adequate evidence | 4 better than average | 5 superior evidence | TOTAL |
|---|---|---|---|---|---|---|
| Attention to neatness and presentation | | | | | | |
| Actively participates in reading discussions | | | | | | |
| Summarizes, asks question, relates personal experience, makes judgments, and makes predictions | | | | | | |
| Recognizes and categorizes types of conflict while reading | | | | | | |
| Illustrates a specific conflict from the story and understands internal vs. external | | | | | | |
| **Total points multiplied by four** | | | | | | |
| **Final grade** | | | | | | |

# Worksheet: Types of Conflict

**Discuss While You Read!** Each group member should read two pages of the biography. After each person takes a turn, the person to the right of the reader should comment about the section read. Use the key below to help stimulate ideas. Put a check beside each kind of response as you participate in the discussion. Your goal is to use all five types.

_____ 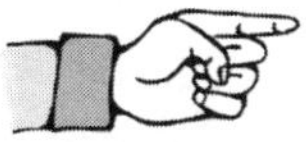 Get to the point! Summarize or restate the section read.

_____  Ask a question to clarify the meaning of a word or idea.

_____  Relate the content to a personal situation or real-life example.

_____ no! yes! React to ideas. Do you agree or disagree with something a character did? Explain.

_____  Predict what will follow in the next section to be read.

**Types of Conflict Chart.** As you read the biography, pay attention to conflicts. As you come across a conflict, record the events under the type of conflict the situation falls under.

| Man vs. Man | Man vs. Nature | Man vs. Himself | Man vs. Society |
|---|---|---|---|
| | | | |
| | | | |
| | | | |
| | | | |

# Teacher Directions: Characterization

## Goals for Student

1. Analyze and describe from various characters' points of view.
2. Identify personality traits that create characterization.
3. Study word meanings consistently.

## Preparation

Your students should begin to understand the basics of characterization. Personality traits that show or describe appearance, display or relate actions, describe the character's thoughts, or describe the reactions of others are all considered when trying to characterize a character in prose.

## Materials

- "Characterization" worksheet
- "Appointment in Samarra" worksheet
- Manila paper

## Focus on the Skill

1. Students will choose one of the personality traits from the list on the "Characterization" worksheet. They should write the word in the middle of the vocabulary web on the worksheet. They will then find the definition in the dictionary and write it on the line provided at the top of the web.
2. Then, they should complete the rest of the web by writing related words and ideas on the "is" side, writing opposite meanings or non-examples on the "is not" side, and drawing a picture that illustrates the word in the box provided.

## Practice the Skill

1. Then, the students will read the "Appointment in Samarra" parable and summarize the events under the story on the "Appointment in Samarra" worksheet.
2. After reading the parable, the students must select the character (the servant, the merchant, or Death) who represents the character trait they mapped. For example, if they mapped the word "compassionate," they might choose the merchant because he lent his servant a horse to escape Death.
3. The students should complete the framed sentence on the "Characterization" worksheet to explain their choice.
4. Have the students create an acrostic poem using *MERCHANT*, *SERVANT*, and *DEATH* as the subjects. They will begin each line with the letter from the character's name, writing words, phrases, mannerisms, or personality traits as descriptions of each character.

## Take It to the Next Level

Have the students fold a piece of manila paper into three sections (try the "Trifold Foldable" from Dinah Zike's website at www.dinah.com). They will draw a picture of each of the three characters from the parable. Under each picture, they should list personality traits that would describe that character.

## Special Considerations

Middle-school-aged children need a lot of practice with characterization. They can describe people, but they do not recognize how that is different from characterizing them. Since I began teaching characterization, my students have been quick to show me trait words in their own reading. This shows me they had little previous understanding of the depth of those terms.

# Student Directions: Characterization

## Focus on the Skill

1. Choose one of the personality traits from the list. Write the word in the middle of the web on the "Characterization" worksheet. Find the definition in the dictionary and write it on the line provided at the top of the web.
2. Complete the vocabulary map by writing related words and ideas on the "is" side, writing opposite meanings or non-examples on the "is not" side, and drawing a picture that illustrates the word in the box provided.

## Practice the Skill

1. Read the "Appointment in Samarra" parable, and summarize the events under the story on the "Appointment in Samarra" worksheet.
2. After reading the parable, select the character (the servant, the merchant, or Death) who represents the character trait you mapped. For example, if you mapped the word "compassionate," you might choose the merchant because he lent his servant a horse to escape Death (that is an example—choose something else).
3. Complete the framed sentence on the "Characterization" worksheet to explain your choice.
4. Create an acrostic poem using *MERCHANT*, *SERVANT*, and *DEATH* as the subjects. You will begin each line with the letter from the character's name, writing words, phrases, mannerisms, or personality traits as descriptions of each character.

## Take It to the Next Level

Fold a piece of manila paper into three sections. Draw a picture of each of the three characters from the parable. Under each picture, list personality traits that would describe that character.

## How You Will Be Graded

| | 1 little or no evidence | 2 below average | 3 adequate evidence | 4 better than average | 5 superior evidence | TOTAL |
|---|---|---|---|---|---|---|
| Attention to neatness and presentation | | | | | | |
| Accurately completes the vocabulary map of a personality trait | | | | | | |
| Summarizes the events of the parable | | | | | | |
| Accurately describes the character who represents the mapped personality trait and provides details and examples to show understanding | | | | | | |
| Creates effective acrostic poems that show an understanding of each character in the parable | | | | | | |
| **Total points multiplied by four** | | | | | | |
| **Final grade** | | | | | | |

# Worksheet: Characterization

## Focus on the Skill

**Mapping a Personality Trait.** Choose one of the personality traits from the list below. Write the word in the middle of the web. Find the definition in the dictionary and write it on the line provided at the top of the web. Then, complete the vocabulary map by writing related words and ideas on the "is" side, writing opposite meanings or non-examples on the "is not" side, and drawing a picture that illustrates the word in the box provided.

| | | |
|---|---|---|
| **Compassionate** | **Dependable** | **Intimidating** |
| **Curious** | **Generous** | **Threatened** |

Definition:________________________________________________

**IS NOT** **IS**

**IS NOT** **IS**

**IS NOT** **IS**

The personality trait I mapped was ____________________, and the character from "Appointment in Samarra" that represented this trait the most was ____________________ because ________________________________________.

## Practice the Skill

**Acrostic Poems.** Begin each line with words, phrases, mannerisms, or personality traits that are descriptions of each character.

**S**ays he saw Death in the market
**E**
**R**
**V**
**A**
**N**
**T**

**M**
**E**
**R**
**C**
**H**
**A**
**N**
**T**

**D**
**E**
**A**
**T**
**H**

## Worksheet: "Appointment in Samarra"

A merchant in Baghdad sent his servant to the market to buy provisions. In a little while the servant came back, white and trembling. The servant told the merchant, "I was shoved in the market, turned around, and saw Death."

"Death made a threatening gesture, and I fled in terror. May I please borrow your horse? I can leave Baghdad and ride to Samarra, where Death will not find me."

The master lent his horse to the servant, who rode away, to Samarra.

Later the merchant went to the market and saw Death in the crowd. "Why did you threaten my servant?" He asked.

Death replied, "I did not threaten your servant. It was merely that I was surprised to see him here in Baghdad, for I have an appointment with him tonight in Samarra."

**Summarize the story.** ____________________________________________

____________________________________________

____________________________________________

____________________________________________

____________________________________________

____________________________________________

____________________________________________

____________________________________________

____________________________________________

# Teacher Directions: Imagery

## Goals for Student

1. Understand how effective word choice, sensory details, or figurative language contribute to the mood or meaning of a poem or a short story.
2. Identify imagery.
3. Create imagery.

## Preparation

1. Your students should begin to understand sensory details and recognize those details during active reading.
2. Collect stories and poems that evoke a lot of imagery, such as Sandra Cisneros's "Eleven," William Wordsworth's "Daffodils," many of Edgar Allen Poe's short stories, etc., for students to analyze.

## Materials

- "Imagery" worksheet
- Story paper
- Colored pencils

## Focus on the Skill

The students will begin by creating their own images on the "Imagery" worksheet. They should choose an event from the list (a volcano that is about to erupt, a shopping mall food court, a Civil War battlefield, a crowded subway train, a stream in the woods, or a busy fast food restaurant) and determine what they would see, hear, smell, and feel if they were there.

## Practice the Skill

1. Students will analyze a paragraph about going to the dentist on the "Imagery" worksheet. They should underline words and phrases that make the event come alive and create imagery in their minds.
2. Looking back at the images they wrote down for the first exercise, they will now write a paragraph. They may use the dentist paragraph as a model for creating their own imagery.

## Take It to the Next Level

Have your students read a short story like "Eleven" or a poem like "Daffodils" and underline the words and phrases that create imagery. You may want to break the story or poem up ahead of time (in the case of "Daffodils," you will only need the first stanza). Each student will draw the imagery from his or her section of the story or poem on story paper with either an excerpt or the complete line of poetry used as a caption. The details are very important for this assignment. In the end, the pictures can be displayed in the hall in the same order as the text to offer a different interpretation of the prose—telling a story with images.

## Special Considerations

It's important that struggling readers practice identifying and creating imagery. This see-it-and-do-it exercise will yield results with enough practice, but the application of the skills has to come from many different angles.

# Student Directions: Imagery

## Focus on the Skill

Begin by creating your own images on the "Imagery" worksheet. You should choose an event from the list (a volcano that is about to erupt, a shopping mall food court, a Civil War battlefield, a crowded subway train, a stream in the woods, or a busy fast food restaurant) and determine what you would see, hear, smell, and feel if you were there. Just brainstorm—do not focus on writing sentences right now.

## Practice the Skill

1. Now you will analyze the paragraph about going to the dentist on the "Imagery" worksheet. Underline words and phrases that make the event come alive and create imagery in your mind.
2. Use the images you created in the first exercise to write one or more paragraphs. You may use the dentist paragraph as a model for creating your own imagery paragraph and, of course, you may invent a story to fit the setting.

## Take It to the Next Level

1. Finally, read a short story like "Eleven" or a poem like "Daffodils," and underline the words and phrases that create imagery.
2. You will draw the imagery from your section of the story or poem on story paper with either an excerpt or the complete line of poetry used as a caption. The details are very important for this assignment, so make sure your drawing captures as many descriptions from the text as possible. In the end, the pictures can be displayed in the hall in the same order as the text to offer a completely different interpretation of the prose—telling a story with images.

## How You Will Be Graded

| | 1 little or no evidence | 2 below average | 3 adequate evidence | 4 better than average | 5 superior evidence | TOTAL |
|---|---|---|---|---|---|---|
| Attention to neatness and presentation | | | | | | |
| Creates sensory images of a particular scene | | | | | | |
| Identifies imagery in a paragraph | | | | | | |
| Creates a well-detailed paragraph that includes sensory images | | | | | | |
| Identifies imagery in a short story or poem and draws a picture that effectively reflects the images from the prose | | | | | | |
| **Total points multiplied by four** | | | | | | |
| **Final grade** | | | | | | |

# Worksheet: Imagery

## Focus on the Skill

**Imagery Practice.** Pick the scene you can describe best. Answer each question below with specific, precise images, smells, and sounds. Zoom in to that image and pick out every small detail you can to show the imagery of the scene. BE SPECIFIC!

A volcano that is about to erupt
A crowded subway train
A shopping mall food court
A stream in the woods
A Civil War battlefield
A busy fast food restaurant

What do you see? ____________________

What do you hear? ____________________

What do you feel? ____________________

What do you smell? ____________________

## Practice the Skill

**Identifying Imagery.** Look back at your imagery. Does it capture the scene? Do you feel like a reader would connect with your observations? Read the following passage, and underline the words and phrases that show strong imagery.

> *Staring up at the evenly-spaced ceiling tiles, Letisha clenched the ends of the chair. She hadn't visited the dentist in months, and as Dr. Jones's masked face entered her field of vision, she squeezed her eyes shut, anticipating a painful shot. Surprisingly, she felt only a small prick. The smell of alcohol and antiseptic filled her nostrils as she felt the whir of the miniature drill on her cavity-covered bicuspid. Within moments, her time in the torture chamber had ended, and she slowly peeked through one eye to make sure the ordeal was truly over.*

**Creating Your Imagery.** Take the images you created from above and create a short paragraph like the one you just read. Remember, you should be able to read over your paragraph and see, hear, feel, and smell the scene.

____________________

____________________

____________________

____________________

____________________

____________________

____________________

____________________

# Teacher Directions: Introduction to Bias

## Goals for Student

1. Identify persuasion techniques in literary works.
2. Differentiate facts from opinions.
3. Recognize how bias affects prose.

## Preparation

1. Your class should feel comfortable with facts and opinions. They should be ready to acknowledge biases in what they read.
2. Collect similar versions of the same story. In the case of the "Three Little Pigs," you could collect Teresa Celsi's *The Fourth Little Pig*, Jean Claverie's *The Three Little Pigs*, Susan Lowell's *The Three Little Javelinas*, Glen Rounds's *Three Little Pigs and the Big Bad Wolf*, Jon Scieszka's *The True Story of the Three Little Pigs*, and Eugene Trivizas's *The Three Little Wolves and the Big Bad Pig*.
3. Make enough copies of Black Hawk's surrender speech to the U.S. Army for each student (provided at the end of this center).

## Materials

- "Introduction to Bias" worksheet
- Black Hawk's surrender speech
- Story paper
- Colored pencils
- Two different-colored highlighters

## Focus on the Skill

1. Have the students turn the worksheet over and create a vocabulary map of the word "bias" (definition at the top, related words on the right/"is" side, unrelated words on the left/"is not" side, and an illustration with a caption of at least eight words using the term to show they understand the meaning).
2. Students will then analyze a picture of a dog on the "Introduction to Bias" worksheet and consider which statements about the dog are facts and which are opinions.

## Practice the Skill

1. Next, students will begin to explore what "bias" is. They should read two or three versions of the same story, "The Three Little Pigs." They will start to see bias in the different versions.
2. On the "Introduction to Bias" worksheet, they will determine if the character who is telling the story has a bias. They will provide one example from the story that shows the character's preference. If the story is told by a narrator, make sure the students recognize that the storyteller is usually neutral.
3. Then students will read Black Hawk's surrender speech to the U.S. Army. As they read the speech, they should highlight statements that are clearly facts (could be proven with evidence) with one color and those that are opinions (probably stem from personal experiences and emotions) with another color.
4. Students will then use what they highlighted to fill in the "Analyzing a Speech for Fact, Opinion, and Bias" chart on the worksheet.

# Teacher Directions: Introduction to Bias (continued)

## Take It to the Next Level

Have the students choose one of the paragraphs from Black Hawk's speech. On story paper, they will draw the images he describes in the speech that are biased. Then, they will choose an excerpt from the paragraph that best reflects the bias of the paragraph to write beneath the picture.

## Special Considerations

There are many fairy tales that have been rewritten from a different perspective, and they are easy reads for all levels. Bias is a tough skill to master, but it is increasingly becoming a staple on standardized tests. You will need to monitor this activity closely. Make sure the students know that most speeches contain a bias but that this doesn't mean the speech maker is bad. The persuasive nature of speeches requires bias and partiality.

# Student Directions: Introduction to Bias

## Focus on the Skill

1. Turn the "Introduction to Bias" worksheet over, and create a vocabulary map of the word "bias" (definition at the top, related words on the right/"is" side, unrelated words on the left/"is not" side, and an illustration with a caption of at least eight words using the term to show you understand the meaning).
2. Then, analyze the picture of a dog on the "Introduction to Bias" worksheet and consider which statements about the dog are facts and which are opinions.

## Practice the Skill

1. Begin to explore what a bias is by reading two or three versions of the same story, "The Three Little Pigs."
2. On the "Introduction to Bias" worksheet, determine if the character who is telling the story has a bias. Provide one example from the story that shows the character's preference. When a narrator tells the story, the bias is usually neutral (does not take a side).
3. Then, read Black Hawk's surrender speech to the U.S. Army. As you read the speech, highlight statements that are clearly facts (could be proven with evidence) with one color and those that are opinions (probably stem from personal experiences and emotions) with another color.
4. Use what you highlighted to fill in the "Analyzing a Speech for Fact, Opinion, and Bias" chart on the worksheet.

## Take It to the Next Level

Choose one of the paragraphs from Black Hawk's speech. On story paper, draw the images he describes in the speech that are biased. Choose an excerpt from the paragraph that best reflects the bias (shows his opinion) and write it on the lines below your picture.

## How You Will Be Graded

| | 1 little or no evidence | 2 below average | 3 adequate evidence | 4 better than average | 5 superior evidence | TOTAL |
|---|---|---|---|---|---|---|
| Attention to neatness and presentation | | | | | | |
| Accurately identifies fact and opinion statements about picture of the dog | | | | | | |
| Recognizes bias in picture books for a common story that is told from alternative points of view | | | | | | |
| Identifies facts and opinions in Black Hawk's speech; begins to see why opinions may be biased | | | | | | |
| Illustrates a passage from the speech and chooses an excerpt that shows a bias in the passage | | | | | | |
| **Total points multiplied by four** | | | | | | |
| **Final grade** | | | | | | |

## Black Hawk's Surrender Speech to the U.S. Army (edited for middle school)

Background: As Americans moved into Indian territories in the nineteenth century, the U.S. Army worked to remove and resettle hundreds of Indian tribes. Few tribes went without a fight. Chief Back Hawk led an armed band of Sauk and Fox to reoccupy the lands of the Illinois and Wisconsin Territory to avoid famine and starvation. In the end, women and children were massacred by U.S. soldiers, and Black Hawk had no choice but to surrender.

*Black Hawk is an Indian. He has done nothing for which an Indian ought to be ashamed. He has fought for his countrymen, the* ***squaws and papooses*** (women and children), *against white men, who came, year after year, to cheat them and take away their lands. You know the cause of our making war. It is known to all white men. They ought to be ashamed of it. The white men* ***despise*** (hate) *the Indians, and drive them from their homes. But the Indians are not* ***deceitful*** (dishonest). *The white men speak bad of the Indian, and look at him* ***spitefully*** (with meanness). *But the Indian does not tell lies; Indians do not steal.*

*An Indian, who is as bad as the white men, could not live in our nation; he would be put to death, and eat up by the wolves. The white men are bad schoolmasters; they carry false looks, and deal in false actions; they smile in the face of the poor Indian to cheat him; they shake them by the hand to gain their confidence, to make them drunk, to deceive them, and ruin our wives. We told them to let us alone, and keep away from us; but they followed on, and* ***beset*** (overtook) *our paths, and they* ***coiled*** (twisted) *themselves among us, like the snake. They poisoned us by their touch. We were not safe. We lived in danger. We were becoming like them,* ***hypocrites*** (frauds) *and liars, lazy* ***drones*** (followers), *all talkers, and no workers.*

*We looked up to the Great Spirit. We went to our great father. We were encouraged. His great council gave us fair words and big promises; but we got no satisfaction. Things were growing worse. There were no deer in the forest. The opossum and beaver were fled; the springs were drying up, and our squaws and papooses without* ***victuals*** (food) *to keep them from starving; we called a great council, and built a large fire. The spirit of our fathers arose and spoke to us to avenge our wrongs or die. We all spoke before the council fire. It was warm and pleasant. We set up the war-whoop, and dug up the tomahawk; our knives were ready, and the heart of Black-hawk swelled high in his bosom, when he led his warriors to battle. He is satisfied. He will go to the world of spirits contented. He has done his duty. His father will meet him there, and commend him.*

*Black Hawk is a true Indian, and* ***disdains*** (does not respect) *to cry like a woman. He feels for his wife, his children and friends. But he does not care for himself. He cares for his nation and the Indians. They will suffer. He* ***laments*** (cries for) *their fate. The white men do not scalp the head; but they do worse-they poison the heart, it is not pure with them. His countrymen will not be scalped, but they will, in a few years, become like the white men, so that you can't trust them, and there must be, as in the white settlements, nearly as many officers as men, to take care of them and keep them in order.*

*Farewell, my nation. Black Hawk tried to save you, and* ***avenge*** (get even) *your wrongs. He drank the blood of some of the whites. He has been taken prisoner, and his plans are stopped. He can do no more. He is near his end. His sun is setting, and he will rise no more. Farewell to Black Hawk.*

Source: Frank E. Stevens, *The Black Hawk War* (1903), 372-73.

# Worksheet: Introduction to Bias

## Focus on the Skill

**The Basics.** Look at the picture and analyze the statements below. Remember, facts are based on evidence, and opinions are based on feelings, emotions, and biases.

This is a brown dog. ___ Fact ___ Opinion
This is a cute dog. ___ Fact ___ Opinion
This dog has two ears. ___ Fact ___ Opinion
This dog has sad eyes. ___ Fact ___ Opinion
The dog is thinking about food. ___ Fact ___ Opinion
The dog has a mean streak. ___ Fact ___ Opinion

**Understanding Bias.** Biases are preferences, and they do not consider both sides of a situation. They are based on personal experience. Read one of the versions of "The Three Little Pigs," and answer the following questions.

Who is telling the story? ___ a pig ___ a wolf ___ a narrator

Is the character who is telling the story *biased*? ___ yes ___ no

If yes, give an example.

---

## Practice the Skill

**Analyzing a Speech for Facts, Opinions, and Bias.** As you read the speech, highlight facts in one color and opinions in another. Then, fill in the chart below.

| Facts from the speech | If this is a fact, can it be proven? Explain. | Opinions from the speech | If this is an opinion, do you think it is biased? If so, explain. |
|---|---|---|---|
| Example: *Black Hawk is an Indian.* | Yes. They could test to find out his ethnic group. | *He has done nothing for which an Indian should be ashamed.* | A white man may not have agreed with him. |
| 1. | | | |
| 2. | | | |
| 3. | | | |
| 4. | | | |
| 5. | | | |
| 6. | | | |
| 7. | | | |

# Teacher Directions: Validity and Accuracy

## Goals for Student

1. Identify persuasion techniques in literary works.
2. Begin to differentiate valid and accurate from unfounded and erroneous information.
3. Begin to recognize how bias affects prose.

## Preparation

1. Your class should begin to use the terms "valid" and "accurate."
2. Collect tabloid articles (with lots of pictures, preferably in color) and newsworthy articles from a legitimate publication.

## Materials

- "Validity and Accuracy" worksheet
- "Validity and Accuracy in Articles" worksheet
- Manila paper
- Colored pencils

## Focus on the Skill

To begin, students should complete a vocabulary map of the terms "valid" (possible) and "accurate" (truth) on the "Validity and Accuracy" worksheet. They should write related words and ideas to the right (*is*) and opposite or non-example words and ideas to the left of the web (*is not*). On the bottom, in the box, they should create a sketch and write a sentence using the term correctly.

## Practice the Skill

1. Next, they will complete the "Analyzing Headlines for Validity and Accuracy" portion of the worksheet. They will read ten headlines and determine which headlines seem valid and accurate. Then, they will answer the questions following the checklist.
2. The students should then analyze two articles you have provided using the "Validity and Accuracy in Articles" worksheet (one tabloid article and one newsworthy article). They will read the articles one at a time and go through the checklist.
3. When they are done, they will complete the four short-answer questions at the bottom of the worksheet.

## Take It to the Next Level

Sometimes, it's easier to understand valid and accurate information by exploring how to write a story that is *invalid* and *inaccurate*. Have the students choose one of the headlines from the "Analyzing Headlines for Validity and Accuracy" section that they determined to be invalid and inaccurate. They will pretend that they are a news reporter and write an informative article using as many absurd, improbable details and elaborations as possible. Encourage them to use their imagination, draw pictures as if they were photos for the article, and to remember—the more outlandish, the better!

## Special Considerations

Again, teaching students to be aware of valid, accurate information is important, but it is not easy. For one thing, they are bombarded with media—twenty-four-hour news shows, commercials with hidden agendas, and magazines that seem interested in selling a certain look or way of life. Be patient, but encourage discussions that get kids talking about respectable vs. yellow journalism.

# Student Directions: Validity and Accuracy

## Focus on the Skill

To begin, complete a vocabulary map of the terms "valid" (possible) and "accurate" (truth) on the "Validity and Accuracy" worksheet. Write related words and ideas to the right (*is*) and opposite or non-example words and ideas to the left of the web (*is not*). On the bottom, in the box, create a sketch and write a sentence using the term correctly.

## Practice the Skill

1. Next, complete the "Analyzing Headlines for Validity and Accuracy" portion of the worksheet. Read the ten headlines and determine which headlines seem valid and accurate. Then, answer the questions following the checklist.
2. Next, analyze two articles that have been provided using the "Validity and Accuracy in Articles" worksheet (one tabloid article and one article from a trusted news source). Read the articles one at a time and go through the checklist.
3. When you are done, complete the four short-answer questions at the bottom of the worksheet.

## Take It to the Next Level

Sometimes, it's easier to understand valid and accurate information by exploring how to write a story that is *invalid* and *inaccurate.* Choose one of the headlines from the "Analyzing Headlines for Validity and Accuracy" section that you determined to be invalid and inaccurate. You will pretend that you are a news reporter and write an informative article using as many absurd, improbable details and elaborations as possible. Use your imagination, draw pictures as if they were photos for the article, and remember—the more outlandish, the better!

## How You Will Be Graded

| | 1<br>little or no evidence | 2<br>below average | 3<br>adequate evidence | 4<br>better than average | 5<br>superior evidence | TOTAL |
|---|---|---|---|---|---|---|
| Attention to neatness and presentation | | | | | | |
| Accurately maps meanings of "valid" and "accurate" | | | | | | |
| Analyzes headlines for validity and accuracy | | | | | | |
| Analyzes articles for validity and accuracy; determines why articles are and are not valid | | | | | | |
| Writes a good example of biased, invalid, inaccurate article; illustrations support biased information | | | | | | |
| **Total points multiplied by four** | | | | | | |
| **Final grade** | | | | | | |

# Worksheet: Validity and Accuracy

## Focus on the Skill

(adj.) strong possibility or conclusion; legitimate

(adj.) Factual; truthful; precise; exact

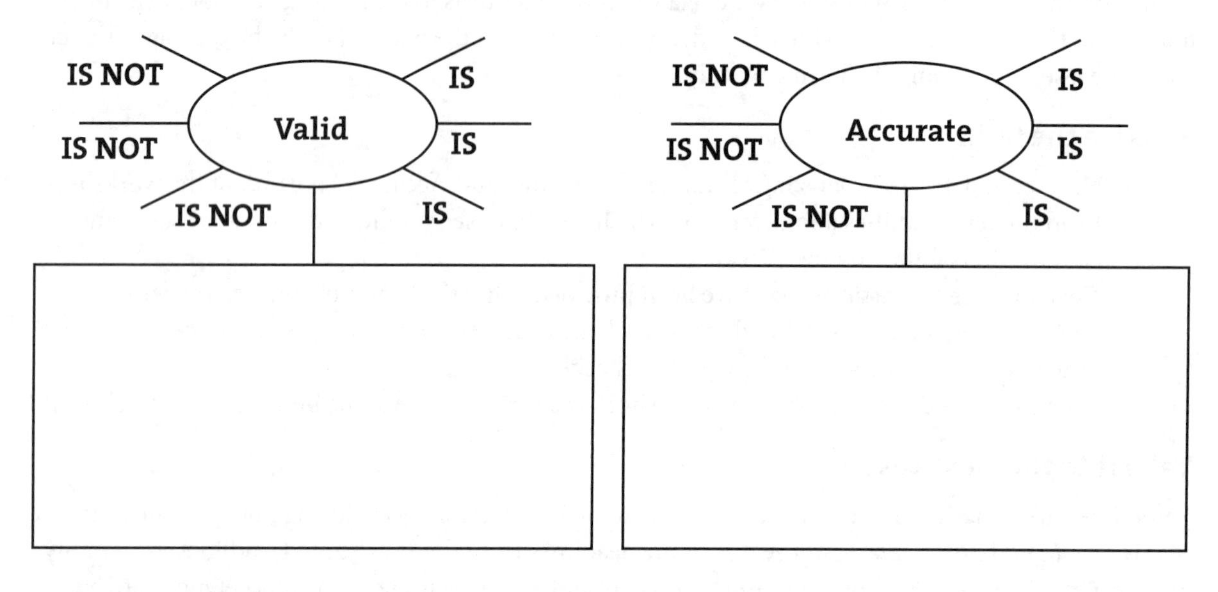


## Practice the Skill

**Analyzing Headlines for Validity and Accuracy.** Read the following headlines. Based on your understanding of the terms "valid" and "accurate," put a check in the appropriate column for each headline.

| | Headline | Valid (possible) | Accurate (true) |
|---|---|---|---|
| 1. | Bomber Strikes Bakery in Israeli Resort Town | ________ | ________ |
| 2. | Chimp Arrested for Reckless Driving | ________ | ________ |
| 3. | China Successfully Tests Anti-Satellite Missile | ________ | ________ |
| 4. | Daydreaming Healthy and Inevitable, Research Finds | ________ | ________ |
| 5. | Elvis Found Alive and Well in Akron, Ohio | ________ | ________ |
| 6. | Man Invents New Bicycle for Horses | ________ | ________ |
| 7. | Our Plane was Hijacked by Aliens | ________ | ________ |
| 8. | Spurs Squeak Past Lakers 96-94 in OT | ________ | ________ |
| 9. | Storm-Battered South Braces for Latest Round of Winter Weather | ________ | ________ |
| 10. | Woman finds Dead Leprechauns in a Jar | ________ | ________ |

Choose one headline that seems accurate. What specifically makes it seem valid? ________________

________________________________________________________________.

Choose one headline that seems inaccurate. What specifically makes it seem invalid?________________

________________________________________________________________.

# Worksheet: Validity and Accuracy in Articles

| Article Analysis | Article #1 Headline: ______ ______ ______ | Article #2 Headline: ______ ______ ______ |
|---|---|---|
| Author seems neutral; just reporting the facts; steers a middle path and shows both sides of a story | ___ no ___ yes (if yes, explain) | ___ no ___ yes (if yes, explain) |
| Colorful adjectives and phrases; "hot," "jealous," "cold shoulder," etc. | ___ no ___ yes (if yes, explain) | ___ no ___ yes (if yes, explain) |
| Events seem unreal or unlikely | ___ no ___ yes (if yes, explain) | ___ no ___ yes (if yes, explain) |
| Facts, opinions, and other information seem to have been verified by another source | ___ no ___ yes (if yes, explain) | ___ no ___ yes (if yes, explain) |
| Information seems based on rumors; uses the phrase "a source close to. . ." | ___ no ___ yes (if yes, explain) | ___ no ___ yes (if yes, explain) |
| Lots of pictures with the article | ___ no ___ yes (if yes, explain) | ___ no ___ yes (if yes, explain) |
| Mostly about rich and famous people; personal information | ___ no ___ yes (if yes, explain) | ___ no ___ yes (if yes, explain) |
| Over-exaggerated story; too silly to be true | ___ no ___ yes (if yes, explain) | ___ no ___ yes (if yes, explain) |
| Shocking headlines | ___ no ___ yes (if yes, explain) | ___ no ___ yes (if yes, explain) |
| The author is reporting the truth; information is honest and meant to inform rather than entertain | ___ no ___ yes (if yes, explain) | ___ no ___ yes (if yes, explain) |

## Worksheet: Validity and Accuracy in Articles (continued)

1. After analyzing Article #1, I have determined that ______________________________

______________________________________________________________________

______________________________________________________________________.

2. After analyzing Article #2, I have determined that ______________________________

______________________________________________________________________

______________________________________________________________________.

3. Of the two articles, which seems more reliable? ______________________________

4. What is it about that article that makes you believe the information is valid and accurate? Be specific.

______________________________________________________________________

______________________________________________________________________

______________________________________________________________________.

# Teacher Directions: Using Facts

## Goals for Student

1. Distinguish between fact and opinion.
2. Begin to use resources to check the validity of information.
3. Separate collected information into useful components using a variety of techniques.

## Preparation

1. Your class should discuss the process of separating facts from fiction.
2. Obtain enough copies of *Cat* (Eyewitness Books), a non-fiction, informational book about cats, for each person in the center.
3. Also, collect fictional picture books about spiders. I suggest Doreen Cronin and Harry Bliss's *Diary of a Spider*, Mary Howitt and Tony DiTerlizzi's *Spider and the Fly*, Gerald McDermott's *Anansi the Spider*, David Kirk's *Miss Spider's Tea Party*, and Judy Allen's *Are You a Spider?*.
4. Provide factual resources about spiders as well.

## Materials

- *Cats* (Eyewitness Books)
- Spider picture books and factual books
- "Using Facts" worksheet
- Manila paper
- Colored pencils

## Focus on the Skill

1. First, the students will complete the "Semantics Chart" on the "Using Facts" worksheet. They will place a "+" in the box where the facts fit and a "-" where the facts do not fit.
2. Students will complete "Drawing Conclusions from the Chart" on the worksheet.

## Practice the Skill

Next, the students will choose one of the picture books about a spider. As they read the books, they are to collect facts about spiders. They will complete the chart on the "Using Facts" worksheet. They should document information that is impossible and factual regarding spiders.

## Take It to the Next Level

1. The students should fold a piece of manila paper in half. They should title one side of the paper "I am a Real Spider" and the other side "I am a Spider from a Picture Book."
2. On the "real" side, they should draw a factual-looking picture of a spider, and on the "fiction" side, they should draw a picture of the fictional spider described in the story. Both pictures should include details about physical characteristics, behavior, and habitat. You may want to provide non-fiction books and articles about spiders for students to validate their information. The details of both drawings should delineate fact from fiction.

## Special Considerations

Struggling readers do not always have the prior knowledge to separate fact from fiction in their own reading. They need to understand that, although this may seem easy, the same skill has to be applied to more complicated information—even when something "sounds" factual, it could be a writer's hidden agenda or personal experiences that motivate the writing.

# Student Directions: Using Facts

## Focus on the Skill

1. First, complete the "Semantics Chart" on the "Using Facts" worksheet. Place a "+" in the box where the facts fit and a "-" where the facts do not fit.
2. Afterwards, complete the sentences in the "Drawing Conclusions from the Chart" section of the worksheet.

## Practice the Skill

Next, choose one of the fictional picture books about a spider. As you read the book, you are to collect facts about spiders that are believable (valid). Complete the chart on the "Using Facts" worksheet. You should document information that is impossible for spiders and factual information about spiders that you could verify.

## Take It to the Next Level

1. Finally, fold a piece of manila paper in half. Title one side of the paper "I am a Real Spider" and the other side "I am a Spider from a Picture Book."
2. On the "real" side, draw a factual-looking picture of a spider, and on the "fiction" side, draw a picture of the fictional spider described in the story. Both pictures should include details about physical characteristics, behavior, and habitat. You can use non-fiction books and articles about spiders to validate your information. The details of both drawings should separate fact from fiction.

## How You Will Be Graded

| | 1 little or no evidence | 2 below average | 3 adequate evidence | 4 better than average | 5 superior evidence | TOTAL |
|---|---|---|---|---|---|---|
| Attention to neatness and presentation | | | | | | |
| Accurately collected facts on a semantic map | | | | | | |
| Draws conclusions from the semantic map that show comprehension of facts | | | | | | |
| Differentiates factual and nonfactual information about spiders from a fictional source | | | | | | |
| Illustrations of real spider and picture-book spider show understanding of factual-versus-fictional details | | | | | | |
| **Total points multiplied by four** | | | | | | |
| **Final grade** | | | | | | |

# Worksheet: Using Facts

## Focus on the Skill

**Semantics Chart.** Use the Eyewitness *Cats* book to complete the following chart. Put a "+" in the box if the species of cat has that feature and a "–" in the box if they do not. If the feature does not apply, put "N/A" in the box.

| | Spotted fur | Hunts alone | Long tail | Licks fur to keep clean | Known for eating men | Rolls on back to show affection | Known as "small" cats | Known for climbing trees |
|---|---|---|---|---|---|---|---|---|
| Black panther | | | | | | | | |
| Bobcat | | | | | | | | |
| Common housecat | | | | | | | | |
| Jaguar | | | | | | | | |
| Leopard | | | | | | | | |
| Lion | | | | | | | | |
| Lynx | | | | | | | | |
| Puma (Cougar) | | | | | | | | |
| Tiger | | | | | | | | |

**Drawing Conclusions from the Chart.** It's not enough to just collect information; you must be able to use it. Think about each species of cat. Draw some conclusions from your chart.

1. Most species of cats have ________________________ fur.
2. Most species of cats like to hunt ______________________.
3. Most species of cats have ___________________ tails.
4. All species of cats ___________________________ and ___________________________.
5. (Circle one) Most species of cats **are/are not** known for eating men.

## Practice the Skill

**Spider Story Chart.** Chart information from one of the fictional spider stories..

| Impossible events from the story | Facts about spiders from the story |
|---|---|
| | |

# Teacher Directions: Analyzing Magazine Articles for Facts

## Goals for Student

1. Read literature about a variety of cultural experiences.
2. Gain a better understanding of self through the reading of literature.
3. Understand the role of point of view or persona in a literary or informational text.

## Preparation

1. Your class should have experience analyzing periodicals.
2. Collect many magazine articles from specific areas of interest: sports, fashion, car racing, hunting, fishing, video games, music, etc. It's best to offer articles that are *outside* of students' normal interests.
3. Make several copies of each article.

## Materials

- "Analyzing Magazine Articles for Facts" worksheet
- Story paper
- Colored pencils

## Focus on the Skill

1. Students will first choose an article and, using the "Previewing an Article" section of the "Analyzing Magazine Articles for Facts" worksheet, they should predict what kind of magazine the article is from.
2. Next, they will brainstorm everything they know about the subject for the "What Do I Know?" portion of the worksheet.
3. Using a highlighter, the students will read the article and highlight terms (jargon) that are probably specific to that area of interest (for instance, in an article about fishing, you might come across terms like "bait," which is anything that a fish will eat; "cast," which is to throw a line and its bait onto the water; "fly," which is an artificial imitation of an insect used for bait; or "hole," which is a deep section of a stream or river). In the "Understanding Jargon" portion of the "Analyzing Magazine Articles for Facts" worksheet, the students will write six of the highlighted words. (If they are not sure if the words are jargon, they may do a quick Internet search to find the definitions.)
4. They should circle one of the jargon words and define it on the lines provided.

## Practice the Skill

Next, the students will use the GLIMMER strategy to analyze the article as a whole. They should make notes about the following: **G**eneral observations; **L**abels, titles, and headings; **I**nteresting words that are unfamiliar; **M**essage; **M**y own words; **E**valuate for bias; and **R**eaction.

# Teacher Directions: Analyzing Magazine Articles for Facts (continued)

## Take It to the Next Level

You'll need to supply students with magazines from the same subject as their article (I have had a lot of luck with surfing and racecars). After they have gone through the GLIMMER process, ask students to create a collage about the subject of the magazine on the blank part of the story paper. At the bottom lined section of the paper, they will write the "My Words" section of the GLIMMER chart. At the top, they will title the paper with the same title as the article's headline.

## Special Considerations

A good activity to precede this one is to go through the very same steps using an article that covers a subject where your students *do* have prior experiences. You could show them how reading is really about interest and motivation—jargon is created by the people who enjoy that pastime and hobby.

While it may seem strange to ask students to read articles about subjects where they lack prior knowledge, the truth is that they will benefit from the experience. It requires them to activate all of the best reading strategies. The side benefit of this activity may be in their willingness to look at other activities outside their scope of interest with a "wondering eye," and they may develop a little tolerance for people who enjoy activities they consider unimportant.

# Student Directions: Analyzing Magazine Articles for Facts

## Focus on the Skill

1. First choose an article and, using the "Previewing an Article" section of the "Analyzing Magazine Articles for Facts" worksheet, predict what kind of magazine the article is from.
2. Next, brainstorm everything you know about the subject for the "What Do I Know?" portion of the worksheet.
3. Using a highlighter, read the article and highlight terms (jargon) that are probably specific to that area of interest (for instance, in an article about fishing, you might come across terms like "bait," which is anything that a fish will eat; "cast," which is to throw a line and its bait onto the water; "fly," which is an artificial imitation of an insect used for bait; or "hole," which is a deep section of a stream or river). In the "Understanding Jargon" portion of the "Analyzing Magazine Articles for Facts" worksheet, write six of the highlighted words. (If you are not sure if the words are jargon, you may do a quick Internet search to find the definitions.)
4. Circle one of the jargon words and define it on the lines provided.

## Practice the Skill

Next, use the GLIMMER strategy to analyze the article as a whole. Make notes about the following: **G**eneral observations; **L**abels, titles, and headings; **I**nteresting words that are unfamiliar; **M**essage; **M**y own words; **E**valuate for bias; and **R**eaction.

## Take It to the Next Level

After you have gone through the GLIMMER process, create a collage about the subject of the magazine on the blank part of the story paper. At the bottom lined section of the paper, write the "My Words" section of the GLIMMER chart. At the top, title the paper with the same title as the article's headline.

## How You Will Be Graded

| | 1 little or no evidence | 2 below average | 3 adequate evidence | 4 better than average | 5 superior evidence | TOTAL |
|---|---|---|---|---|---|---|
| Attention to neatness and presentation | | | | | | |
| Identifies jargon related to the subject of a magazine article | | | | | | |
| Brainstorms as an active reading strategy | | | | | | |
| Uses the GLIMMER strategy effectively to evaluate a magazine article | | | | | | |
| "My Own Words" effectively summarizes the main idea of the article | | | | | | |
| **Total points multiplied by four** | | | | | | |
| **Final grade** | | | | | | |

# Worksheet: Analyzing Magazine Articles for Facts

## Focus on the Skill

**Previewing an Article.** Before you begin reading the article, look at the overall presentation, headline, captions, pictures, etc. Decide what kind of magazine this article came out of.

*This article, obviously, came out of a* ________________________________ *magazine.*

**What Do I Know?** Before you read the article, determine what you know about the subject of the article (put the name of that subject in the middle of the web). If it's an article about boxing, what do you know about the words, rules, and clothing related to boxing? If it's surfing, what do you know about the moves, weather, scoring, and equipment related to surfing? Think of every possible related idea.

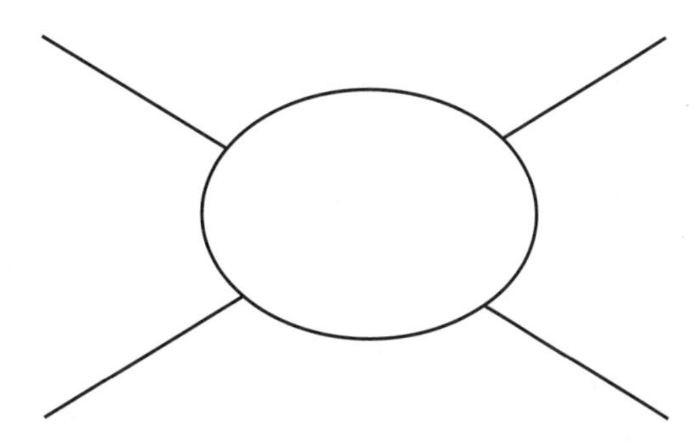

**Understanding Jargon.** As you read the magazine article, you should highlight words that are specific to people who read this kind of magazine. Those words are "jargon." Different sports use jargon. For example, baseball players know the "diamond" is the layout of the bases, "junk" is a breaking ball or knuckle ball, and a "save" is when the relief pitcher manages to keep the lead for a win at the end of a game. People who live in a particular place may share jargon. A "Benjamin" may be a one-hundred dollar bill, "chill" might be to relax, and your "ride" might be the car you drive.

Some words that may be jargon, or words that are used by people who enjoy this activity, are:

______________________________ ______________________________

______________________________ ______________________________

______________________________ ______________________________

One jargon word from this article that I defined is ____________________________, and it means

________________________________________________________________________

________________________________________________________________________

# Worksheet: Analyzing Magazine Articles for Facts (continued)

## Practice the Skill

A great way to analyze magazine articles is the GLIMMER strategy.

| | |
|---|---|
| General observations: pictures, captions, charts, graphs, etc. | |
| Labels, titles, and headings | |
| Interesting words that are unfamiliar | |
| Message—what seems to be the point? | |
| My own words—summarize the information | |
| Evaluate for bias—is this article meant for a certain type of audience, or is it designed to capture the attention of all readers? Explain. | |
| Reaction | |

# Teacher Directions: Tone Words

## Goals for Student

1. Learn ways the tone of a literary work is used to support its intention.
2. Understand the impact on the reader of specific word choices.
3. Begin to recognize how the author's purpose is revealed through the tone of words he/she chooses.

## Preparation

Your class should begin to connect tone words with author's purpose.

## Materials

- 'Tone Words" worksheet
- Story paper
- Colored pencils
- Dictionary

## Focus on the Skill

1. Have the students choose one of the words from the list in the "Introducing Tone Words" section of the "Tone Words" worksheet.
2. Each person at the center should select a different word. They will do a vocabulary map for the words and discuss their meanings with the rest of the group.

## Practice the Skill

1. Next, they will consider the list of fifteen words in the "Categorizing Tone Meanings" section of the worksheet. They will determine whether each of the words shares its connotation with the words "happy," "sad," or "angry" (three overused words when discussing tone).
2. Finally, have the students read Meriwether Lewis's journal entry from 1906 in the "Analyzing Tone in Literature" section of the worksheet. They are to circle the words that show that Lewis felt the group was *satisfied.*
3. Then, the students should complete the framed sentence that proves Lewis's group felt satisfied. This statement could also be called a thesis statement.

## Take It to the Next Level

Have the students consider how the original words from the "Introducing Tone Words" section might apply to them. Everyone in the group should choose a different word from the list. They may discuss incidents when a person feels each of these words. On story paper, they will create a sentence with the tone word they chose about themselves that shows when they feel or behave this way. (Example for the tone word "obnoxious": *Lynn hated that she lost the game of Pictionary and said, 'I think you are cheating!' She was definitely being obnoxious.*" On the top of the paper, they will draw a picture that expresses the meaning of the sentence.

# Teacher Directions: Tone Words (continued)

## Special Considerations

Tone words are vital to good reading, and studying emotions is a good place to start. Low-level readers (and most middle schoolers) do not go much further than your basic "happy," "sad," and "angry." They have to see there are stronger words to connote those feelings, and they must apply those words to themselves and the literature they read. You might find that your students start showing you the tone words in their own reading if you get excited enough about the concept.

The other consideration is the framed sentence. This could be presented as a thesis statement. If low-level readers are consistently taught the value of writing effective thesis statements, they will begin to understand that analyzing literature is a constant search for details and evidence to *prove* something. It is a higher step, but with practice, they will gain proficiency.

# Student Directions: Tone Words

## Focus on the Skill

1. Choose one of the words from the list in the "Introducing Tone Words" section of the "Tone Words" worksheet.
2. Each person at the center should select a different word. Everyone will create a vocabulary map of his or her word and discuss their meanings with the rest of the group.

## Practice the Skill

1. Next, consider the list of fifteen words in the "Categorizing Tone Meanings" section of the worksheet. Determine whether each of the words shares its connotation with the words "happy," "sad," or "angry" (three overused words when discussing tone).
2. Read Meriwether Lewis's journal entry from 1906 in the "Analyzing Tone in Literature" section of the worksheet. Circle the words that show that Lewis felt the group was *satisfied*.
3. Then, complete the framed sentence that proves Lewis's group felt satisfied. This statement could also be called a thesis statement.

## Take It to the Next Level

1. Consider how the original words form the "Introducing Tone Words" section might apply to your life.
2. Everyone in the group should choose a different word from the list. You may discuss incidents when a person feels each of these words. On story paper, create a sentence with the tone word you chose that shows yourself feeling or behaving this way. (Example for the tone word "obnoxious": *Lynn hated that she lost the game of Pictionary and said, 'I think you are cheating!' She was definitely being obnoxious.")* On the top of the paper, draw a picture that expresses the meaning of the sentence.

## How You Will Be Graded

| | 1 little or no evidence | 2 below average | 3 adequate evidence | 4 better than average | 5 superior evidence | TOTAL |
|---|---|---|---|---|---|---|
| Attention to neatness and presentation | | | | | | |
| Vocabulary map accurately reflects meaning of the tone word | | | | | | |
| Categorizes the tone words correctly | | | | | | |
| Identifies tone words from a primary source and creates a framed sentence that shows comprehension | | | | | | |
| Story paper accurately reflects meaning and use of a tone word; effectively shows personal experience | | | | | | |
| **Total points multiplied by four** | | | | | | |
| **Final grade** | | | | | | |

## Worksheet: Tone Words

**Introducing Tone Words.** Each person at the center should choose one of the tone words and create a vocabulary web. Each person at the center should choose a different word.

annoyed
relaxed
restless
hostile
amused
fascinated

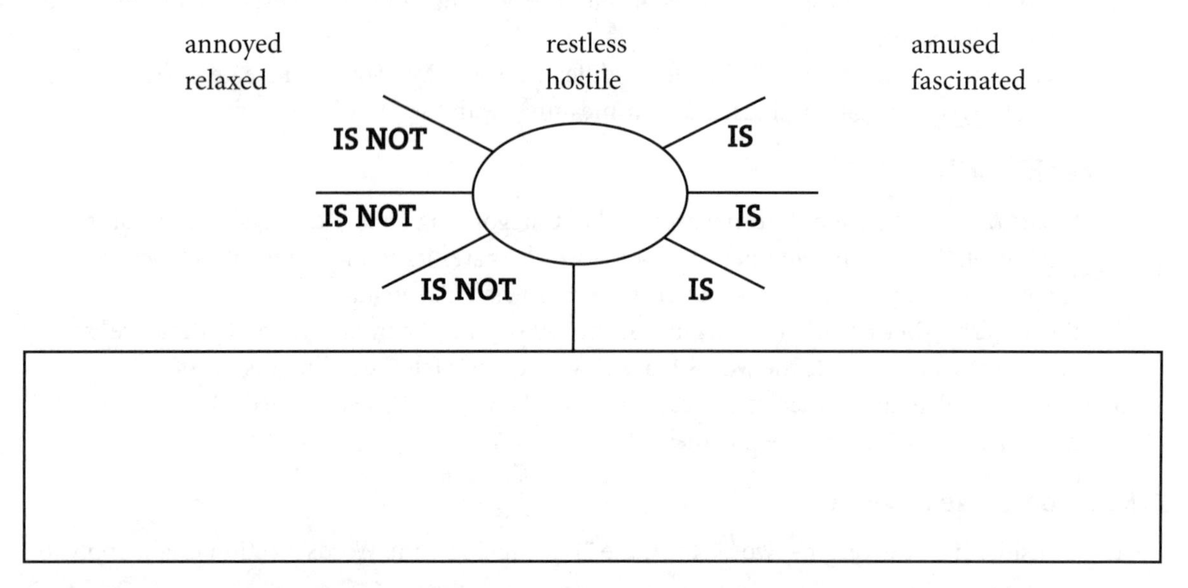


**Categorizing Tone Meanings.** Look at the list of tone words below. Place each word in the chart under the word that shares its similar tone.

annoyed
blissful
cheerless
content
depressed
ecstatic
enraged
furious
gloomy
heartbroken
irate
irritated
joyful
miserable
pleased

| happy | sad | glad |
|---|---|---|
| | | |
| | | |
| | | |
| | | |
| | | |

**Analyzing Tone in Literature.** The following journal entry was written by Meriwether Lewis in the last year of the Lewis and Clark Expedition West. Circle the words that show that Lewis is satisfied.

***January 16, 1806***
*Meriwether Lewis*

*We have plenty of Elk beef for the present and a little salt, our houses dry and comfortable, and having made up our minds to remain until the 1st of April, every one appears content with his situation and his fare.*

Complete the following sentence. Make sure you include at least three of the words and phrases from the journal entry.

Because ________________________________________, it is clear that the group is ________________________________________.

# Teacher Directions: Warnings as Persuasion

## Goals for Student

1. Identify persuasion techniques in literary works.
2. Identify strong verbs and phrases that create tone.
3. Analyze literature for strong arguments.

## Preparation

Your class should feel comfortable with facts and opinions. They should be ready to acknowledge biases in what they read.

## Materials

- "Persuasion" worksheet
- "The Dangers of Gossip" essay
- Manila paper
- Colored pencils
- Two different colored highlighters
- Dictionary

## Focus on the Skill

1. Have the students consider what a warning is designed to do. They will evaluate three warning signs on the "Persuasion" worksheet. They should determine what it is about the pictures and the words that make the warning effective.
2. Then, the students must decide which warning seems most effective and explain why. Does it evoke a certain feeling? Is there something about the image that seems persuasive?

## Practice the Skill

1. Have the students read the essay, "The Dangers of Gossip." They will read the essay twice. The first time, they will look only for strong, vivid verbs. They should underline these verbs and move three of them to the "Evaluating Essays That Warn" part of the worksheet. They will write each verb and use the dictionary to define the meaning.
2. For the second reading, students will look for evidence of two different types of arguments. They will use two different colored highlighters and, with one color, they will highlight words and phrases used as evidence in the essay to show that gossip is bad. With the other color, they will find words and phrases used as evidence in the essay to show that bad things happen to those who gossip.
3. Finally, the students will use the chart to log their findings. After looking at both columns, they should decide which argument is strongest and explain their answer on the lines provided.

## Take It to the Next Level

Have the students think of a warning they could create—perhaps about cheating, lying, or something related to health. Using manila paper, they will write their warning at the bottom of a paper and create an illustration that effectively supports their caption.

## Special Considerations

Struggling readers do not recognize the elements of persuasion. They fail to see that they are often the targets for persuasive ads and provocative commercials. It is important to help struggling readers recognize how the powers of influence can affect their opinions and judgments.

# Student Directions: Warnings as Persuasion

## Focus on the Skill

1. Consider what a warning is designed to do. Evaluate the three warning signs on the "Persuasion" worksheet. Determine what it is about the pictures and the words that make the warning effective.
2. Then, decide which warning seems most effective and explain why. Does it evoke a certain feeling? Is there something about the image that seems persuasive?

## Practice the Skill

1. Read the essay, "The Dangers of Gossip" (actually, you will read the essay twice). The first time, look only for strong, vivid verbs. Underline these verbs, and move three of them to the "Evaluating Essays That Warn" part of the worksheet. Write each verb and use the dictionary to define the meaning.
2. For the second reading, look for evidence of two different types of arguments. Use two different colored highlighters and, with one color, highlight words and phrases used as evidence in the essay to show that gossip is bad. With the other color, find words and phrases used as evidence in the essay to show that bad things happen to those who gossip.
3. Finally, use the chart to log your findings. After looking at both columns, you should decide which argument is strongest and explain your answer on the lines provided.

## Take It to the Next Level

Think of a warning you could create—perhaps about cheating, lying, or something related to health. Using manila paper, write the warning at the bottom of a paper and create an illustration that effectively supports your caption.

## How You Will Be Graded

| | 1 little or no evidence | 2 below average | 3 adequate evidence | 4 better than average | 5 superior evidence | **TOTAL** |
|---|---|---|---|---|---|---|
| Attention to neatness and presentation | | | | | | |
| Accurately identifies elements of persuasion in a warning sign | | | | | | |
| Recognizes strong verbs in a persuasive essay | | | | | | |
| Identifies words and phrases that support arguments | | | | | | |
| Creates an effective warning with pictures and words | | | | | | |
| **Total points multiplied by four** | | | | | | |
| **Final grade** | | | | | | |

## The Dangers of Gossip

Tessa leaned into Lourdes' ear and you could tell the tale was definitely juicy. Lourdes bent back and covered her mouth to laugh, "Oh girl! That is crazy!" As Rosa closed her top locker, she caught a glare from Tessa, who seemed satisfied with how well she had retold the story. Rosa nervously gathered her papers and rushed to math – a tear caught in the corner of her eye. Rosa thought in despair, "Now, everybody knows!" The truth is, gossip is never far from pain and sorrow.

Our society has become a legion of drones, programmed to seek out the filth and darkest secrets of every celebrity and entertainer. We sit, cornered in our living rooms, taking in every detail of the latest starlet who tripped on the red carpet, and we demand to know who is dating whom. The media traps us with their constant stream of "revealing" news stories and shocking features. Before you know it, we are all more concerned with the newest designer outfit purchased for some spoiled pooch who sits in a purse all day than we are with peace, justice, and friendship.

Consequently, we begin to imagine we have the right to judge and condemn others for doing and saying what we have done and thought many times before. For instance, we are consumed with weight and wrinkles. More than half of all Americans are overweight, and inevitably, we are all going to age. Furthermore, as soon as we catch sight of some famous person wearing an outfit we might not like or a hairdo that seems strange, we sit back and laugh. Haven't we all been guilty of bad fashion and problem hair days?

"Who gossips with you will gossip of you," wisely warns the old Irish quote. Our true friends protect and defend our honor. Are your secrets becoming entertainment at the lunch table? Is your most embarrassing moment being ridiculed at P.E.? Too often, "friends" are all too ready to reveal the secrets they were told in private just to get some attention. When rumors and hearsay are more important than being true to a pal, it's probably time to consider finding a new friend.

Be aware of the dangers of gossip. What may seem entertaining may really be corrupt. None of us has the right to judge others, despite our faulty sense of entitlement. Besides, if you are the type who makes a habit of judging, you can be certain you are being judged. Live a gossip-free life and live a happy life.

# Worksheet: Warnings as Persuasion

**Warning Signs.** Consider each of the following warnings. On the lines below each warning, describe what images and words are used to persuade the reader.

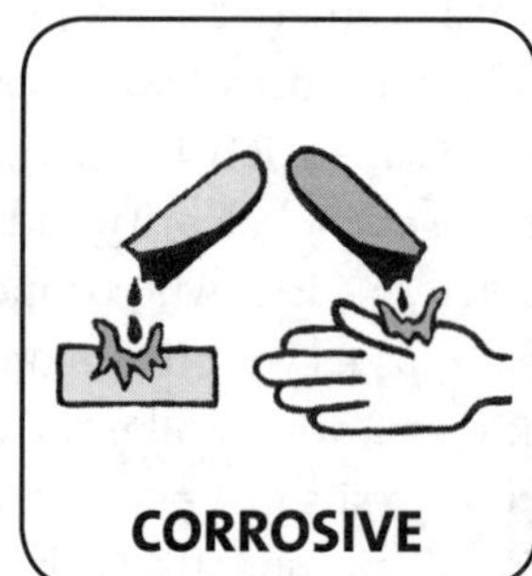


______________________ ______________________ ______________________
______________________ ______________________ ______________________
______________________ ______________________ ______________________

Of the three signs, which one seems most effective and why? Be specific. ______________________
____________________________________________________________
____________________________________________________________.

**Evaluating Essays That Warn**

Strong verbs Definitions

______________________: ______________________________________
______________________: ______________________________________
______________________: ______________________________________

| Words and phrases that show gossip is bad | Words and phrases that show bad things happen to gossipers |
|---|---|
| | |
| | |
| | |
| | |
| | |
| | |

Which argument seems stronger? Use the words and phrases you collected to explain.

____________________________________________________________
____________________________________________________________
____________________________________________________________
____________________________________________________________.

# Teacher Directions: Persuasion

## Goals for Student

1. Identify persuasion techniques in literary works.
2. Recognize what makes writing persuasive.
3. Evaluate purpose in a variety of persuasive texts

## Preparation

Your class should begin to see how persuasion relies on purpose.

## Materials

- "Persuasion" worksheet
- Jackie Robinson letter
- Story paper
- Colored pencils
- Two different colored highlighters

## Focus on the Skill

1. Have the students analyze the slogans of four social activist groups that are passionate about their cause on the "Persuasion" worksheet. Then, have the students study the names of the groups. Without knowing anything about their causes, have the students try to match the group with one of its slogans.
2. After the students put the group and the slogan together, have the students explain how each message is persuasive. What is about these slogans that gets their attention?

## Practice the Skill

1. Next, the students will read the "Analyzing a Letter for Persuasion" section of the worksheet. They will highlight the words and phrases in the letter that Jackie Robinson wrote to persuade the president to take a stand for African Americans in 1958.
2. Using the PERM tool and chart, the students will analyze the letter for persuasion. They will determine the **P**urpose, **E**motional words, **R**ealization (what you learned), and the **M**essage intended. Then, they should complete the sentence to explain how Robinson used persuasion to convince President Eisenhower of his convictions.

## Take It to the Next Level

Have the students write their own persuasive letter demanding better food in the cafeteria. Have them consider ways that the social groups and Jackie Robinson tried to get their messages across. They will then use the PERM tool to analyze their own letter.

## Special Considerations

Help your students to brainstorm strong verbs that would be effective for persuasive writing ("insist," "assert," "challenge," "require," etc.).

# Student Directions: Persuasion

## Focus on the Skill

1. Analyze the slogans of four social activist groups that are passionate about their cause on the "Persuasion" worksheet. Then, study the names of the groups. Without knowing anything about their causes, try to match the group with its slogan.
2. Now, explain how each message is persuasive. What is about these slogans that gets your attention?

## Practice the Skill

1. Next, read the "Analyzing a Letter for Persuasion" section of the worksheet. Highlight the words and phrases in the letter that Jackie Robinson used to persuade the president to take a stand for African Americans in 1958.
2. Using the PERM tool and chart, analyze the letter for persuasion. You will determine the **P**urpose, **E**motional words, **R**ealization (what you learned), and the **M**essage intended. Then, complete the sentence to explain how Robinson used persuasion to convince President Eisenhower of his convictions.

## Take It to the Next Level

Now, write your own persuasive letter demanding better food in the cafeteria. Consider ways that the social groups and Jackie Robinson tried to get their messages across. Afterwards, use the PERM tool to analyze your own letter.

## How You Will Be Graded

| | 1 little or no evidence | 2 below average | 3 adequate evidence | 4 better than average | 5 superior evidence | **TOTAL** |
|---|---|---|---|---|---|---|
| Attention to neatness and presentation | | | | | | |
| Accurately matches slogans with activist groups | | | | | | |
| Explains meaning of slogans and how they are persuasive | | | | | | |
| Analyzes letter for persuasion and purpose using PERM chart | | | | | | |
| Creates a persuasive letter and accurately analyzes the letter for effective persuasion | | | | | | |
| **Total points multiplied by four** | | | | | | |
| **Final grade** | | | | | | |

## Letter from Jackie Robinson to President Eisenhower

May 13, 1958
The President (Dwight D. Eisenhower)
The White House
Washington, D.C.

My Dear Mr. President:

I was sitting in the audience at the Summit Meeting of Negro Leaders yesterday when you said we must have patience. On hearing you say this, I felt like standing up and saying, "Oh no! Not again."

I respectfully remind you sir, that we have been the most patient of all people. When you say we must have self-respect, I wondered how we could have self-respect and remain patient considering the treatment accorded us through the years.

17 million Negroes cannot do as you suggest and wait for the hearts of men to change. We want to enjoy now the rights that we feel we are entitled to as Americans. This we cannot do unless we pursue aggressively goals which all other Americans achieved over 150 years ago.

As the chief executive of our nation, I respectfully suggest that you unwittingly crush the spirit of freedom in Negroes by constantly urging forbearance and give hope to those pro-segregation leaders like Governor Faubus who would take from us those freedoms we now enjoy. Your own experience with Governor Faubus is proof enough that forbearance and not eventual integration is the goal the pro-segregation leaders seek.

In my view, an unequivocal statement backed up by action such as you demonstrated you could take last fall in dealing with Governor Faubus (in Little Rock, Arkansas) if it became necessary, would let it be known that America is determined to provide—in the near future—for Negroes—the freedoms we are entitled to under the constitution.

Respectfully yours,

Jackie Robinson

(National Archives & Records Administration, http://www.archives.gov)

# Worksheet: Persuasion

## Focus on the Skill

**Slogans as Persuasion.** Many activist groups are passionate about their cause. Study the names of these groups and, without knowing anything about their causes, try to match the group with its slogan.

| Slogans | Groups |
|---|---|
| a. *Global Warming. It's the Real Thing!* | ___ People for the Ethical Treatment of Animals (PETA) |
| b. *Over the limit? Under Arrest.* | ___ Truth |
| c. *Every eight seconds, someone in the world dies from tobacco-related illness.* | ___ Mothers Against Drunk Driving (MADD) |
| d. *Beef: It's what's rotting in your colon.* | ___ Greenpeace |

**Identify the Message.** Look at the slogans above. Now that you recognize the group and the slogan together, explain how each message is persuasive.

a. ______________________________

b. ______________________________

c. ______________________________

d. ______________________________

## Practice the Skill

**Analyzing a Letter for Persuasion.** Highlight the words and phrases in the letter that Jackie Robinson uses to persuade the president to take a stand for African Americans in 1958.

Then, use the PERM tool to analyze the letter.

| Purpose for writing | Emotional words that make a difference | Realization by you, the reader (what you learned) | Message to the recipient (intended) |
|---|---|---|---|
| | | | |

Overall, Jackie Robinson's letter is persuasive because ______________________________

______________________________.

# Teacher Directions: Autobiographies

## Goals for Student

1. Analyze and describe from a historical characters' points of view.
2. Explain or demonstrate how phrases, sentences, and passages relate to personal life.
3. Explain the influence of a person's experiences on personal growth and development.

## Preparation

Your class should begin to analyze primary sources.

## Materials

- "Autobiographies" worksheet
- Excerpt from *The Autobiography of Ben Franklin*
- Dictionary
- Highlighter
- Internet access

## Focus on the Skill

Have students analyze *The Autobiography of Ben Franklin* for order of events. On the "Recognizing the Chronology of Autobiographies" section of the "Autobiographies" worksheet, they will record five events and illustrate those events to show they understand the meaning of each.

## Practice the Skill

1. Next, students will read through the excerpt and highlight words that are unfamiliar. They will look these words up and write the words and definitions on the back of the worksheet.
2. The students will use the "ESQC: Events, Surprises, Questions, Conclusions" chart to analyze the excerpt. You want your students' conclusions to be detailed and reflect an understanding of what Franklin revealed about his childhood.
3. In the "Bio Poem" section of the worksheet, the students will use each letter of Franklin's last name to reflect what they have learned about the famous American. The first letter has been used as an example. A good bio poem should be full of details and examples from the excerpt.
4. If Internet access is available, the students should complete the "Internet Search" section of the worksheet to understand what tallow-chandlers and sope-boilers do for a living.

## Take It to the Next Level

Have the students write a RAFT (**R**ole, **A**udience, **F**ormat, **T**opic). The author might be an older Ben (role) writing to his father (audience) a letter (format) criticizing his parenting (topic). Or, perhaps Ben's teacher (role) could write for newspaper readers (audience) a tell-all news article (format) bragging about his relationship with the younger Ben (topic).

## Special Considerations

Middle-school-aged kids are rarely asked to read non-fiction that is historic and full of terms that may no longer exist. This provides struggling readers with a lot of opportunities to analyze words in context and the personalities of historical figures in their own words (rather than having someone else do it for them). Again, yes, it takes effort to get them through these experiences, but they must practice with literature that challenges their skills as readers.

# Student Directions: Autobiographies

## Focus on the Skill

1. Read the excerpt from *The Autobiography of Ben Franklin*, and highlight words that are unfamiliar. Look these words up, and write the words and definitions on the back of the "Autobiographies" worksheet.
2. In the "Recognizing the Chronology of Autobiographies" section of the worksheet, record five events and illustrate those events to show you understand the meaning of each.

## Practice the Skill

1. You will use the "ESQC: Events, Surprises, Questions, Conclusions" chart to analyze the excerpt. Your conclusions should be detailed and reflect an understanding of what Franklin revealed about his childhood.
2. In the "Bio Poem" section of the worksheet, use each letter of Franklin's last name to create a poem that reflects what you have learned about the famous American. The first letter has been used as an example. A good bio poem should be full of details and examples from the excerpt.
3. If Internet access is available, complete the "Internet Search" section of the worksheet to understand what tallow-chandlers and sope-boilers do for a living.

## Take It to the Next Level

You will write a RAFT (**R**ole, **A**udience, **F**ormat, **T**opic). The author might be an older Ben (role) writing to his father (audience) a letter (format) criticizing his parenting (topic). Or, perhaps Ben's teacher (role) could write for newspaper readers (audience) a tell-all news article (format) bragging about his relationship with the younger Ben (topic).

## How You Will Be Graded

| | 1 little or no evidence | 2 below average | 3 adequate evidence | 4 better than average | 5 superior evidence | **TOTAL** |
|---|---|---|---|---|---|---|
| Attention to neatness and presentation | | | | | | |
| Highlights and defines unfamiliar words; including "tallow-chandler" and "sope-boiler" | | | | | | |
| Creates accurate timeline of Franklin's childhood from a primary document; bio poem is detailed | | | | | | |
| Evaluates excerpt effectively with "ESQC" chart; conclusions show understanding | | | | | | |
| Creates a RAFT that shows comprehension of the primary document in an alternative format | | | | | | |
| **Total points multiplied by four** | | | | | | |
| **Final grade** | | | | | | |

# Worksheet: Autobiographies

The purpose of journals and autobiographies is for people to chronicle their lives. This allows for future generations to study the progression of a person's success; however, for the writer, it may just be a way to reflect on their lives. Analyze an excerpt from *The Autobiography of Ben Franklin* for purpose and effect.

**Recognizing the Chronology of Autobiographies.** Read the excerpt from *The Autobiography of Ben Franklin*. Identify five events in Franklin's young life to create a timeline, and illustrate your events on the back of this sheet.

--------------------- → --------------------- → --------------------- → --------------------- → ---------------------

**ESQC: Events, Surprises, Questions, Conclusions.** Use the chart to analyze the excerpt.

| | |
|---|---|
| **Events from the passage** | |
| **Something that surprises me** | |
| **Questions I would like to ask Ben** | |
| **Conclusions** | |

**Bio Poem.** Create a bio poem using just the information from this excerpt.

**F***ailed arithmetic in school*

**R**

**A**

**N**

**K**

**L**

**I**

**N**

## Worksheet: Autobiographies (continued)

**Internet Search.** Describe the job of a "tallow-chandler" and "sope-boiler" using information from the Internet.

Tallow-chandler: ____________________________________________

____________________________________________

Sope-boiler: ____________________________________________

____________________________________________

## Excerpt from *The Autobiography of Ben Franklin*

My elder brothers were all put apprentices to different trades. I was put to the grammar-school at eight years of age, my father intending to devote me, as the tithe of his sons, to the service of the Church. My early readiness in learning to read (which must have been very early, as I do not remember when I could not read), and the opinion of all his friends, that I should certainly make a good scholar, encouraged him in this purpose of his. My uncle Benjamin, too, approved of it, and proposed to give me all his short-hand volumes of sermons, I suppose as a stock to set up with, if I would learn his character.

I continued, however, at the grammar-school not quite one year, though in that time I had risen gradually from the middle of the class of that year to be the head of it, and farther was removed into the next class above it, in order to go with that into the third at the end of the year. But my father, in the meantime, from a view of the expense of a college education, which having so large a family he could not well afford, and the mean living many so educated were afterwards able to obtain--reasons that be gave to his friends in my hearing--altered his first intention, took me from the grammar-school, and sent me to a school for writing and arithmetic, kept by a then famous man, Mr. George Brownell, very successful in his profession generally, and that by mild, encouraging methods.

Under him I acquired fair writing pretty soon, but I failed in the arithmetic, and made no progress in it. At ten years old I was taken home to assist my father in his business, which was that of a tallow-chandler and sope-boiler; a business he was not bred to, but had assumed on his arrival in New England, and on finding his dying trade would not maintain his family, being in little request. Accordingly, I was employed in cutting wick for the candles, filling the dipping mold and the molds for cast candles, attending the shop, going of errands, etc.

(*The Autobiography of Ben Franklin*)

# Teacher Directions: Graphs

## Goals for Student

1. Record information (e.g., observations, notes, lists, charts, legends) related to a topic.
2. Organize information to show understanding of or relationships among facts by representing key points within text through charting or graphing.
3. Synthesize and use information from the text to state the main idea or provide relevant details.

## Preparation

1. Students must be aware of visual representations, such as charts and graphs, as easily overlooked text structures.
2. Collect three different candy bar wrappers (one set for each student) with the nutritional information on the back.
3. Collect *USA Today* charts and graphs—they are found on the front cover of the papers and usually cover a topic related to a survey or scientific study.

## Materials

- Candy bar wrappers with nutritional information
- *USA Today* charts and graphs
- "Graphs" worksheet

## Focus on the Skill

1. The students will turn the worksheet over and draw a T-chart (two-column chart). They will label the left side "Electric Bill Bar Graph" and the right side "Food Pyramid."
2. They will brainstorm all of the details, measurements, and inferred information that can be gathered from each type of chart.

## Practice the Skill

1. Using the candy bar wrapper information, students will create a bar graph that reflects the fat, carbohydrates, and protein in each brand.
2. After they have created the graph, they should analyze their findings to determine the "healthiest" candy—that would be the candy with the least amount of fat and the most protein.
3. Finally, they will evaluate the grid at the bottom of the worksheet and answer the questions.

## Take It to the Next Level

Have the students create a flip book (try the "Bound Book Foldable" from Dinah Zike's website at www.dinah.com) where they can display five examples of charts or graphs from *USA Today*. On each page of the flip book, they should explain what the chart is comparing and all of the features of the chart or graph that make it effective or interesting.

## Special Considerations

While charts and graphs are usually studied in math, they are often featured in reading selections. If we do not alert students to their significance, they will not include them in their active reading.

# Student Directions: Graphs

## Focus on the Skill

1. Turn the worksheet over and draw a T-chart (two-column chart). Label the left side "Electric Bill Bar Graph" and the right side "Food Pyramid."
2. Brainstorm all of the details, measurements, and inferred information that can be gathered from each type of chart.

## Practice the Skill

1. Using the candy bar wrapper information, create a bar graph that reflects the fat, carbohydrates, and protein in each one—fats in red, carbohydrates in blue, and protein in green.
2. After you have created the graph, you should analyze your findings to determine the "healthiest" candy—that would be the candy with the least amount of fat and the most protein.
3. Finally, evaluate the grid at the bottom of the worksheet and answer the questions.

## Take It to the Next Level

*USA Today* often features a chart or graph on the front page. Create a flip book of graphs and charts with five examples of charts or graphs from *USA Today*. On each page of the flip book, you will explain what the chart is comparing, how it is informative, and all of the features of the chart or graph that make it effective or interesting.

## How You Will Be Graded

| | 1 little or no evidence | 2 below average | 3 adequate evidence | 4 better than average | 5 superior evidence | TOTAL |
|---|---|---|---|---|---|---|
| Attention to neatness and presentation | | | | | | |
| Interprets detail and purpose from charts and graphs | | | | | | |
| Accurately creates a bar graph using nutrition information and evaluates information | | | | | | |
| Analyzes a grid for information | | | | | | |
| Creates a flip book that displays a variety of visual representations and accurately assesses their functions | | | | | | |
| **Total points multiplied by four** | | | | | | |
| **Final grade** | | | | | | |

# Worksheet: Graphs

## Practice the Skill

Turn the worksheet over and draw a T-chart (two-column chart). Label the left side "Electric Bill Bar Graph" and the right side "Food Pyramid." Brainstorm all of the details, measurements, and inferred information that can be gathered from each type of chart.

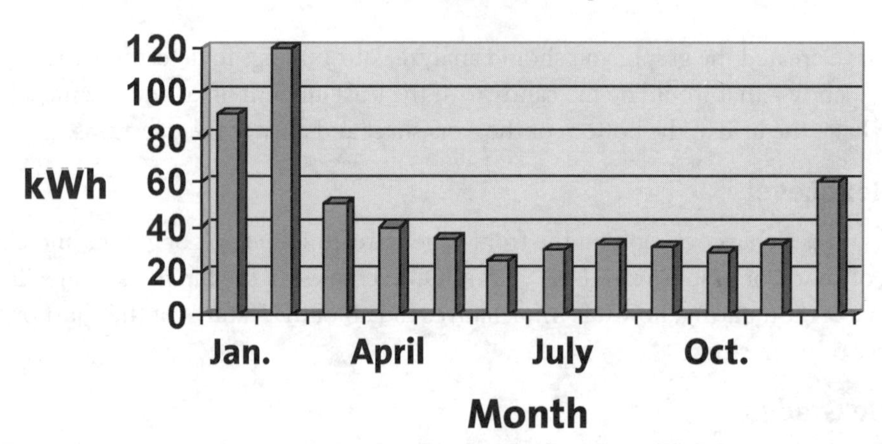


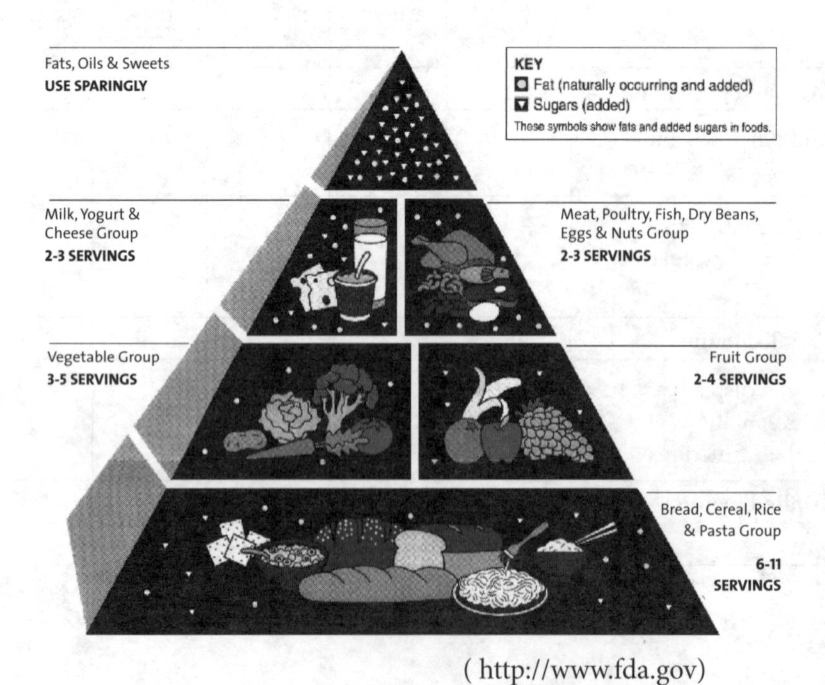


( http://www.fda.gov)

# Worksheet: Graphs (continued)

**Creating Bar Graphs Using Candy Bar Wrappers.** Three important pieces of information on a food label are the amounts of fat, carbohydrates, and protein (in grams) the food contains. For each candy bar, show the grams of fat in red, carbohydrates in blue, and protein in green.

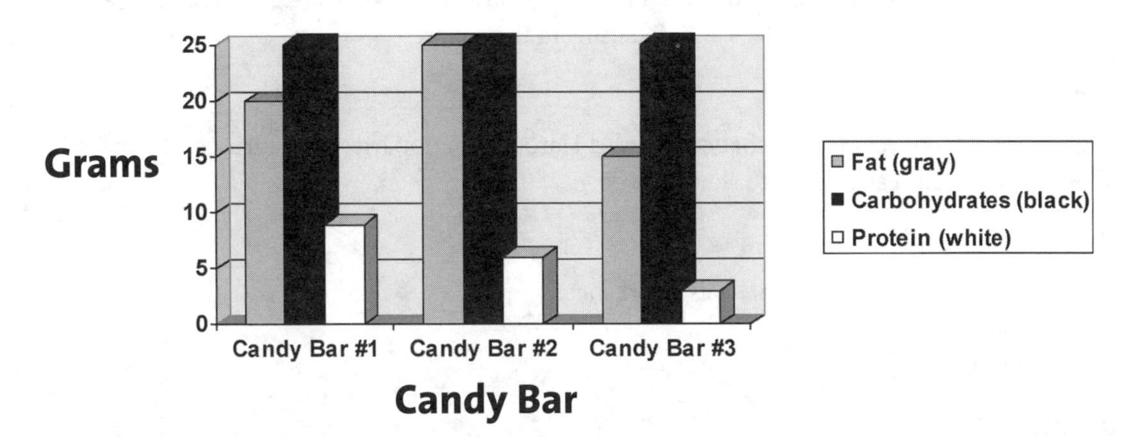


According to nutritionists, the "healthiest" candies will contain the least amount of fat and more protein. Using the information you graphed, which candy bar is the healthiest?

**Reading a Grid: Basketball**

**Eastern Conference—Atlantic Division (2006)**

| Team | Wins | Losses | Pct. of Wins | GB* |
|---|---|---|---|---|
| New Jersey Nets | 49 | 33 | .598 | - |
| Philadelphia 76ers | 38 | 44 | .463 | 11 |
| Boston Celtics | 33 | 49 | .402 | 16 |
| Toronto Raptors | 27 | 27 | .329 | 22 |
| New York Knicks | 23 | 23 | .280 | 26 |

http://www.nba.com

* "GB" means "Games Back," which represents the number of games each team would have had to win in order to be tied with team in first place.

Is the following information found in this grid chart?

| | No | Yes |
|---|---|---|
| Sixth-place team | _______ | _______ |
| Total games played | _______ | _______ |
| Team roster | _______ | _______ |
| Mascots | _______ | _______ |
| Number of three-point shots | _______ | _______ |

# Teacher Directions: Using a Variety of Reference Materials

## Goals for Student

1. Examine and gather information from several sources, both primary and secondary.
2. Collect, evaluate, and summarize information using a variety of sources (e.g., encyclopedias, websites, experts); paraphrase ideas and details from the source.

## Preparation

You should have enough encyclopedias (that cover Pearl Harbor), dictionaries, thesauruses, almanacs, and United States atlases for each group to share.

## Materials

- "Using a Variety of Reference Materials" worksheet
- Manila paper
- Colored pencils

## Focus on the Skill

1. On the back of the worksheet, students will brainstorm everything they know about Pearl Harbor.
2. They will skim the worksheet and place a "P" next to the sources they think are primary and an "S" next to the sources they believe are secondary. Reveal to the group that the survivor's interview is the only primary source as he was a witness to the event.

## Practice the Skill

Now the students will utilize each of the sources to fill out the worksheet and collect information about Pearl Harbor.

## Take It to the Next Level

1. On the bottom of the back side of the manila paper where students drew a map and flag (as directed on the worksheet), they will write a one-sentence summary about the events at Pearl Harbor using no less than fifteen words.
2. Then, at the top, they will draw a detailed picture that captures as many details from their researched information as possible

## Special Considerations

Struggling readers are not often asked to research, and they rely heavily on the Internet to answer their questions. If it becomes clear that something cannot be located in a reference book, allow them to use Internet references as an alternative they feel comfortable with and can use successfully.

## Student Directions: Using a Variety of Reference Materials

### Focus on the Skill

1. On the back of the worksheet (at the top), brainstorm everything you know about Pearl Harbor.
2. Skim the worksheet and place a "P" next to the sources you think are primary and an "S" next to the sources you believe are secondary.

### Practice the Skill

Now, utilize each of the sources to fill out the worksheet and collect information about Pearl Harbor.

### Take It to the Next Level

1. On the bottom of the back side of the manila paper where you drew the map and the flag (as directed on the worksheet), you will write a one-sentence summary about the events at Pearl Harbor using no less than fifteen words.
2. Then, at the top, draw a detailed picture that captures as many details from your researched information as possible.

### How You Will Be Graded

| | 1 little or no evidence | 2 below average | 3 adequate evidence | 4 better than average | 5 superior evidence | TOTAL |
|---|---|---|---|---|---|---|
| Attention to neatness and presentation | | | | | | |
| Brainstorms background information | | | | | | |
| Effectively uses reference materials to research a topic | | | | | | |
| Summarizes events using researched information | | | | | | |
| Details an illustration that includes researched information | | | | | | |
| **Total points multiplied by four** | | | | | | |
| **Final grade** | | | | | | |

# Worksheet: Using a Variety of Reference Materials

______ **Encyclopedia.** Look up **Pearl Harbor**, and answer the following questions.

Who: ______________________________

What: ______________________________

Where: ______________________________

When: ______________________________

Why: ______________________________

How: ______________________________

______ **Dictionary.** Use the dictionary to define the following words related to the subject of Pearl Harbor. On the bottom of the back of this worksheet, draw a picture that accurately depicts one of the words you looked up the dictionary. Your drawing should reflect an understanding for the term and its significance in the attack. Make sure everyone at the center chooses a different word.

**bomber** ______________________________

**depth charge** ______________________________

**destroyer** ______________________________

**dispatch** ______________________________

**Imperialists** ______________________________

**Kamikaze** ______________________________

**radar**______________________________

**raid** ______________________________

**strafing** ______________________________

**torpedo** ______________________________

______ **Atlas.** Find a map of the Hawaiian Islands. On a piece of manila paper, draw the islands, the location of the Harbor, and the location of four other towns on the islands on the left side of the paper. Also, draw the flag of Hawaii.

______ **Personal Account from a Survivor.** (John Kunel, 1942, www.kunel.org/pearl_harbor.htm)

**War in Hawaii: A Personal Account of Pearl Harbor**

*The news about the fleet was worse, if anything. Many ships had been sunk or damaged. Seven battleships had been in the harbor. Five were on the bottom just with the superstructure showing. Another was badly hit and listing against the wharf. Many soldiers and sailors were dead. The Island could not be held against a serious invasion attempt. We had been so confident just 12 hours previous that no enemy could ever capture these islands, and now we realized it might be done within a few hours.*

*I spent one of the longest nights I have ever experienced. It was rainy and cold out, not being dressed for such weather, I nearly froze. I would gaze into the night trying to see the approaching enemy. My mind was in a turmoil of thoughts. If I was not killed immediately, what should I do. Try to regain my family and protect them? Or kill them? Memories of what I had read of the treatment of white people in the Boxer Rebellion came to my mind. After all, even at best, conquered people usually get poor treatment. Then, 80% of our food was imported from the Mainland. The Japanese couldn't begin to feed that population even if they were so inclined. My wife was five months' pregnant. My son was not yet two years of age. If I was killed, who would look out for them? To kill them appeared best but what an ending of all my plans and dreams!*

## Worksheet: Using a Variety of Reference Materials (continued)

**Complete the sentence using information from the personal account.**

Right after the attack it seems Mr. Kunel was most concerned about ____________________________,

____________________________________, and ______________________________________________.

______**Almanac (Book of Facts).** Look up the following in the almanac. After reading about each, summarize the important information on the lines below.

Franklin D. Roosevelt ______________________________________________________________

USS Arizona ______________________________________________________________________

WWII ____________________________________________________________________________

______**Thesaurus.** Use the thesaurus to locate two or three words that share a similar meaning with the following.

dispatch ____________________ infamy ____________________ vessel __________________

salvage ____________________ raid ______________________ munitions _______________

# Teacher Directions: The Phone Book

## Goals for Student

1. Comprehend the wide array of informational text that is part of our day-to-day experiences.
2. Use information from the text to answer questions.
3. Locate, organize, and interpret written information for a real-world task.

## Preparation

1. Your students must understand how a phone book is organized into different sections—residential, governmental, and business.
2. Collect local phone books with local, state, and federal information. Make sure the phone book has *Yellow Pages*.

## Materials

- Phone books with *Yellow Pages* (enough for each student)
- "The Phone Book" worksheet
- Colored pencils

## Focus on the Skill

1. Have students turn the worksheet over and brainstorm all of the information that can be found in a phone book.
2. They should open the first informational pages of the phone book and list three headings from the first few pages. You might want to direct them through this and point out area codes, time zones, important/emergency numbers, etc.
3. Finally, at the bottom of the page, have them explain the difference between "governmental" and "residential" in a one-sentence summary of no less than eight words.

## Practice the Skill

Now the students will follow the directions on the worksheet and locate each of the phone numbers for each of the organizations.

## Take It to the Next Level

At the bottom of the worksheet, they should locate information from the *Yellow Pages*. They will draw an advertisement for each example (you might want to require that they draw one for a business that does not already feature an advertisement).

## Special Considerations

Struggling readers need to experience the everyday woes of being a literate citizen. They must recognize the importance of being able to find and retrieve information from sources that are available to help address and solve their personal needs.

# Student Directions: The Phone Book

## Focus on the Skill

1. On the back of the worksheet, brainstorm all of the information you can find in a phone book.
2. Then, open the first informational pages of the phone book and list three headings from the first few pages.
3. Finally, at the bottom of the page, explain the difference between "governmental" and "residential" in a one-sentence summary of no less than eight words.

## Practice the Skill

Now follow the directions on the worksheet and locate each of the phone numbers for each of the organizations.

## Take It to the Next Level

At the bottom of "The Phone Book" worksheet, you will record information from the *Yellow Pages*. Draw an advertisement for each example (try to draw an ad for a business that does not already feature an advertisement). Make sure your ads are detailed and specific.

## How You Will Be Graded

| | 1 little or no evidence | 2 below average | 3 adequate evidence | 4 better than average | 5 superior evidence | TOTAL |
|---|---|---|---|---|---|---|
| Attention to neatness and presentation | | | | | | |
| Effectively brainstorms uses for a phone book; able to tell the difference between residential and governmental | | | | | | |
| Locates phone numbers for a variety of agencies, businesses, and organizations. | | | | | | |
| Records *Yellow Pages* information | | | | | | |
| Illustrates *Yellow Pages* information effectively | | | | | | |
| **Total points multiplied by four** | | | | | | |
| **Final grade** | | | | | | |

# Worksheet: The Phone Book

## Practice the Skill

**Using the Phone Book to Locate Information.** What number would you call if you needed the following information?

**Federal Organizations/Services**
Immigration Services ____________________
Internal Revenue Service____________________
Social Security ____________________
Your district's U.S. senator ____________________
Your district's congressmen ____________________
Marine Corps recruiting ____________________
Airport information ____________________
Federal Bureau of Investigations____________________
Post Office Branch ____________________

**Local Organizations/Services**
Local public library____________________
Public health clinic ____________________
Animal shelter____________________

**State Organizations/Services**
Governor's office ____________________
State senator's office____________________
Department of Aging ____________________
Child abuse ____________________

**Yellow Pages Ads.** Find an advertisement for each of the following: a dentist, pest control, and a locksmith. Draw the advertisements and all of the accompanying information for each business.

| Dentist | Pest Control | Locksmith |
|---|---|---|
| | | |

# Teacher Directions: Using an Almanac

## Goals for Student

1. Comprehend the wide array of informational text that is part of our day-to-day experiences.
2. Use information from the text to answer questions.
3. Understand the function of an index.

## Preparation

1. Your students should recognize an almanac as a reference material. I strongly recommend playing "World Almania," a classroom game distributed by World Almanac Education (http://www.waebooks.com/), to familiarize students with almanacs. Being able to effectively use an index and recognize how to generalize information is an invaluable skill!
2. Supply world almanacs for each student.

## Materials

- World almanacs (one for each student)
- "Using an Almanac" worksheet

## Focus on the Skill

1. The students will begin by recognizing how American almanacs got their start.
2. They will explain the meanings of Ben Franklin's quotes from *Poor Richard's Almanac.*

## Practice the Skill

Now the students will follow the directions on the worksheets and locate information from the world almanac. The directions are listed on the worksheets.

## Take It to the Next Level

At the bottom of the second page, they will draw an interpretation of one of the facts they located in the almanac. Their captions and details should reflect understanding.

## Special Considerations

The almanac is simply an overlooked resource! Middle schoolers who are exposed to the resource will learn its value and return to read its contents again and again.

# Student Directions: Using an Almanac

## Focus on the Skill

1. Begin by recognizing how American almanacs got their start.
2. Read and explain the meanings of Ben Franklin's quotes from *Poor Richard's Almanac.*

## Practice the Skill

Follow the directions on the worksheets and locate information from the world almanac.

## Take It to the Next Level

At the bottom of the second page, you will draw an interpretation of one of the facts you located in the almanac. Your captions and details should reflect understanding.

## How You Will Be Graded

| | 1 little or no evidence | 2 below average | 3 adequate evidence | 4 better than average | 5 superior evidence | TOTAL |
|---|---|---|---|---|---|---|
| Attention to neatness and presentation | | | | | | |
| Analyzes and interprets Ben Franklin's quotes | | | | | | |
| Identifies world map information from the almanac | | | | | | |
| Locates facts from the almanac | | | | | | |
| Interprets facts and creates detailed illustration of an interesting fact from the almanac | | | | | | |
| **Total points multiplied by four** | | | | | | |
| **Final grade** | | | | | | |

# Worksheet: Using an Almanac

## Focus on the Skill

One of the first American almanacs was *Poor Richard's Almanac*, and it was first published in 1732 by Ben Franklin. Franklin included many insightful proverbs in the almanac. A proverb is a popular saying which contains advice. Analyze each of the proverbs and determine what advice Franklin is providing. Write your explanation on the lines provided.

"At a working man's house, hunger looks in, but does not enter."

____________________________________________________________

___________________________________________________________.

"No gains without pains."

____________________________________________________________

___________________________________________________________.

"Beware of little expenses; a small leak will sink a great ship."

____________________________________________________________

___________________________________________________________.

## Practice the Skill

**World Almanac (Book of Facts).** Label the world map with the locations of Iceland, Brazil, and Japan. Use the information from the almanac to complete the information below.

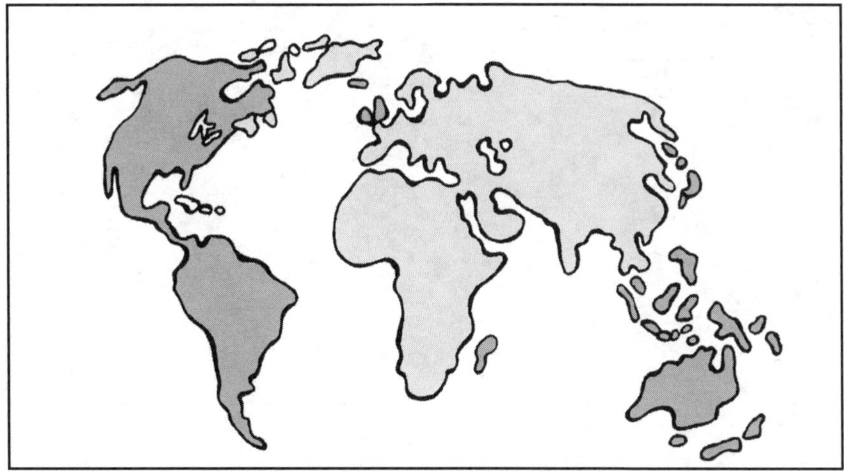

**Iceland**
Bordered by what countries? ____________________________________
Is in the Northern or Southern Hemisphere? ____________________________
Borders what body/bodies of water? ________________________________
Population: ________________
Capital city: _______________
Type of currency: _______________
Languages spoken: _______________
Draw their flag

# Worksheet: Using an Almanac (continued)

**Brazil**

Bordered by what countries? ____________________

Is in the Northern or Southern Hemisphere? ____________________

Borders what body/bodies of water? ____________________

Population: ____________________

Capital city: ____________________

Type of currency: ____________________

Languages spoken: ____________________

Draw their flag

**Japan**

Bordered by what countries? ____________________

Is in the Northern or Southern Hemisphere? ____________________

Borders what body/bodies of water? ____________________

Population: ____________________

Capital city: ____________________

Type of currency: ____________________

Languages spoken: ____________________

Draw their flag

**What does the world almanac say about the following?**

Robert E. Lee ____________________

"The Gettysburg Address" ____________________

Lincoln's assassination ____________________

In your own words, explain the relationship all three share with one another. ____________________

____________________

____________________

# Worksheet: Using an Almanac (continued)

**Find the following information in the world almanac:**

Disaster with the most deaths ______________________________
Last two teams in men's NCAA basketball tournament
____________________ and ____________________
Population of the state of Vermont ________________
Area code for state of Delaware ____________
Year Clara Barton founded the Red Cross __________
Slowest animal and speed ___________________________
Who won the Nobel Peace Prize in 1984?___________________________
Wealthiest American and income ____________________________

**Fill in the blanks for the Presidential Oath of Office.**

*I do so solemnly swear that I will faithfully execute the office of President of the United States, and will, to the best of my ability, __________, __________, and __________ the Constitution of the United States.*

## Take It to the Next Level

**Almanac Illustration.** Choose one of the facts from the worksheet that you find interesting, and draw a picture below to show you comprehend what it means. Make sure your picture is detailed and reflects understanding.

# Teacher Directions: Travel Brochures

## Goals for Student

1. Use pre-reading knowledge with complex reading texts.
2. Synthesize and use information from the text to state the main idea or provide relevant details.
3. Determine the main idea or essential message by inferring, paraphrasing, summarizing, and identifying relevant details.

## Preparation

1. Provide three to five different destination brochures per center (at least one per student)—foreign countries, cities in the U.S., theme parks, museums, or even shopping centers. Welcome centers or chambers of commerce often have these, and most places are willing to send several copies for free.
2. Your students are going to cut these brochures up, so have extras on hand.

## Materials

- "Travel Brochures" worksheet
- A variety of brochures
- Scissors
- Glue stick
- Manila drawing paper

## Focus on the Skill

1. The students will choose a brochure to analyze and summarize.
2. On the "Pre-Reading a Brochure" section of the "Travel Brochures" worksheet, have students answer the questions about the text and non-text clues of their brochure. The goal is for them to recognize brochures as a persuasive piece of literature.

## Practice the Skill

1. First, students will complete the "3-2-1 Summarizing" section of the worksheet. They will brainstorm **three** of the best reasons to visit the destination, **two** kinds of people who might enjoy this place, and **one** word or big idea that captures the importance of this destination.
2. Next, they will create a "quality summary statement." They should use the information from the 3-2-1 summary to create an original, to-the-point sentence that would convince others to visit the location described in the brochure. Emphasize that most of the 3-2-1 information should be included in their sentence. An example has been provided.

## Take It to the Next Level

The students will complete a "brochure scavenger hunt." Have them draw a line down the middle of a piece of manila paper. Label the left side "Visuals" and the right side "Language." The students should try to find an example in their brochure for each of the text and non-text clues listed. They will cut each example out, glue it to the manila paper, and label it accordingly.

## Special Considerations

It's good to offer a variety of brochures. For example, if your students have never been to a rural location (the mountains of Tennessee, white water rafting in the Grand Canyon, or camping in Wyoming), locate brochures that are different from their own experiences. Also, travel brochures may contain terms and vocabulary that are foreign to your students. You may want to provide sticky notes to create a "parking lot" of unknown words to spur discussion.

# Student Directions: Travel Brochures

## Focus on the Skill

1. Choose a brochure to analyze and summarize.
2. On the "Pre-Reading a Brochure" section of the "Travel Brochures" worksheet, answer the questions about the text and non-text clues of your brochure.

## Practice the Skill

1. Now, complete the "3-2-1 Summarizing" section of the worksheet. Brainstorm **three** of the best reasons to visit the destination, **two** kinds of people who might enjoy this place, and **one** word or big idea that captures the importance of this destination.
2. Next, create a "quality summary statement." Use the information from the 3-2-1 summary to create an original, to-the-point sentence that would convince others to visit the location described in your brochure. Most of the 3-2-1 information should be included in your sentence. An example has been provided.

## Take It to the Next Level

Finally, complete a "brochure scavenger hunt." Draw a line down the middle of a piece of manila paper. Label the left side "Visuals" and the right side "Language." You should try to find an example in your brochure for each of the text and non-text clues listed. Cut each example out, glue it to the manila paper, and label accordingly.

## How You Will Be Graded

| | 1 little or no evidence | 2 below average | 3 adequate evidence | 4 better than average | 5 superior evidence | TOTAL |
|---|---|---|---|---|---|---|
| Attention to neatness and presentation | | | | | | |
| Able to recognize purpose of a brochure using text and non-text clues | | | | | | |
| Brainstorms effective ideas that reflects ideas presented in brochure | | | | | | |
| Creates an original, to-the-point summary sentence that is convincing and thoughtful | | | | | | |
| Effectively identifies and classifies text and non-text elements of the brochure | | | | | | |
| **Total points multiplied by four** | | | | | | |
| **Final grade** | | | | | | |

# Worksheet: Travel Brochures

## Focus on the Skill

**Pre-Reading a Brochure**

Are there appealing pictures? If so, of what? ______

Is the layout attractive? If so, how? ______

Does the brochure contain testimonials? If so, what do they say? ______

______

What seems to be the goal of this brochure, and how do you know? ______

______

## Practice the Skill

a. **3-2-1 Summarizing**

**3** of the best reasons to visit this destination

**2** kinds of people who might enjoy this place

**1** word or big idea that captures the importance of this destination

b. **Creating a Quality Summary Statement.** Use the information from the 3-2-1 summary to create an original, to-the-point sentence that would convince others to visit your location. Make sure your 3-2-1 information is included in your sentence.

Example: *Capture history, patriotism, and architecture in an up-close visit to an important American symbol—the Statue of Liberty!*

______

______

______

## Take It to the Next Level

**Brochure Scavenger Hunt.** Divide a piece of manila paper in half by drawing a line down the middle. Write "Visuals" on the top of the left side and "Language" on the top of the right. Try to find an example of each of the following in your brochure. Cut each example out, glue it to the manila paper, and label it.

## Worksheet: Travel Brochures (continued)

Visuals

1. Heading with a interesting font or style
2. Bolded words
3. Italicized words
4. Important photos
5. Clip art, sketches, or graphics
6. Map

Language

1. Interesting headings
2. Convincing words or sentences
3. Good description or imagery
4. Captions
5. Testimonials

# Teacher Directions: Movie Posters and Cases

## Goals for Students

1. Use pre-reading knowledge with complex reading texts.
2. Synthesize and use information from the text to state the main idea or provide relevant details.
3. Determine the main idea or essential message by inferring, paraphrasing, summarizing, and identifying relevant details.

## Preparation

1. Find three to five movie posters. It's okay if the students have seen the movie. However, be mindful of the rating and content.
2. Provide a variety of movie cases (DVD or VHS) that contain well-written summaries on the back. Movie rental stores and theatres are very willing to help teachers.

## Materials

- "Movie Posters and Cases" worksheet
- Manila drawing paper
- Colored pencils

## Focus on the Skill

Have students create small sketches that capture the meaning of the different types of movies (comedy, science-fiction, action/adventure, romance, western, drama, and war). The goal is to help students see that summaries are concise yet provide the most important information.

## Practice the Skill

1. Students will analyze their movie poster using the "out, in, and conclude" strategy.
2. Have students carefully look at a poster. As a whole, what do they notice? What are their first observations? They will write their responses on the "Movie Posters and Cases" worksheet.
3. Now, have them imagine that the poster is divided into four quarters. They will begin at the top right corner and examine each section for the smallest details—words, characters, settings, expressions, objects, etc. Again, they should reflect their observations on the worksheet.
4. Finally, they should consider the poster as a whole and in its smaller parts. They will assume the role of the designer of this poster and create a summary statement about the movie that includes all of the major ideas from the poster (remember *who*, *what*, *where*, *when*, *why*, and *how*).

## Take It to the Next Level

1. Have students analyze several movie cases (front and back). They should notice how the designers were able to summarize the events of the movie while still making the movie seem intriguing and motivating people to see it.
2. Using the information from just the case, students will try to answer as many of the questions as possible on the "Movie Posters and Cases" worksheet.
3. Finally, students will create a comic strip that shows the events or plot of the movie. Encourage them to use creative license to fill in any information not provided on the case (in other words, make it up!). If it's a movie they have already seen, ask them to rely on the information from the covers only.

## Special Considerations

Help students focus on the analysis activity, not an exciting plot or cool graphic.

# Student Directions: Movie Posters and Cases

## Focus on the Skill

Think of what you know about the different types of movies. Sketch the meaning of each of the following movie types: comedy, science-fiction, action/adventure, romance, western, drama and war.

## Practice the Skill

1. Analyze your movie poster using the "out, in, and conclude" strategy.
2. Step back and look carefully at the poster carefully. As a whole, what do you notice? What are your first observations? Write your responses on the "Movie Posters and Cases" worksheet.
3. Now, imagine that the poster is divided into four quarters. Begin at the top right corner and examine the section for the smallest details—words, characters, settings, expressions, objects, etc. Again, you should reflect your observations on the worksheet.
4. Go clockwise around the poster to each quarter and write your observations on the worksheet.
5. Think about all of the information you have collected. Assume the role of the designer of this poster. Create a summary statement about the movie that includes all of the major ideas from the poster (remember *who*, *what*, *where*, *when*, *why*, and *how*).

## Take It to the Next Level

1. Finally, look at several movie cases (front and back). Notice how the designers were able to summarize the events of the movie while still making it intriguing and motivating people to see it.
2. Using the information from just the case, try to answer as many of the questions as possible on the worksheet about the characters, setting, and plot of the movie.
3. Then, create a comic strip that shows the events or plot of the movie. You may use creative license to fill in any information not provided on the case (in other words, make it up!).

## How You Will Be Graded

| | 1<br>little or no evidence | 2<br>below average | 3<br>adequate evidence | 4<br>better than average | 5<br>superior evidence | TOTAL |
|---|---|---|---|---|---|---|
| Attention to neatness and presentation | | | | | | |
| Effectively sketches meaning of each movie type; sketches show understanding | | | | | | |
| Observes movie poster for overall meaning and successfully locates smaller, less obvious details | | | | | | |
| Able to create a well-written summary that uses all of the "out, in, and conclude" information | | | | | | |
| Creates a detailed comic strip that adequately reflects the information provided on a movie case | | | | | | |
| **Total points multiplied by four** | | | | | | |
| **Final grade** | | | | | | |

# Worksheet: Movie Posters and Cases

## Focus on the Skill

**Symbols.** Summaries are short descriptions of a larger idea. Often, a symbol can summarize the meaning of a larger idea. Consider the following types of movies. Think of an image that would accurately represent each category, and draw that image with the category labeled on the back of this sheet.

Comedy
Science-fiction
Action/adventure
Romance
Western
Drama
War

## Practice the Skill

**Out, In, and Conclude.** When you look at a poster, you are creating small summaries in your mind by forming the big picture from the smaller, specific parts.

*Out.* Step back and look at the movie poster. As a whole, what do you notice? What are your first observations?

___

___

*In.* Imagine that the poster is divided into four quarters. Begin at the top right corner. Examine each section for the smallest details—words, characters, settings, expressions, objects, etc.

Top right quarter: ___

Bottom right quarter: ___

Bottom left quarter: ___

Top left quarter: ___

*Conclude.* Consider the "out" and "in" information. Pretend you designed this poster. Create a summary statement that informs movie-goers of what to expect (remember to include the *who, what, where, when, why,* and *how*).

___

___

# Worksheet: Movie Posters and Cases (continued)

## Take It to the Next Level

Analyze several movie cases (front and back). Notice how the designers were able to summarize the events of the movie while still making the movie intriguing and motivating people to see it. Try to answer as many of the following questions as possible with just the information you find on the case.

Who is the main character of this movie?

What is this movie about?

Where does this movie take place?

When does it take place?

Now, create a comic strip that shows the events or plot of the movie. You may use creative license to fill in any information not provided on the case (in other words, make it up!).

# Teacher Directions: Menus

## Goals for Students

1. Use pre-reading knowledge with complex reading texts.
2. Synthesize and use information from the text to state the main idea or provide relevant details.
3. Determine the main idea or essential message by inferring, paraphrasing, summarizing, and identifying relevant details

## Preparation

Provide three to five different menus from a variety of restaurants (local or from the Internet).

## Materials

- "Menus" worksheet
- Manila drawing paper
- Colored pencils

## Focus on the Skill

1. Have students brainstorm a list of as many different types of restaurants as they can (based on food type, ethnic influence, formality, or any number of ways we describe restaurants today).
2. Students will then study the menu they have been given. Based on the information on the menu, they should determine the most important word on this menu. It *cannot* be an opinion word.
3. Then, students should compile a list of the details that support their word choice. They must be specific. For example, if they choose the word "Cajun," they must provide details from the menu that support that word being the most important feature of this restaurant.

## Practice the Skill

1. Have students read the menu carefully and complete the questions on the worksheet. They should evaluate how the information is organized, what kinds of meals are served, the graphic details of the menu, and any other interesting information they can locate.
2. Next, students will consider all of the information they have gathered from the menu. They will write a short, summarizing advertisement that would appeal to restaurant-goers. An example has been provided.

## Take It to the Next Level

Students will create a free-form map that captures the details of the menu and the restaurant. On a blank sheet of manila paper, they should create as many sketches as possible to show the various features of this restaurant (ingredients, themes, traditions, ethnic influence, etc.). They should not use words, but they may caption their sketches.

## Special Considerations

Try to provide a wide assortment of menus. Many low-performing students do not have varied restaurant experiences, and this is a real opportunity to expose them to something different. Any words or phrases that seem strange should be written on sticky notes and placed in a "parking lot" for unknown words.

# Student Directions: Menus

## Focus on the Skill

1. First, brainstorm a list of as many different types of restaurants as you can. Your ideas can be based on food type, ethnic influence, formality, or any number of ways we describe restaurants today.
2. Next, study the menu you have been given. Based on the information on the menu, determine the most important word or phrase on this menu. It *cannot* be an opinion word.
3. Then, on the worksheet, compile a list of the details that support your choice. You must be specific. For example, if you choose the word "Cajun," you must provide details from the menu that support this word being the most important feature in this restaurant.

## Practice the Skill

1. Now, read the menu carefully and complete the questions on the worksheet. Evaluate how the information is organized, what kinds of meals are served, the graphic details of the menu, and any other interesting information you can locate.
2. Consider all of the information you have gathered from the menu. Write a short, summarizing advertisement that would appeal to restaurant-goers. An example has been provided.

## Take It to the Next Level

Finally, create a free-form map that captures the details of the menu and the restaurant. On a blank sheet of manila paper, create as many sketches as possible to show the various features of this restaurant (ingredients, themes, traditions, ethnic influence, etc.). Do not use words, but you may caption your sketches.

## How You Will Be Graded

| | 1 little or no evidence | 2 below average | 3 adequate evidence | 4 better than average | 5 superior evidence | TOTAL |
|---|---|---|---|---|---|---|
| Attention to neatness and presentation | | | | | | |
| Effectively brainstorms different types of restaurants and classifies a restaurant by using a menu only | | | | | | |
| Able to support the "most important word" with details from the menu; shows comprehension of the big picture | | | | | | |
| Writes an appealing advertisement that summarizes | | | | | | |
| Creates a free-form map of sketches that captures the various features of the restaurant's menu | | | | | | |
| **Total points multiplied by four** | | | | | | |
| **Final grade** | | | | | | |

# Worksheet: Menus

## Focus on the Skill

1. List as many different types of restaurants as you can.

2. Now, study the menu you have been given. Based on the information on the menu, determine the most important word on this menu.

3. What are the details that support your choice? Be specific.

## Practice the Skill

**Studying the Menu.** Read the menu carefully and complete the following questions.

1. How is the menu organized (appetizers, entrees, desserts, beverages, etc.)?

2. Look at the individual meals. What are the ingredients (specific meats, vegetables, spices, etc.)?

3. Examine the non-text details—photos, clip art, captions, etc. What can you conclude about the atmosphere of the restaurant (fine dining, family, casual, home cooking, etc.)?

4. Is there anything else about the menu that makes the restaurant seem interesting? If so, what?

**Summarizing the Menu.** Consider all of the information you have gathered from the menu. Now, write a short, summarizing advertisement to appeal to restaurant-goers.

Example: *Love seafood? Then reward yourself with a trip to Red Lobster. Indulge in tender Rock Lobster, succulent shrimp, and your favorite fish, grilled to absolute perfection. Every day is an occasion to celebrate at Red Lobster with friends and family. (Red Lobster, 2007)*

______________________________________________________________________

______________________________________________________________________

______________________________________________________________________

## Take It to the Next Level

**Free-Form Mapping.** See if you can capture the feeling of the restaurant without using words! On a blank sheet of manila paper, create as many sketches as you can that would show the various features of this restaurant (ingredients, themes, traditions, ethnic influence, etc.). Be specific and detailed.

# Teacher Directions: Recipes

## Goals for Students

1. Use pre-reading knowledge with complex reading texts.
2. Synthesize and use information from the text to state the main idea or provide relevant details.
3. Determine the main idea or essential message by inferring, paraphrasing, summarizing, and identifying relevant details.

## Preparation

1. Find three to five different recipes. Depending on your students' background, this may be a good opportunity to integrate their cultures into the lesson. Find recipes that may contain ingredients familiar to your students—this is a good talking point that makes them the "experts."
2. You may also want to use recipes that are completely different from your students' experiences. A good resource is Allrecipes.com.

## Materials

- "Recipes" worksheet
- Manila drawing paper

## Focus on the Skill

1. Have students make a list of all of the ingredients necessary to create the dish for their recipe.
2. Next, they should classify each of the ingredients according to categories (seasonings, meat, etc.).

## Practice the Skill

1. Students should examine how the recipe is worded and think about the steps necessary to creating the dish.
2. Next, they should use the "25 to 10" strategy to summarize the instructions. They will attempt to condense the directions for making this dish into a twenty-five-word explanation. Though grammar may go to the wayside, students must realize that a general understanding of the process must be provided by their directions.
3. To step up the challenge, students will then take their twenty-five-word description and abbreviate it even further into a ten-word description.

## Take It to the Next Level

A recipe is a set of instructions. To summarize this recipe in a different way, have students draw the directions on manila paper. Students may write short captions for their illustrations, but the goal is for a reader to understand the main ideas of the recipe without the use of words.

## Special Considerations

The "25 to 20" strategy can be tough. It forces students to evaluate what they consider important information. They may have to categorize words ("salt," "pepper," "garlic," etc. may become "seasonings") to condense the instructions. Obviously, the goal here isn't specificity; it is about helping students see that, when creating summaries, they need look for ways to combine information and get to the point.

# Student Directions: Recipes

## Focus on the Skill

1. Make a list of all of the ingredients necessary to create the dish for your recipe.
2. Next, classify each of the ingredients according to categories on the "Menus" worksheet.

## Practice the Skill

1. Examine how the recipe is worded and think about the steps necessary to create the dish.
2. Use the "25 to 10" strategy to summarize the instructions. To do this, attempt to condense the directions for making this dish into a twenty-five-word explanation. Though grammar may go to the wayside, it is important for you to provide a general understanding of the process with your new directions.
3. To step up the challenge, take your twenty-five-word description and abbreviate the instructions even further into a ten-word description.

## Take It to the Next Level

A recipe is a set of instructions. To summarize this recipe in a different way, draw the directions on manila paper. You may write short captions for your illustrations, but the goal is for a reader to understand the main ideas of the recipe without the use of words. The more detailed, the better!

## How You Will Be Graded

| | 1 little or no evidence | 2 below average | 3 adequate evidence | 4 better than average | 5 superior evidence | TOTAL |
|---|---|---|---|---|---|---|
| Attention to neatness and presentation | | | | | | |
| Able to classify the ingredients of a recipe into recognizable categories | | | | | | |
| Effectively condenses a detailed recipe into 25 and then 10 words that capture the main ideas | | | | | | |
| Creates a wordless set of directions that captures the most important ingredients, steps, and processes for creating this dish | | | | | | |
| **Total points multiplied by five** | | | | | | |
| **Final grade** | | | | | | |

# Worksheet: Recipes

## Focus on the Skill

**Classifying.** List all of the ingredients in this recipe.

Now, classify all of the ingredients into categories (meats, dairy products, seasonings, etc.).

## Practice the Skill

**25 to 10.** Read the recipe carefully. See if you can explain how to cook this dish using only TWENTY-FIVE words!

________________________________________

________________________________________

________________________________________

Read your summarized version of the instructions. Now, think about the most important points and see if you can reduce the description to TEN words!

________________________________________

________________________________________

## Take It to the Next Level

A recipe is a set of instructions. To summarize this recipe in a different way, draw the directions on a piece of manila paper. You may write short captions for your illustrations, but the goal is for a reader to understand the main ideas of the recipe without having to read.

# Teacher Directions: Brainstorming

## Goals for Student

1. Generate ideas from multiple sources based upon teacher-directed topics and personal interests.
2. Create precision and interest by elaborating ideas through supporting details.
3. Use organizational strategies and tools to develop a personal organizational style.

## Preparation

1. Your class should practice some form of brainstorming before just about every reading lesson. Whether it's free-form mapping, one-minute free talks, or some formal brainstorming technique, your students must learn to create "inventory"—a student-created source for ideas.
2. Collect Americana photos at the Travel Channel (http://travel.discovery.com/yourshot/americana/americana.html) or similar website. Categories include nature, wildlife, and sunsets.
3. Supply ordinary office supplies: a rubber band, paper clip, pen, etc.

## Materials

- "Brainstorming" worksheet
- Americana photos
- Ordinary office supplies (rubber band, paper clip, etc.)

## Focus on the Skill

1. Students will head each of the four columns on the worksheet with a category from the list above the chart. Their goal is to try to fill the chart in with words that fit each of the columns.
2. Allow them to choose one of the photos you found and, for three minutes, list words, phrases, or ideas that come to mind on the back of the worksheet.
3. Next, students will circle three of the best ideas they came up with and create three sentences using each of the words or phrases in their sentences.

## Practice the Skill

Now, they will look at another one of the photos. They will use "ABC Brainstorming" to create as many words and phrases as they can, using the alphabet to guide their answers.

## Take It to the Next Level

To understand how higher-level thinking works, the students may enjoy the following activity. Each student will choose an ordinary item they brought to class or one of the items on the table. Working with the other members of the group, they will answer the following questions (based on Bloom's Taxonomy) and write their answers on the back of the worksheet in complete sentences.

1. Knowledge: Name this item.
2. Comprehension: Describe what this item was designed to do.
3. Application: Think of as many alternative uses for your item as possible. Be creative!
4. Analysis: Put all of the items from the group in the middle, and create three categories for the items. You may separate and combine items as you like to make the categories work
5. Synthesis: Combine your item with one other person's item (or more than one other item), and create a new invention. What could this new item be used for?
6. Evaluation: Create an advertisement for your new item. Your goal is to persuade others that they need your invention in their lives.

# Student Directions: Brainstorming

## Focus on the Skill

1. Title each of the four columns on the worksheet with a category from the list above the chart. Your goal is to try to fill the chart with words that fit each of the columns.
2. Now, choose one of the pictures at the center. Turn the worksheet over. Keeping an eye on the clock, you should take three minutes to brainstorm as many words, phrases, or ideas that come to mind after looking at that photo.
3. Go back and circle three of the best ideas you came up with, and create three *creative* sentences using each of the words or phrases (no less than eight words each).

## Practice the Skill

Now, look at another one of the photos. You will use "ABC Brainstorming" to create as many words and phrases as you can, using the alphabet to guide your answers.

## Take It to the Next Level

Find an ordinary item (or one that is interesting and different) that you brought to class or choose one of the items on the table. Working with the other members of your group, you will answer the following questions on the back of the worksheet in complete sentences.

1. Knowledge: Name this item.
2. Comprehension: Describe what this item was designed to do.
3. Application: Think of as many alternative uses for your item as possible. Be creative!
4. Analysis: Put all of the items from the group in the middle, and create three categories for the items. You may separate and combine items as you like to make the categories work
5. Synthesis: Combine your item with one other person's item (or more than one other item), and create a new invention. What could this new item be used for?
6. Evaluation: Create an advertisement for your new item. Your goal is to persuade others that they need your invention in their lives.

## How You Will Be Graded

| | 1 little or no evidence | 2 below average | 3 adequate evidence | 4 better than average | 5 superior evidence | TOTAL |
|---|---|---|---|---|---|---|
| Attention to neatness and presentation | | | | | | |
| Able to brainstorm categories with good examples to fit each | | | | | | |
| Uses a picture to stimulate creative sentences with no less than eight words each | | | | | | |
| Uses "ABC Brainstorming" to effectively list words, ideas, and phrases inspired by a photograph | | | | | | |
| Works in a group to go through the six steps of Bloom's Taxonomy; ideas are diverse and reflect creativity | | | | | | |
| **Total points multiplied by four** | | | | | | |
| **Final grade** | | | | | | |

# Worksheet: Brainstorming

## Focus on the Skill

Choose four of the categories from the list. Write the four categories you chose in the columns below. Set the timer for five minutes and see if you can fill the chart. The words in the column must match the topic.

fast-food words
Halloween words
hair words
things that grow
weather words
cooking words
animal words
words related to money
hospital words
words related to flying

| Category 1: | Category 2: | Category 3: | Category 4: |
|---|---|---|---|
| | | | |
| | | | |
| | | | |
| | | | |
| | | | |
| | | | |
| | | | |
| | | | |
| | | | |
| | | | |

**Americana Photos.** Choose one of the photographs at the center. Give yourself three minutes, and brainstorm as many words and phrases as you can about the photo on the back of the worksheet. Next, look at your list of words and phrases. Circle the three that seem most interesting to you, and create three sentences (with at least eight words each) using each of the words or phrases in your sentences.

1. ______________________________
2. ______________________________
3. ______________________________

## Practice the Skill

**ABC Brainstorming.** Now, look at another photo, and brainstorm words, phrases, and ideas that begin with each letter of the alphabet. You may have to get mighty creative!

A ____________
B ____________
C ____________
D ____________
E ____________
F ____________
G ____________
H ____________
I ____________
J ____________
K ____________
L ____________
M ____________
N ____________
O ____________
P ____________
Q ____________
R ____________
S ____________
T ____________
U ____________
V ____________
W ____________
X ____________
Y ____________
Z ____________

# Teacher Directions: Inference

## Goals for Student

1. Use context and word-structure clues to make inferences and generalizations.
2. Complete assignments and tasks using complex reading texts.
3. Recognize inference in quotations.

## Preparation

1. Your students should readily use the word "inference." They simply have to understand the scope of the word. It can be applied to a variety of situations, and a good reader must feel comfortable with its meaning.
2. Supply a book of quotes or a healthy supply of quotes from a good Internet source, such as "The Quotations Page" at http://www.quotationspage.com.

## Materials

- "Inference" worksheet
- Manila paper
- Colored pencils
- Books of quotations/quote lists from Internet

### Focus on the Skill

1. Students will begin by reading the sentences at the top of the page and determining what is going on. They should complete the framed sentence to reflect that a baseball game is being lost.
2. Then, they must create a similar paragraph that gives clues about a particular situation: a monkey on the loose, being lost on the subway, getting a gift for Valentine's Day, finding a lost dog, winning a football championship, or being in a wedding. Their writing must only *imply* what's going on.

## Practice the Skill

1. Now the students will follow the directions on the worksheet and determine the purpose and meaning for each of the quotes on the chart.
2. On the bottom chart, they will use the "TREE (**T**he quote, **R**ephrased, **E**xamples, and **E**ffect) Strategy" to analyze a quote they find in one of the quotation books.

## Take It to the Next Level

On a piece of manila paper, students will write their quote at the bottom and draw an illustration that effectively captures the meaning. Their details should show they have made a personal connection with the quotation.

## Special Considerations

I have found a neat Internet resource to use with this center for students who finish early. They can play "Inference Battleship" in which the computer won't let you get a hit until you respond to a question that tests your inference skills. You can find it at http://www.quia.com/ba/41785.html.

# Student Directions: Inference

## Focus on the Skill

1. Begin by reading the sentences at the top of the page and determining what is going on. Complete the framed sentence to reflect the problem and its effects.
2. Then, create a similar paragraph that gives clues about a particular situation: a monkey on the loose, being lost on the subway, getting a gift for Valentine's Day, finding a lost dog, winning a football championship, or being in a wedding. Your writing must only *imply* what's going on. If we were to send your paragraph to another class, would they be able to figure it out? Don't make it *too* easy on them!

## Practice the Skill

1. Now follow the directions on the worksheets and determine the purpose and meaning for each of the quotes on the chart.
2. Find a quote that you like from the quotes your teacher has supplied. You want to find one you can identify with.
3. On the bottom chart, you will use the "TREE (**T**he quote, **R**ephrased, **E**xamples, and **E**ffect) Strategy" to analyze that quote.

## Take It to the Next Level

On a piece of manila paper, you will write your quote at the bottom and draw an illustration that effectively captures the meaning. Your details should show you have made a personal connection with the quotation.

## How You Will Be Graded

| | 1 little or no evidence | 2 below average | 3 adequate evidence | 4 better than average | 5 superior evidence | TOTAL |
|---|---|---|---|---|---|---|
| Attention to neatness and presentation | | | | | | |
| Interprets a paragraph using inference skills | | | | | | |
| Effectively creates a paragraph that infers a situation | | | | | | |
| Determines meaning of quotes using the "TREE Strategy" | | | | | | |
| Creates a detailed illustration that reflects a personal quotation choice | | | | | | |
| **Total points multiplied by four** | | | | | | |
| **Final grade** | | | | | | |

# Worksheet: Inference

## Focus on the Skill

Begin by reading the sentences below, and determine what is going on. Complete the framed sentence to reflect the problem and its effects.

*Their hopes for a 9-inning contest were disappearing with each new cloud that formed in the sky. The coach checked his watch and disappointedly began to stow the bats into the team's bags. Each boy followed suit, picking up storm-drenched gloves and muddy balls off of the dugout floor. So, a bid for the championship would have to wait. With so much water on the field, there would be no hope for victory this day.*

Using inference, I know the sport is ______________________________ and the problem is
________________________________________________________________________________
________________________________________________________________________________.

**Creating Inference.** Now, you have to create a situation where the reader would have to use inference to figure out what's going on. Consider each of the following, and create a five-sentence paragraph that shows the situation. DO NOT use the words you are inferring in your writing.

A monkey on the loose
Getting a gift for Valentine's Day
Winning a football championship
Being lost on the subway
Finding a lost dog
Being in a wedding

________________________________________________________________________________
________________________________________________________________________________
________________________________________________________________________________
________________________________________________________________________________
________________________________________________________________________________.

## Practice the Skill

**Inference and Quotes.** Read each quote and determine the author's purpose. Is it *to explain, to encourage, to teach, to criticize,* or *to warn*? Could the purpose fit more than one category? Explain your answer.

| QUOTE | AUTHOR'S PURPOSE AND EXPLANATION |
|---|---|
| *"Measure wealth not by things you have, but by the things you have for which you would not take money."* -Anonymous | |
| *"Some folks pay a compliment like they went down in their pocket for it."* -Kin Hubbard | |
| *"There are lots of people who mistake their imagination for their memory."* -Josh Billings | |
| *"There are no secrets to success. It is the result of preparation, hard work, learning from failure."* -General Colin Powell | |
| *"To carry a grudge is like being stung to death by one bee."* -William H. Walton | |

## Worksheet: Inference (continued)

**Analyzing Quotes/Aphorisms.** Choose a significant quote or quotes, and analyze the meaning using the "TREE (**T**he quote, **R**ephrased, **E**xamples, and **E**ffect) Strategy."

| The quote | Rephrased in my own words | Examples from my world | Effect on the reader |
|---|---|---|---|
| *"Genius is 1 percent inspiration, 99 percent perspiration."* -Thomas Edison | The really successful people are the ones who are willing to work hard. | Making good grades is not easy for me because I struggle with school. But, I work hard, so I make good grades. | Edison's quote helps me remember that I can't quit if I want to be successful. |
| | | | |

# Teacher Directions: Test Words

## Goals for Student

1. Use new vocabulary that is introduced and taught directly.
2. Recognize double meanings of new vocabulary.
3. Confirms meaning of new vocabulary.

## Preparation

1. Point out the need for understanding the directions and the questions on a test. For example, a word like "illustrate" may bring to mind a drawing, but the test makers intended the meaning to be a form of "show" or "indicate."
2. Practice underlining the part of the question that is specific and should be answered. Have your students practice rephrasing the question by mentally saying, "This question is asking me . . ."
3. Supply your students with a copy of a released version of the standardized test from a previous year.

## Materials

- Previous year's standardized test
- "Test Words" worksheet
- Dictionaries and thesauruses
- Colored paper
- Colored pencils

## Focus on the Skill

1. Students will begin by going through the instructions and questions on the test. They will circle words that are confusing or unfamiliar. They will make a list of those words on the back of the worksheet.
2. The students will circle one of the words and create a vocabulary map for the term under the list they just created.

## Practice the Skill

1. Now, introduce the test words to your students. It may be valuable to say the words for your students and have them repeat the words back to you. Pronunciation is very important when taking a test.
2. Students will now create a vocabulary book (try the "Vocabulary Book Foldable" from Dinah Zike's website at www.dinah.com). They will write each word in the first column. Then, they will use a dictionary to find the meaning, list a synonym and an antonym, and create a sentence (no less than eight words) that shows they understand the meanings.

## Take It to the Next Level

A fun way to get to the bottom of easily confused test words is to create an "Author's Purpose Cartoon Book" (try the "Bound Book Foldable" from Dinah Zike's website at www.dinah.com). Students choose ten words from the list and create a flip book where each phrase is featured in a drawing and caption. The best books can be shared with elementary-school students as study guides for their own tests!

## Special Considerations

When I realized how confusing the terminology used to ask questions and give directions were on standardized tests, I knew my students were missing a huge piece to being successful. They needed clarification and an opportunity to differentiate meanings.

# Student Directions: Test Words

## Focus on the Skill

1. Begin by going through the *instructions* and *questions* of the test. Circle words that are confusing or unfamiliar. Make a list of those words on the back of the worksheet.
2. Circle one of the words and create a vocabulary map for the term under the list you just created.

## Practice the Skill

1. Say each of the twenty-five test words at the top of the "Test Words" worksheet. Pronunciation is very important when taking a test.
2. Write each word in the first column. Then, use a dictionary to find the meaning, list a synonym and an antonym, and create a sentence (no less than eight words) that shows you understand the meanings.

## Take It to the Next Level

A fun way to get to the bottom of easily confused test words is to create an "Author's Purpose Cartoon Book." Choose ten of the phrases from the list and create a flip book where each phrase is featured in a drawing and caption to show comprehension. The best books can be shared with elementary-school students as study guides for their own tests!

## How You Will Be Graded

| | 1 little or no evidence | 2 below average | 3 adequate evidence | 4 better than average | 5 superior evidence | TOTAL |
|---|---|---|---|---|---|---|
| Attention to neatness and presentation | | | | | | |
| Finds easily confused words in the instructions and questions of the test | | | | | | |
| Accurately completes a vocabulary map that shows comprehension of one of the confusing terms | | | | | | |
| Determines synonyms and antonyms and writes a well-written sentence for each of the twenty-five test words | | | | | | |
| Creates a detailed "Author's Purpose Cartoon Book" that effectively expresses each phrase | | | | | | |
| **Total points multiplied by four** | | | | | | |
| **Final grade** | | | | | | |

# Worksheet: Test Words

## Focus on the Skill

1. alternative
2. appropriate
3. aspect
4. assume
5. bias
6. caption
7. column
8. consistent
9. concept
10. derive
11. display
12. evidence
13. express
14. factor
15. function
16. illustrate
17. indicate
18. interpret
19. least accurate
20. most likely
21. primarily
22. row
23. significant
24. suggest
25. tendency

## Practice the Skill

**Chart for Analyzing Test Words**

| Original word or phrase | Synonyms | Antonyms | A sentence that shows meaning is understood (at least eight words) |
|---|---|---|---|
| 1. | | | |
| 2. | | | |
| 3. | | | |
| 4. | | | |
| 5. | | | |
| 6. | | | |
| 7. | | | |
| 8. | | | |
| 9. | | | |
| 10. | | | |
| 11. | | | |
| 12. | | | |
| 13. | | | |
| 14. | | | |
| 15. | | | |
| 16. | | | |
| 17. | | | |
| 18. | | | |
| 19. | | | |
| 20. | | | |
| 21. | | | |
| 22. | | | |
| 23. | | | |
| 24. | | | |
| 25. | | | |

## Take It to the Next Level

Choose ten of the phrases below and create an "Author's Purpose Comic Book."

To explain
To predict
To persuade
To identify
To highlight
To analyze
To entertain
To describe
To categorize
To teach
To convince
To inform
To encourage
To share
To compare
To verify
To emphasize
To outline

# Teacher Directions: Elaborations

## Goals for Student

1. Use active reading strategies to self-correct comprehension problems.
2. Use an effective organizational pattern and substantial support to achieve a sense of completeness or wholeness in writing.
3. Explore ways that elaborations can be useful for test taking.

## Preparation

1. Your students should be comfortable working in small groups while using active reading strategies.
2. Supply each student with a copy of *Dear Mrs. LaRue* by Mark Teague

## Materials

- "Elaborations" worksheet
- Colored pencils
- *Dear Mrs. LaRue*

## Focus on the Skill

1. Students will begin by turning the worksheet over and completing a vocabulary map on the word "elaboration."
2. They will begin by focusing on how they should be elaborating while they read—actively working to make good connections and comprehend the text.
3. They will all read *Dear Mrs. LaRue*, following the directions on the worksheet and participating in active reading with the other members of the group.

## Practice the Skill

Now the students will complete the "Elaborating What We Write" part of the worksheet. They should read the directions and begin focusing on how elaborations can improve writing.

## Take It to the Next Level

At the bottom of the worksheet, they will draw an interpretation of an extended sentence they wrote. It should reflect all of the details and imagery from their new sentence.

## Special Considerations

Most standardized tests are requiring extended-response questions. Students who do not have a full understanding for what elaborations are and how they can help improve their scores are at a grave disadvantage to those who do. Elaborations are the product of good details, so it is vital that your students become detail hunters for evidence they can use in their written responses. Often, I liken the extended response question to an Easter egg hunt. If there are twelve eggs hidden, there must be twelve eggs found. Assessors score extended-response questions according to the number of details found, and they know how many to look for. Students that recognize a need to search and elaborate will be better prepared for the experience.

# Student Directions: Elaborations

## Focus on the Skill

1. Begin by turning the worksheet over and completing a vocabulary map for the word "elaboration."
2. You should understand that good reading skills require elaborating—actively working to make good connections and comprehend the text details.
3. You will read *Dear Mrs. LaRue*, following the directions on the worksheet and participating in active reading with the other members of the group.

## Practice the Skill

1. Now complete the "Elaborating What We Write" part of the worksheet. You should read the directions and begin focusing on how elaborations can improve writing.
2. Try to follow the model provided for you. It's very important that you really try to EXPAND your sentence.

## Take It to the Next Level

At the bottom of the worksheet, you will draw an interpretation of the extended sentence you created. It should reflect all of the details and imagery from your new sentence.

## How You Will Be Graded

| | 1 little or no evidence | 2 below average | 3 adequate evidence | 4 better than average | 5 superior evidence | TOTAL |
|---|---|---|---|---|---|---|
| Attention to neatness and presentation | | | | | | |
| Completes an accurate vocabulary map for "elaboration" | | | | | | |
| Participates well in active reading with group | | | | | | |
| Focuses on how to elaborate a sentence effectively | | | | | | |
| Interprets the extended sentence in a detailed illustration | | | | | | |
| **Total points multiplied by four** | | | | | | |
| **Final grade** | | | | | | |

# Worksheet: Elaborations

## Focus on the Skill

We have to practice ELABORATING what we read. Read *Dear Mrs. LaRue.* Go through all of the steps of good reading. Sometimes, kids who struggle to read well would rather say what they don't understand. These are the steps good readers use to comprehend (maybe not with a worksheet, but in their heads). It takes practice, but if you can go through these steps with an easy book, you may remember the process when the reading is more difficult.

**Step One:** Think about what you read! Read thoroughly, and think about the main ideas.

I've thought about it, and I believe the main idea behind *Dear Mrs. LaRue* is ______________
______________________________________________________________
_____________________________________________________________.

**Step Two:** Ask yourself questions about the main ideas and main points in the story. Decide if you agree with the way the author presented the information. Try to imagine if the characters were different.

One question I have about the story is "_______________________________________
_____________________________________________________________?"

**Step Three:** Try to find ways to apply the material to events, people, or things in your life. Is there any way the events in this story can connect to my life—someone trying to persuade someone to do something, a funny pet, an experience away from home that wasn't fun, etc.? BE SPECIFIC!

One connection I can make with *Dear Mrs. LaRue* is ______________________________
______________________________________________________________
_____________________________________________________________.

**STOP! Wait for another person in the center to arrive at this step!**

**Step Four:** Talk with others. Ask other people what they think about the story you read. Take turns talking for twenty seconds (time each other) about the story. Don't interrupt if you're listening, and do not stop to breath if it's your turn to talk! Talk about the author's point of view, your opinion, and why you agree or disagree with way the events unfolded.

After talking about the story, we agreed _______________________________________
_____________________________________________________________.

**Step Five:** Teach somebody about a subject in the story. Pretend you are teaching the material. As a teacher, what would you say or do to help others understand? Literally pretend you are in front of a class of children. What would you say to help them if they just didn't understand? Choose one of the subjects below and see how well you can teach the topic!

| obedience school | pet ownership | misbehaving animals |
|---|---|---|
| being misunderstood | visiting a new place | charity work or community service |

## Worksheet: Elaborations (continued)

I think I can explain ______________________ best. ______________
________________________________________
________________________________________
________________________________________
________________________________________

### Practice the Skill

**Elaborating What You Write.** Aside from expanding how you think about what you read, you can also expand what you write. The sample chart below EXPANDS the simple sentence, "We made some tea."

| We | made | some | tea |
|---|---|---|---|
| My best friend, Michelle, and I | prepared | a pot of | fragrant leaves steeped in boiling water |
| Two silly girls who always giggle out loud | readied | more than enough | the perfect mix of ice, sugar, and golden-colored refreshment |
| The easygoing one and her hyper sidekick | simmered | a nip of | the hot beverage to be served in the afternoon. |
| A pair of lost, little eighth graders | brewed | a taste of | the drink infused with oolong and other exotic herbs |

My favorite expanded sentence from the chart is: *"The easygoing one and her hyper sidekick brewed a pot of fragrant leaves steeped in boiling water."*

**Your Turn.** Use the sentence, "Ike wrote a letter to Mrs. LaRue," and see if you can expand its meaning. Use a thesaurus for verbs, and really define each of the nouns and pronouns.

| Ike | wrote | a letter | to Mrs. LaRue |
|---|---|---|---|
| | | | |
| | | | |

Write your favorite expanded sentence from the chart. ______________________
________________________________________
________________________________________.

### Take It to the Next Level

Now take your new, expanded sentence and draw a picture on the back of this sheet to represent its details.

# Bibliography


Alvermann, D. E. (2001). Reading Adolescents' Reading identities: Looking back to see ahead. *Journal of Adolescent & Adult Literacy*, Vol. 44, 676-690.

Batstone, P. B. (2004). Focused anecdotal records assessment: A tool for standards-based, authentic assessment. *The Reading Teacher*, Vol. 58, No. 3.

Bonner, B. L. (2004). Expertise in group problem solving: Recognition, social combination, and performance. *Group Dynamics: Theory, Research, and Practice*, 4, 277–290.

Boston, C. (2002). The concept of formative assessment. *Practical Assessment, Research & Evaluation*, 8(9).

Bray, R. M., Kerr, N. L., & Atkin, R. S (1978). Effects of group size, problem difficulty, and sex on group performance and member reactions. *Journal of Personality and Social Psychology*, 36, 1224–1240.

"Crime, Violence, Discipline, and Safety in U.S. Public Schools: Findings from the School Survey on Crime and Safety." National Center for Education Statistics, 2003–04.

Elkind, D. H. and Sweet, F., Ph.D. (1997). The Socratic approach to character education. *Educational Leadership*, 54, 56-59.

Farkas, R. D. (2003). Effects of traditional versus learning-styles instructional methods on middle school students. *The Journal of Educational Research*, 97, no. 1, 42-51.

Fisher, J.B., Schumaker, J.B., & Deshler, D.D (2002). *Improving the Reading Comprehension of At-Risk Adolescents*. New York: Guildford Press.

Gard, C. (April/May 2000). What is he/she saying? *Current Health*, No.8, 18-19.

Garvin, D. A. and Christensen, C. R. (1992). *Education for Judgement: The Artistry of Discussion Leadership.* Boston: Harvard Business School Press.

"Groups Perform Better Than the Best Individuals at Solving Complex Problems" (2006). APA Press Release. American Psychological Association.

Guild, P.B., and Garger, S. (1998). *Marching to Different Drummers*. Alexandria, VA: Association for Supervision and Curriculum Development.

Gurian, M., Henely, P., Trueman, T. (2002). *Boys and Girls Learn Differently! A Guide for Teachers and Parents.* San Francisco: Jossey-Bass.

Hall, T. (2002). Differentiated instruction. Wakefield, MA: National Center on Accessing the General Curriculum. Retrieved October 4, 2006 from http://www.cast.org/publications/ncac/ncac_diffinstruc.html

Langer, J. A., Close, E., Angelis, J., Preller, P. (2000). Guidelines for Teaching Middle and High School Students to Read and Write Well: Six Features of Effective Instruction. Albany, NY: National Research Center On English Learning & Achievement.

Laughlin, P., Hatch, E., Silver, J., & Boh, L. (2006). Groups perform better than the best individuals on letters-to-numbers problems: Effects of group size. *Journal of Personality and Social Psychology*, Vol. 90, No. 4.

Moon, T. R., Tomlinson, C. A., & Callahan, C. M. (1995). *Academic diversity in the middle school: Results of a national survey of middle school administrators and teachers* (Research Monograph 95124). Storrs, CT: The National Research Center on the Gifted and Talented, University of Connecticut.

Rasmussen, R. V. (1984). Practical discussion techniques for instructors. *Alberta Association for Continuing Education Journal*, 12(2), 38-47.

"Reading Next: A Vision for Action and Research in Middle and High School Literacy. A Report to Carnegie Corporation of New York." Alliance for Excellent Education, 2004.

Tyre, P. (2006, January 30). The trouble with boys: They're kinetic, maddening and failing at school. *Newsweek*.

# Professional Resources

## Classroom Management

Emmer, E. T., Everston, C. M., Worsham, M. E. (2005). *Classroom Management for Middle and High School Teachers*. Boston: Allyn & Bacon.

Jones, F. H. (2000). *Fred Jones Tools for Teaching*. Santa Cruz, CA: Fredric H. Jones & Associates.

Rubenstein, G. (1999). *Reluctant Disciplinarian: Advice on Classroom Management from a Softy Who Became (Eventually) a Successful* Teacher. Fort Collins, CO: Cottonwood Press.

## General Internet Resources

Project CRISS: Creating Independence through Student-owned Strategies, http://www.projectcriss.com

Dinah Zike's Foldables, http://www.dinah.com

Teachers.net Middle School Chatboard, http://teachers.net/mentors/middle_school

## Suggested Resources for Use with Literacy Centers

### Cause and Effect

Dean, J. "Big Bad John," re-released in Bear Family Records, 1994, CD 1.

Jennings, P. (2000). "Strapbox Flyer." *Unreal: Eight Surprising Stories!* New York: Puffin Books.

### Vocabulary

Barrett, J. (1985). *Cloudy with a Chance of Meatballs*. New York: Aladdin.

Gwynne, F (2006). *The King Who Rained*. New York: Aladdin.

Parish, P. *Amelia Beldelia* Lectorum Publications (April 2000)

### Sequence of Events

Bryant, J. (2004). *The Trial*. New York: Knopf Books for Young Readers.

Cronin, D. and Lewin, B. (2003). *Click, Clack, Moo: Cows That* Type. New York: Simon & Schuster.

Gerstein, M. (2007). *The Man Who Walked Between the Towers*. New York: Square Fish.

Leaf, M. (2000). *The Story of Ferdinand*. New York: Grosset & Dunlap.

Lester, J. (1999). *John Henry*. New York: Puffin Books.

McCully, E. A. (2006). *Marvelous Mattie: How Margaret E. Knight Became an Inventor*. New York: Farrar, Straus and Giroux.

Sendak, M. (2001). *Where the Wild Things Are*. New York: Galison Books.

Winter, H. (2006). *39 Apartments of Ludwig Van Beethoven*. New York: Schwartz & Wade.

### Literature Terms

Cisneros, S. (1992). "Eleven." *Woman Hollering Creek: And Other Stories*. New York: Vintage.

Wordsworth, W. (1963). "Daffodils." *The Oxford Book of English Verse, 1250-1918*. Quiller-Couch, ed. Oxford: Oxford University Press.

### Fact and Opinion

Allen, J. (2000). *Are You a Spider?* New York: Kingfisher.

Celsi, T., Cushman, D. (1992). *The Fourth Little Pig*. Orlando, FL: Steck-Vaughn.

Claverie, J. (1992). *The Three Little Pigs*. New York: North South Books.

Clutton-Brock, J. (1991). *Cat (Eyewitness Books)*. New York: Knopf Books for Young Readers.

Cronin, D., Bliss, H. (2005). *Diary of a Spider*. New York: Joanna Cotler.

Howitt, M., DiTerlizzi, T. (2002). *Spider and the Fly*. New York: Simon & Schuster.

Kirk, D. (2007). *Miss Spider's Tea Party*. New York: Scholastic.

Lowell, S. (1992). *The Three Little Javelinas*. Flagstaff, AZ: Rising Moon Books.

McDermott, G. (1999). *Anansi the Spider: A Tale from Ashanti*. Austin, TX: Holt, Rinehart and Winston.

Rounds, G. (1992). *The Three Little Pigs and the Big Bad Wolf*. New York: Holiday House.

Scieszka, J., Smith, L. (1999). *The True Story of the Three Little Pigs*. New York: Viking Juvenile.

Trivizas, E. (2004). *The Three Little Wolves and the Big Bad Pig*. London: Egmont Books.

### Reference and Research

World Almanac Education. "World Almania" game. Strongsville, OH: World Almanac Education.

### Standardized Testing Must-Have Skills

Discovery Communications, Inc. (2007). "Travel Channel: Americana Photos," http://travel.discovery.com/yourshot/americana/americana.html.

Moncur, M. (1994-2007). "The Quotations Page," http://www.quotationspage.com.